CONCEIVING A NATION

Mira Morgenstern

CONCEIVING A NATION

THE DEVELOPMENT OF POLITICAL DISCOURSE
IN THE HEBREW BIBLE

The Pennsylvania State University Press
University Park, Pennsylvania

Library of Congress Cataloging-in-Publication Data

Morgenstern, Mira.
Conceiving a nation : the development of political discourse in the
Hebrew Bible / Mira Morgenstern.
p.   cm.
Includes bibliographical references and index.
Summary: "Interprets the Bible as a text concerned with the
political reality of conceiving and nurturing a nation. Highlights
the emphasis that the Bible places on women's contribution to
what it takes to make a nation"—Provided by publisher.
ISBN 978-0-271-03473-7 (cloth : alk. paper)
1. Bible. O.T.—Language, style.
2. Hebrew language—Discourse analysis.
3. Rhetoric—Political aspects.
4. Political oratory.
I. Title.

BS1171.3.M67 2009
221.8'32—dc22
2008037773

CONTENTS

PREFACE

This book is the product of many years of study and thought, and many people from the diverse areas of life in which I work have supported it. I have received important personal support from Shuly Parkoff, Sarah Rosen, Susan Weissman, and Dr. Shoshana Rybak, women who have been active in local Bible study groups, where some of the ideas presented in this book received early exposure. Special thanks are due also to Rabbi Chaim Wasserman and Rabbi Shlomo Rybak, particularly as they encouraged my work by officially making their pulpits available for early presentation of some of the themes of this book. On the (more narrowly couched) academic side, I owe great thanks to Professor Marshall Berman (CCNY/CUNY), Professor Nicole Fermon (Fordham University), and Professor Carole Lambert (Azusa), all of whom have, throughout the years, supported the intellectual importance of explicating the political discourse within the Hebrew Bible. Special thanks go to Professor Gordon Schochet (Rutgers University) and Professor Steven Grosby (Clemson University), who nurtured early drafts of work that appeared in *Hebraic Political Studies*. I take this opportunity to thank the Memorial Foundation for Jewish Culture, whose grant financed an early version of the chapter on Ruth and political difference, published in the spring 1999 edition of *Judaism*. Likewise, I gratefully acknowledge the opportunities afforded me by two NEH grants, which financed summers of thought and writing: first at the Jewish Theological Seminary, under the leadership of Professor Jonathan Boyarin (Kansas University) and Professor Daniel Boyarin (University of California, Berkeley), and subsequently at Yale University (Professor Leslie Brisman). Special thanks go to Sanford Thatcher for supporting the publication of this book and to Nicholas Taylor for carefully copyediting it.

Of overriding importance is the debt that I owe to the teachers who developed in me the important skills in Biblical hermeneutics, without which this project could not even have been conceived. I refer specifically to the master classes of the late Rabbi Dr. Isaac Suna (Yeshiva University) and of Rabbi Dr. Walter Orenstein (Yeshiva University). Finally, my families of origin and of formation have played central roles in my own understanding of the Biblical text as quotidian counterpoint. My husband has supported my scholarship, even in circles and circumstances where this activity is denigrated and ignored. My parents in their home created an atmosphere of scholarship and careful critical attention to texts in general, and to Biblical texts in particular, which extends with great hope and happiness to the children and grandchildren of the succeeding generations.

INTRODUCTION

This book uses the Bible as a springboard to explore the role that discourse plays in forming a nation. The Bible is an ancient text with modern tonalities: it is one of the first works in which the tensions of the complex relationships between personal and communal life are presented, not as inevitably tragic (as reflected in ancient Greek thought), but rather as part of a intricate system whose ongoing comprehension yields its participants a richer and more deeply human experience.

In its analysis of the political process of forming a nation, *Conceiving a Nation* does not emphasize the better-known and obviously contentious confrontations in the Bible over the course of Israelite nation formation (for example, the civil war between Saul and David is not discussed here). Rather, this book focuses on the development of *political discourse* in the process of defining a nation. Central to the Bible's presentation of political discourse is that this process always remains open-ended: there is no one "correct" solution to the challenges of national existence. The Bible's pluralistic understanding of different models of political development for different nations, along with its depiction of the changing concepts of national identity over time, provides a much-needed corrective to the current tendency to view the Bible as a text of uniform and univalent meaning. Indeed, the ambiguity and the laconic quality of the Hebrew Bible render it constantly open to new interpretations, and its texts therefore always speak to changing circumstances.[1] In her book on Biblical hermeneutics, Susan

---

1. Cf. "Odysseus' Scar" in Erich Auerbach's *Mimesis* (Princeton: Princeton University Press, 1953).

Handelman expresses it this way: "Thus in speaking of *Torah*, the act of interpretation is included and integral. . . . The boundaries between text and interpretation are fluid."[2]

The fluid quality of interpretation is an important part of the concept of national identity presented in this book. This understanding of national belonging is influenced by what Benedict Anderson has called "imagined communities."[3] Although Anderson consciously writes of the "modern culture of nationalism," much of what Anderson describes regarding the power of the imagination to distill a coherent and dynamic sense of nationhood already exists in the text of one of the most ancient of written documents.[4] The Hebrew Bible portrays the development of Israelite nationhood as a thing that is imagined before it is realized. Significantly, the Bible does not conceptualize a nation's development as the product of just one person or group. In order to attain an existence that is both stable and dynamic—that is to say, partaking of the qualities of both permanence and ongoing development—the Bible demonstrates that the imagination of the nation must be the product of both a leader and a people. As the Bible understands it, a nation must be "conceived," in both senses of that word, before it can be successfully born. As I will discuss later, it is no accident that the process of nurturing national identity in the Hebrew Bible holds women at its core.

The narratives that I highlight all focus on the conflicts that lie at the core of every nation. In all of these stories—the dreams of Joseph and the quarrels with his brothers, the "storybook" tale of the arch foreigner Ruth, the shocking parable of Jotham, the riddling exploits of Samson, the metaphors of the triply estranged Esther—the central themes reach beyond what are commonly considered to be the "political" concerns of a leader for his/her own power position. That is why I do not focus on the travails of power as experienced by Biblical kings like Saul, David, or Solomon. Instead, the highlighted Biblical narratives underscore a different kind of conflict, one that encompasses the larger social and national tensions whose energies those leaders must harness if they are to nurture a national entity that will survive beyond their own charismatic authority. As portrayed in the Bible, not all of these leaders completely accomplish their self-appointed tasks: as even the most successful of them realize, establishing a political

2. *Torah* is the Hebrew expression for the "the Hebrew Bible." Susan A. Handelman, *The Slayers of Moses* (Albany: SUNY Press, 1982), 40–41.

3. Benedict Anderson, *Imagined Communities* (New York: Verso, 1983).

4. Ibid., 9, 13, 36; also chap. 3, "The Origins of National Consciousness," 37–46.

discourse is an undertaking that can never be finally "achieved," but instead remains a project of perennial negotiation. The Bible emphasizes the commonality of effort between people and leader needed to provide for the emergence of a vibrant national discourse and political identity.

In this book, *discourse* denotes the conversation that establishes the concept of national commonality and hence a sense of political identity. In the course of outlining the development of a nation's self-understanding, I emphasize the conversations constituting this discourse rather than the particulars of the legal code that reflect/impel this dialogue.[5] In this context, the texts that are the focus of sustained analysis depict periods of flux, or crisis, in Israelite development. These texts are scattered throughout the Hebrew Bible, and certainly not every one of these texts is treated in this book. (In fact, the argument can be made that every episode that results in writing is by definition a text of crisis.) With two major exceptions, the texts treated in this book focus largely on the period depicted in the Biblical Book of Judges, which is chronologically post-conquest (of the Promised Land) and pre-monarchical: that is to say, when the Israelite nation is portrayed as growing out of one mode (a newly established nation) and into another (settling on a particular mode of political leadership). Any period of protracted searching for self-definition is easily recognized as one of crisis, although that crisis is generally appreciated only retrospectively, after it has produced fundamental change. (At the moment of crisis, individuals and groups are generally too busy coping with the actualities of change to recognize its wider theoretical and practical implications.) Because the crises depicted in these texts are national (or at least trans-tribal) in character, they give rise to a renewed interest in national self-definition. As a result, a new approach to dialogue on a national level takes place, which I identify as the national discourse that establishes a polity.

In describing the development of the Israelites into a nation, the term *political* is used to denote the development of a communal sense of identity and general welfare, both of which result from the establishment of a common sense of meaning through the promotion of a shared civil discourse. In this connection, it is important to note the particular sense of the word *development* as it is utilized in this book. While development may be defined as a practice with a discrete beginning, middle, and end, I employ a

---

5. This explains why the part of the Bible conventionally described as the "legal code" receives scant mention in the pages of this book. I focus on the discourse that makes the common sense of politics possible, rather than the details of the legal code itself.

more open-ended concept of development, one that emphasizes process rather than final closure (this approach is familiar when dealing with the concept of love, or of intellectual development). The Biblical presentation of the development of this political discourse becomes difficult to comprehend, however, because there is no obvious "sweep" or resolution to this conversation. It evolves—and sometimes backslides—in fits and starts; it is very much a function of the people and circumstances of a particular era. Although this book's chapters are arranged in a loosely historical fashion—the placement of Ruth toward the beginning of the book takes seriously the Hebrew Bible's situation of these events during the period of the judges, and relies also on some of the historical details scattered about the text—this does not imply that there is a smooth trajectory of growth in the development of political discourse from start to finish. To be sure, the location of Esther's contribution at the end of the book may give the impression that some final resolution has been "achieved," particularly as the Book of Esther appears much later in the chronology of the Biblical text. What this chapter actually signals, however, is the ability of national discourse to operate even when the obvious trappings of nationality—independence, freedom, statehood—no longer obtain. This may be *interpreted* as an advance; what the Biblical text actually *shows*, however, is that national discourse may exist in a vast array of circumstances, and it need not be a function of traditionally defined power concerns or political struggles.

Thus, I read the Bible as the source of a dynamic critique of the concepts conventionally considered fundamental to national identity. The Biblical text interrogates and problematizes these accepted categorizations of nationality: the ethnic (Ruth), the cultural (Samson), the political (Jotham), and the territorial (Esther). Consequently, this book highlights the Bible's contribution to a conversation that, in contrast to the "organic" conception of nationhood so vaunted in the nineteenth century, is once again coming to be viewed as highly problematic and unsettled.[6] The Bible has a central role to play in the conversation about the nation within the current stream of political and ethical discord. The nuanced understanding of the Bible advanced in this book is a reminder that, even for those uninterested in the ancient religious provenance or even in particular narrative tales of the Bible, this text remains of central importance in constructing contemporary political discourse.

6. Cf. Colin Kidd, *British Identities Before Nationalism* (Cambridge: Cambridge University Press, 1999), especially 1–33.

The Bible structures its analysis of political discourse by focusing on a nation whose political development is atypical, especially when contrasted with surrounding empires (e.g., those of the ancient Egyptians, Hittites, and Babylonians of the time). This renders the Israelite experience particularly interesting for theoretical analysis, because it provides an unusual vantage point from which to analyze common (historical and current) assumptions about nation formation and national identity. Biblical narratives reflect this singular perspective by refracting the development of Israelite nationhood and the background of discord against which it developed through the concept of *strangeness/difference*. Consequently, I utilize the concept of strangeness to interpret the development of Israelite nationhood and the political discourse that impels it.

In the Biblical texts, strangeness is evident in both the structure and the quality of Israelite political existence. Structurally, for example, the strangeness of Israelite nationhood is apparent in how the text describes the Israelite delineation of the political sphere. Unlike many of its cultural contemporaries, Israelite political discourse does not develop exclusively (or even mainly) in venues specifically or traditionally recognized as public: there is no institutionalized agora in which to situate a growing awareness of the public commonality.[7] Instead, in the Biblical text, national awareness develops in settings that are both quotidian and domestic, such as Gideon's granary, Samson's parties, or Ruth's conversations in privately owned farms or walking along a dusty path. Furthermore, the Israelites are depicted, unlike many nations of the time, as articulating their own political identity through people who are generally considered domestic and alien to "public" space: women, or else leaders who are presented as women. This portrayal is subtle and may not be immediately apparent to the casual reader. It is only after absorbing the Bible's litany of leaders that are each

---

7. To be sure, one can speak of the space "at the gates" as one area of common discussion: the elders of the city sit there to render legal judgment in the cases that come before them. Interestingly enough, however, these gates are not depicted as places where political discourse/self-awareness develops. One might suppose the structures of the king's palace or of the Holy Temple to be (public) locations lending themselves to the expression of political discourse. In the Biblical text, however, these identities are not automatically equated: the king's palace is typically presented as a place where the king projects either his own personality (e.g., David's nocturnal walks, or the judicial decisions of Solomon) or his preoccupations with his own power position; the Holy Temple is portrayed largely as a place of public/private prayerful reflection, not as a locale of public discourse. To the extent that behavior in the Temple is seen as affecting the public life of the Israelites, this is portrayed negatively, as embodied in the corrupt behavior of the sons of Eli the High Priest (1 Sam. 2:12–17; 22–26).

described as possessing characteristics that normally would disqualify them from leadership—being lame (Ehud's right hand never seems to work properly), being preoccupied with the disposition of his hair coupled with seemingly unpredictable and arbitrary displays of temper (Samson), being a tattletale and a clotheshorse (Joseph)—that the careful reader comes to realize that the text utilizes these adjectives purposefully. The Bible's choice of words deliberately associates leadership with attributes conventionally utilized pejoratively to label women: weak, mercurial, overly talkative, and fashion conscious. The disconcerting attribution of political power to people who are described with socially and sexually fraught terms makes the reader understand that the Bible presents power as intrinsically alienated and alienating. Thus, the estrangement of the Israelite leaders from the standard conception of political power means that these rulers are in no position to impose their own concept of national identity on the people. Indeed, the text implicitly argues that national distinctiveness can be attained only through ongoing negotiation and conversations among people who are likely to be strange to each other; even more importantly, these people may well also be strange to themselves.

The concept of strangeness that dominates the quality of Israelite national existence is manifest textually both in the external relations between the Israelites and their surrounding environment, and by the internal connections among the constituent parts of the Israelite nation. Importantly, both of these arenas are marked by conflict. These clashes increase the uncertainty that accompanies the process of hammering out a national identity, which then heightens the implicit tensions evoked by the real possibility of failure. Although the moral connotations of the socioeconomic gaps within Israelite society form a major theme in the Biblical writings of the Later Prophets, the political implications of these dissonances manifest themselves early on in Israelite political development.[8] As such, these consequences have been less thoroughly analyzed, even though these are central to understanding both the complicated nature of Israelite identity and the polyphonic quality of the discourse(s) that create Israelite national identity.

As the Bible describes it, because the Israelite community is fractured by the conflicts engendered by strangeness, it is clear that the Israelites' sense

---

8. These themes are expressed particularly in the Book of Hosea (chaps. 4 and 8) and the Book of Amos (chaps. 1 and 2).

of themselves as one nation does not develop in a uniform manner. By the same token, the level and quality of the estrangement evinced by different parts of the Israelite community continues to fluctuate. The different parts of this community—rich and poor, urban dwellers and farmers, plains dwellers and mountain folk, judges and plebeians—are variously affected by the structures important to their particular experiences of daily life; consequently, they view the imperatives of national identity in different and often contrasting ways.[9] Because the Israelites' sense of national identity develops against the background of this and other conflicts, their (in/)ability to easily articulate a national discourse mirrors their contentious conceptions of the substance of their national identity. As depicted in the Bible, the evolution of this discourse becomes the sticking point for much of Biblical Israelite history in their Promised Land.

The persistence of the theme of strangeness in Israelite political development implies that dissonance and nonconventional thinking are the hallmarks of Israelite nation formation. The Biblical text presents nationhood in general as a concept that is fundamentally "uncanny"—and even, in Kierkegaard's sense, absurd. In the Tower of Babel episode, for example, the origins of nationhood are depicted as both humanly engendered and Divinely directed. This confluence of causes is the result of a complex irony exposed in the narrative: the success of human cooperation, perceived as upsetting the Divinely bestowed world order, itself inspires the Divine dispersal of humankind. Tellingly, this diffusion is embodied in different linguistic constructions that, previously understood as alternate enunciations of individuality, now become markers of incomprehensibility to all "others."[10] In an "absurd" move, nationhood exaggerates the essence of human distinctiveness into the source of human estrangement and, ultimately, destructive violence.

Countering this, the Bible introduces a new way of analyzing both the traditional constellations of power and conventional arguments centered on traditional raison d'état or national imperatives. Instead of viewing nationhood as a convenient method of organizing power relations within (one's corner of) the world, the Bible introduces another possible understanding

9. This is an important argument that Weber makes in his *Ancient Judaism*, trans. and ed. Jans H. Gerth and Don Martindale (1952; New York: Free Press, 1967), particularly part I.

10. "And the entire earth was of one tongue and several expressions" (Gen. 11:1; unless otherwise noted, all translations are my own).

of national definition: nationhood representing the opportunity to interrogate existing power relations and their accompanying moral implications.[11] Textually, the Bible highlights this counterintuitive approach by
providing a different literary style to anchor crucial episodes centering on
the interrogation and exploration of political discourse. In this way, the
Bible's particulars of literary style reveals the political implications of the
available choices in the development of political discourse.

To be sure, it is easy to mock strangeness as a concept that winds up
painting everybody with the same broad brush: if everyone is estranged,
then no one is really any different. However, it is important to note that
the Biblical text presents the notion of estrangement as a counterweight
to the commonly accepted, even if unacknowledged, idea that people and
their makeup and desires are essentially unchanging. In its treatment of
Israelite political development, the Biblical text points out that as circumstances alter, so do people. Consequently, part of what makes a polity
both dynamic and stable is the ability of its national discourse to adapt to
these changes. Otherwise, the polity becomes a thinly disguised dictator-
ship with no claim to moral coherence. As different narratives in these
various Biblical texts make clear, moral coherence is central to the continuing vitality of both individuals and communities. This is highlighted most
obviously in the famous counterexamples of the political and personal
tragedies brought about by the absence of this coherence: the narratives
of David and Bathsheba, and Jephtah and his daughter, to name just two.
By contrast, the final (historical) narrative in the Hebrew Bible presented
in this book highlights both the achievements of Esther in reimagining a
community and the ability of that community to renew itself. While the
vast majority of Biblical texts essentially present moral coherence as fealty
to the word of God, in the Book of Esther moral coherence is not overtly
presented as a function of God-centered activity. Rather, moral probity is
portrayed in the willingness to identify and oppose baseless evil (what in
today's parlance would be called a "hate crime") in circumstances that are
inconvenient and even dangerous. In that context, "estrangement," in the
sense highlighted by this book, is not understood as a sense of personal
discomfort or adolescent alienation; rather, it is the ability both to look at
oneself as one among many of the players that are on the scene, and to

11. An early depiction of just this approach to political power occurs in Genesis with the
description of the first identified strongman ruler, Nimrod: "Mighty . . . and the beginning of
his kingdom was Babylonia" (Gen. 10:8–12).

realize that the moral and political horizon stretches beyond the tip of one's own nose.[12]

In keeping with this understanding, the development of political discourse among the Israelites is depicted in the Bible as an ongoing exchange. The parameters of this discussion are not imposed from above, and no one leader ever is heralded as the quintessential arbiter of what this discourse should entail. In the course of this conversation, the essence of the ongoing source of national unity itself comes into question. At times, a kind of concord about this core principle seems to be tentatively established. At other times, however, national solidarity is expressed largely in the communal identification and alienation of particular groups, leading to their subsequent victimization. It is worth noting that this purposive estrangement allows the Israelites to project the very strangeness with which they are taxed by other peoples—Weber's "pariah" community—onto a part of their own society. In other words, as the Israelites are defined by other nations as an entity that is excised from accepted social and political communal bonds, the Bible depicts the Israelites themselves as excluding parts of their own community from themselves. The Bible alerts us to the fact that this purposive estrangement—the intentional act of rendering others alien—indicates more than the presence of a significant social/political problem. For the target group of this alienation, the feeling of estrangement can and does also serve as a valuable and critical vantage point. With this analysis, the Bible reveals itself as an ancient document that paradoxically—and uniquely—for its time addresses a central modern concern. In an era where nations are conceived as organically tied to their own portion of the earth (think of Socrates' description in *The Republic* of the myth in which citizens are to be [falsely] inculcated in the belief that they have emerged from the earth), the Bible opens up a new vista on all individuals and all nations as being (at least to some degree) fundamentally estranged. To be sure, the Bible indicates that this estrangement may (in some measure) be overcome, but this requires ongoing and dynamic interpersonal

12. An analogy from Rousseau's political writings may be helpful here: in *The Social Contract*, Rousseau understands the citizen to be constantly negotiating between his personal desires (the private interest) and his apprehension of what would be best for the community as a whole (the General Will). Importantly, the ideal citizen is not one who has destroyed all sense of self ("the good husband, the good father . . . make the good citizen"). *Émile*, bk. 5, in *Oeuvres complètes* (Paris: Gallimard, 1955–). See also Harold Bloom, *The Anxiety of Influence* (Oxford: Oxford University Press, 1973), 363. Rather, it is the ability to control these desires at the same time that promotes at once the best citizen and the most fulfilled individual.

interchange—even, and especially, with strangers—conducted in (existential) good faith.

Reading Biblical texts through the lens of nation formation helps the modern reader recognize the centrality of the Biblical narrative to the implications of political discourse for both communal life and personal existence. Not everyone today is interested in Bible stories, but the Biblical narrative as presented here makes us realize that, in its larger political ramifications, this text encapsulates the vicissitudes of modern political and personal struggle. Read as the complex document that it is, the Bible embodies not the untrammeled expression of arbitrary violence, but the development of humanity in all its varied incarnations.

A Note on Textual Hermeneutics

Paradoxically for what one might expect from such an ancient text, time has not settled the meaning of the Bible. The complicated implications of the text continue to arouse its readers, and even to incite multitudinous quarrels among them. One reason for this may well be that the Bible is often viewed as more than just a narrative presentation of events. Many readers see it also as a religious text commanding various aspects of belief/practice. Particularly (although not exclusively) in modern times, this has resulted in a peculiar, if largely unacknowledged, type of "test" that links the acceptance of a particular reading or interpretation of a Biblical text to the level and direction of the author's perceived commitment to the relevant belief system connected to the text. This "test" applies both to the traditionally "religious" or analytically "scholarly" types, as those terms are themselves variously glossed. In other words, the ostensible confessional approach of the writer of interpretational texts on the Bible is often taken as sufficient reason either to accept or, alternatively, to reject the particular reading advanced.[13] Far from resolving issues of interpretation, this attitude raises the question of why a belief system (of the author) should determine the textual interpretation (of a reader). Is the meaning of a text reducible

13. Thus, in one review of James Kugel's recent *How to Read the Bible* (New York: Free Press, 2007), the comments of the reviewer highlight Kugel's religious beliefs/practices at the very top of the review: "Kugel . . . *mark this, an Orthodox Jew*, aims to prove that you can read the Bible rationally [i.e., as 'the Bible is understood by modern scholars . . . Kugel points out the Bible's plagiarism from non-Israelite sources']." David Plotz, "Reading Is Believing, or Not," *New York Times Book Review*, September 16, 2007, 12; emphasis mine.

to just a matter of (dis)belief? Yet today, interpretational/critical works on the Bible are still routinely (if unconsciously) subjected to similar multi-pronged faith examinations: can the critical work be taken seriously if the author believes/rejects the Divine/multiply authored/multiply sourced origins of the Biblical text/s?

The critical perspective of my book derives from my lifelong study of the various Biblical texts, and particularly from the more recent changes within the enterprise of writing on the Biblical text. Many of these transformations embody central feminist concerns that have largely reshaped the field of Biblical hermeneutics. Some of the most imaginative writing on knotty Biblical issues in the past fifty years has been done by women, regardless of whether or not they are writing from a standpoint of faith: examples range from Phyllis Trible to Athalya Brenner to Mieke Bal. In my own modern Orthodox tradition, the newly public nature (and hence, the inevitable "discovery" of the political nature) of women's voices in the interpretation of important Biblical and legal texts central to religious/communal life is highlighted by a recent news article focusing on the advent of women to positions of religious and textual leadership.[14] In addition, previous years have also seen the publication of well-received, serious exegetical works by Orthodox women such as Nechama Leibowitz and, in a more literary style, Avivah Zornberg.

Thus, the themes that inform this book have grown out of my own engagement with texts. Like most works centering on complex discourses, the origins of my book are multiple in nature. My own writing on eighteenth-century political theory—particularly on the works of Rousseau, highlighting his distinctive contribution to the radical critique of tradition, democracy, and modernity—coupled with the study of its political texts that closely read specific Biblical narratives, have increased my awareness of the important role played by the Biblical text in the formation of modern political discourse. Similarly, the central part played by eighteenth-century political theory to the development of modern feminist discourse likewise reveals the significance of a proto-feminist sensibility in certain key Biblical texts, which allude to the conscious development of national identity, political dialogue, and discursive exchange.

As already noted, my engagement with Biblical texts has led me to comprehend them as fundamental to human concerns in areas of life that may not always have been identified with the traditionally understood "religious"

---

14. See, for example, Michael Luo, "An Orthodox Jewish Woman, and Soon, a Spiritual Leader," *New York Times*, August 21, 2006, B1.

sphere. Particularly in recent years, religiously motivated actors on the political scene have highlighted the centrality of the Biblical text to self-consciously political concerns. To a large degree, these actors have viewed the Enlightenment, conventionally seen as sundering religious and political concerns, as a baneful influence on human development (this is the point of Mark Lilla's recent *The Still-born God*).[15] In fact, while the Enlightenment separates religious *power* from political *might*, sensitive reading of Enlightenment texts, particularly those of Jean-Jacques Rousseau (probably the most misunderstood of Enlightenment philosophes in this area), demonstrates that the Enlightenment makes room for religious concerns, even while guaranteeing no one group an inevitable lock on political power. Lilla's more pessimistic view, stated in appropriately multicultural language, essentially recasts the discussion of politics and religion in a way that problematizes the philosophical acceptability of the universality of liberty. In so doing, he effectively cedes the discussion to those who view human freedom as little more than culturally tangential.

Similarly, although it is conventionally assumed that modernist critical concerns and classical Biblical commentaries are mutually contradictory, I have found that both methods are rooted in an enduring search for meaning that views the life of Biblical texts as embodied in unending, active interpretation. To the extent that the details of these various readings may differ from and even contradict one another, their dissonances serve to highlight the more nuanced approach of the Bible itself—which is often more subtle than those offered by more contemporary commentators— to the issues that continue to energize and bedevil contemporary culture and politics. Although the provenance of the interpretational sources utilized in this book ranges widely—historically and religiously, these may emerge from oppositional belief systems—they as often respond with great sensitivity and in not incongruous ways to the linguistic and substantive issues laid out by the text. This book concentrates on the larger political understandings undergirding the Biblical text, particularly in the demonstrated linkage of long-term political survival to the continuous examination and extension of political discourse. Consequently, I take seriously the current political implications of this theoretical understanding of the Biblical text. These implications are what renders the Biblical text perennially relevant and consistently insightful even, and especially, in contemporary times.

15. Mark Lilla, *The Still-born God* (New York: Knopf, 2007).

The novelty of my book is to foreground the Biblical presentation of political discourse as central to constituting a nation, and to do this in a way that highlights the centrality of political issues like political responsibility, communal discourse, and moral/intellectual autonomy, topics that are conventionally seen as belonging to the democratic tradition rather than to a Biblical/religious one. And that is precisely the point. The mutually exclusive designations of conventional thinking are the product of powerful interests reading the Bible, rather than a true reflection of the concerns of the Biblical text itself. The Bible, even if not recognized as such, forms an integral part of current political discourse; it deserves to be made accessible to everyone who holds a stake in its consequences.

I

JOSEPH: THE POLITICS OF DREAMING

Conventional thought for the most part classifies dreams as having little connection with the empirical politics of nationhood: viewed as nothing more than imaginative ephemera, dreams do not seem to have anything to contribute to the concrete challenges of political reality. The Biblical narrative, however, interrogates this standard divide between what is commonly understood as "real" and what is taken to be "imaginary." In the story of one of the most prolific dreamers of the Bible, the Biblical text advances a new understanding of the process of shaping a nation as it is realized in the development of the Children of Israel.

As this chronicle unfolds, we are introduced not to a (prototypical) nation, but to a troubled family. The length of this narrative focusing on the story of Joseph and his brothers—it occupies fully one-third of the Book of Genesis—seems to indicate its centrality within the Biblical text. For the most part, however, this story has been construed largely as backward looking and summarizing: traditionally, Joseph has been described as the last of the patriarchs, a figure whose life and fortunes bring to a close the patriarchal era of the development of the Israelite nation.[1] For critics

---

1. See, for example, Ackerman's "Joseph, Judah, and Jacob," where he mentions "the theme of favoritism" as a theme running through Genesis (96). Like most commentaries on Genesis, Lowenthal's *The Joseph Narrative in Genesis* does not even consider the Joseph story in any relationship except to his family and patriarchal forebears. In a similar vein, Sarna's *Understanding Genesis* considers the Joseph narrative to be one of the "patriarchal biographies" (211). Von Rad's *Genesis: A Commentary* also classifies the Joseph story as part of the "Biblical patriarchal history" (347). Westermann's *Genesis: A Practical Commentary* specifically divides the Joseph story from the patriarchal history (255–56). James S. Ackerman, "Joseph,

following the redactional hypothesis, the tendency is to attribute the Joseph story to Israel's wisdom literature and to describe it as a self-contained "novella," all the while not neglecting to point out the various places in which the P, E, and J narratives intertwine or become detached from one another.[2] For their part, the more contemporary self-proclaimed "literary critics" view the Joseph saga as a stylistically and psychologically integrated whole, but they still present the story's major import as the resolution of the personal themes and questions first adumbrated in earlier parts of Genesis.[3] This emphasis seems to emanate from the story itself, which is apparently nothing more than the account of a dysfunctional family, or, in Freud's terms, a family romance gone wrong. In this context, the resolution of these issues, allowing the members of Jacob's family to live in harmony once again, is no small accomplishment. Indeed, if Genesis were just an anthropological account of early families on this planet, this in itself would suffice to render it an important object of study.

Genesis, however, purports to be more than just a family history of personal interrelationships. It quite clearly proclaims itself to be the historic overture to the formation of a textually described, Divinely established

---

Judah, and Jacob," in *Literary Interpretations of Biblical Narratives*, ed. Kenneth R. R. Gros Louis, vol. 2 (Nashville: Abingdon, 1992); Eric Lowenthal, *The Joseph Narrative in Genesis* (New York: Ktav, 1973); Nahum Sarna, *Understanding Genesis* (New York: McGraw-Hill, 1966), 211; Gerhard von Rad, *Genesis: A Commentary* (Philadelphia: Westminster, 1972); Claus Westermann, *Genesis: A Practical Commentary*, trans. David E. Green (Grand Rapids, Mich.: Eerdmans, 1987).

2. Westermann, *Genesis*, 257; von Rad, *Genesis*, 347–48, 386, 402–4, 406–8, 414–19, 429–36. Cf. E. A. Speiser, ed., *The Anchor Bible: Genesis* (New York: Doubleday, 1964), especially 292–94, 299–302, 303–4, 307–8, 315–17, 318–20, 329–30, 334–35, 339–41, 346–47, 352–53, 358–60, 370–72, 377–78. As can be seen, Speiser reports on nearly every verse with what he considers its documentary provenance.

3. Thus, Ackerman points to the literary and psychological unity of the Joseph story as a primary starting point for its interpretation (specifically not dealing with the alternate explanation offered by the documentary hypothesis). "Joseph, Judah, and Jacob," 85. Similarly, Robert Alter focuses on the technique of repetition (and its use in the Joseph story) as an example of the "ultimate coherence of meaning through language." *The Art of Biblical Narrative* (New York: Basic, 1981), 112. Without really entering into the question of the relevance of the Joseph story to the larger national implications of the Biblical narrative, Meir Sternberg utilizes his subtle analysis of Biblical literary technique to focus on the psychological motivations of Joseph and the relationship to his brothers. *The Poetics of Biblical Narrative* (1985; Bloomington: Indiana University Press, 1987). (Sternberg's repeated emphasis on "Biblical indeterminacy" is more of a theme regarding the moral implications of Biblical literary technique than a commentary on the relationship of the Joseph story to the national corporate identity of the Children of Israel.) James L. Kugel concentrates on the interpretive life of Biblical texts, focusing primarily on those interpretive glosses that detail Joseph's beauty,

nation.[4] But that aspect of Genesis is largely absent from the critical literature focusing on the Joseph narrative.[5] There seems to be no sustained analysis of the relationship of this narrative to the larger saga of which it forms a part: the development of the Israelite nation as a self-conscious people with a specific role to play in social and political affairs.

This chapter starts where the aforementioned commentaries on the Joseph story leave off, demonstrating that the Joseph saga occupies a central place in the narrative of the development of national self-consciousness. To this end, I analyze Joseph's contribution to the moral and political formation of the Israelite nation.[6] In view of the prominent place that the Joseph narrative occupies in the Genesis text, this is an issue of no small moment.

It is easy to understand the Joseph story merely as providing the historical and geographical background to explain the foreign location of the Children of Israel preparatory to their liberation from Egypt.[7] This approach by itself, however, does not explain Joseph's historical and political impact on his people, because it does not take into account the ending of the Book of Genesis. Significantly, this narrative does not terminate at the time that Jacob collectively blesses his sons, which itself emphasizes their existence not just as a family, but also as a larger, corporate grouping. Instead, the final verses of Genesis detail both the tentative nature of the

---

attraction to women, and actual predilection to sin (with Potiphar's wife). Interestingly, even when dealing with the question of Joseph's bones, Kugel chooses to limit himself exclusively to when and how Joseph's bones are finally taken out of Egypt rather than considering the differing political implications attaching to each interpretational choice. "Inaccessible Bones," in *In Potiphar's House* (1990; Cambridge, Mass.: Harvard University Press, 1994), 125–55. Thus, for example, the difference between a mere "forgetting of Joseph's bones" (the version of the Tebat Marqa) and their absence provoking a halting of the redemptive process (according to the version of Mekhilta Beshallah 1) can be understood as diametrically different approaches to the future national implications of taking Joseph's bones up from Egypt.

4. In Gen. 12:2, God promises Abraham that his descendants will form "a great nation."

5. This is not to say that hints in that direction are not provided. For example, Westermann, *Genesis*, remarks that the Joseph story is pre-monarchical and reflects the "author's attitude towards the conflict of his own day, the rejection or affirmation of monarchy at the time of its beginnings in Israel" (336). Similarly, in *Narration and Discourse in the Book of Genesis* (Cambridge: Cambridge University Press, 1991), Hugh C. White writes of the Joseph story as providing a reconciliation between the familial perspective of the patriarchal period with the political perspective of the monarchical state (235). These authors, however, do not explore the implications of these statements.

6. Aspects of the Biblical treatment of political power and hierarchy are dealt with in subsequent chapters.

7. An important textual support for this approach is that the Biblical text introduces the enslaving Pharaoh as the ruler "who did not know Joseph" (Exod. 1:8).

relationship between the brothers and Joseph, and the palpable unease and lack of frankness among them. In other words, the ending of Genesis indicates that it is the unfinished business between Joseph and his brothers that forms the real drama of the story. This conflict will presumably come to closure when their future descendants physically (perhaps forcibly) fulfill Joseph's deathbed charge to liberate his bones from interment in Egypt and return them to their (common) ancestral land (Gen. 50:25). The last spoken words in the Book of Genesis are Joseph's charge regarding a future time in altered circumstances: on his deathbed, Joseph presages a future when his and his brothers' descendants will retain a common memory of the promise exacted by Joseph. The projected fulfillment of that promise is based on the development of a common identity and the hoped-for realization of a shared destiny (the eventual interment of Joseph's bones in Canaan presupposes the Israelite return to and conquest of their ancestral land). Thus, the ending of Genesis indicates that the guiding theme of the Joseph narrative all along has been Joseph's larger project to transform the band of quarrelling brothers into a unified nation. In concentrating on Joseph's contribution to the formation of that nation, it is apparent that the concept of Israelite nationhood derives its provenance from more than one source: in its historical expression, Joseph's contribution to the self-conscious awareness of Israelite nationhood becomes fully operational in the context of a different conception of leadership, embodied by his brother Judah.

At first glance, the claim that Joseph makes a unique contribution to the formation of Israelite nationhood seems counterintuitive, both in terms of the historical milieu against which the Joseph narrative takes place, as well as the psychological makeup of the main actors in the unfolding drama. First, the Biblical text depicts God, and not any particular set of human beings, as instituting the Israelite nation: Abraham, in particular, is informed that he will become a great nation, blessed by God (Gen. 12:2–3). Subsequent to this promise, Abraham's life—and, to a large extent, Isaac's as well—is portrayed as bound up with the minute details of survival in a strange, new land, embroiled in the political complications of local power struggles. In this context, the small size of the Abrahamitic clan seems further to mitigate against its national realization: in the cases of both Abraham and Isaac, only one son is chosen to carry on the task of engendering God's select nation. Larger issues relating to population growth and the accommodation of different personality strands become salient only with the appearance of Jacob's twelve sons, whose recorded births and names indicate their importance within the new nation-in-formation. It is precisely at this point, however, that the text falls curiously silent regarding the larger national destiny of the family. Jacob exhibits few overt signs of transmitting his sense of national future or of nation building to his sons: on the contrary, it is at this juncture that Jacob's family is shown to be riven with strife and jealousy, directed mainly at Jacob's favored son, Joseph.[8] In that connection, it seems additionally strange to highlight *Joseph's* role in formulating Israelite self-conscious awareness as a nation: he seems instead to provoke increasing hatred and division within the family proclaimed to be the nucleus of that new nation.

In the plethora of seemingly inconsequent detail in the depiction of the mature development of Jacob's family, the Biblical text offers us one clue regarding the larger extent of Joseph's enterprise.[9] This appears in the guise of a destabilizing and strange new structural element: the recounting of Joseph's dreams, which, as we will see, do more than propel the narrative strand of the story. In addition, these dreams have an important part to play in Joseph's own political development as he deals with both friend and foe, in his native land and on foreign soil. In essence, dreams, and the dissonances that they evoke, furnish Joseph with the opportunity to grow into a statesman.

The Presentation of Dreams

Particularly striking about Joseph's first dreams is that they are very short, described in a few terse phrases: the brothers' sheaves bow to Joseph's sheaf (the first dream, Gen. 37:7); and the sun, moon, and eleven stars bow down to Joseph himself (the second dream, Gen. 37:9). It is not hard to account for this brevity: nothing much happens in either dream. One dominant image overrides each dream (the bowing sheaves, the bowing celestial bodies), and that single action seems to be a continuous one, endlessly repeating itself until cut off by the brothers' scornful reaction.[10] Joseph's

---

8. "And they could not speak to him peacefully" (Gen. 37:4).

9. "Mature" is used in this context to indicate that all of Jacob's progeny have now been born: all subsequent development will proceed from people already placed within the family.

10. This occurs after the first dream of the sheaves, when the brothers immediately surmise that this dream is about Joseph's projected wish to rule over them (Gen. 37:8).

dreams are characterized by their imagic/iconic quality, focusing on the repetition of one image.[11] It is the apparent simplicity of the dreams that seems to indicate that not much interpretation is necessary at all: Joseph appears to predict his future dominance over all of his brothers, and even over his father.[12] Perhaps due to the selfishness of youth, Joseph does not seem much disturbed by the notion of his future ascendancy, but both his brothers and his father (for different reasons) denigrate what looks like Joseph's idea of self-aggrandizement.[13]

At any rate, it is clear that these dreams get Joseph into trouble, not least because the dreams identify him as obviously different and even strange: when plotting to kill him, the brothers identify Joseph derisively as the "dream expert."[14] In this context, it is surprising to find that dreams also serve as the vehicle that gets Joseph out of trouble. To be sure, this does not happen right away.[15] At first, even Joseph's hard-won success as a superior servant (slave?) in Potiphar's house seems imperiled, as Joseph is falsely accused and once again jailed (the first time that Joseph is incarcerated, it is in a pit in the field). It is there that he meets with Pharaoh's Chief Butler and Chief Baker and develops the opportunity to interpret their dreams. But there are some crucial differences that distinguish the

11. The grammatical hint for this is the dreams' verbal structure in the present continuous "v'hinei anahnu m'almim" (37:7) and "mishtahavim" (37:9). Compare the Butler's dream, where the verbs are structured in the future pluperfect (with "vav ha'hipukh"), denoting the finite past ("va'ekah; va'esh'hat; va'etain," 40:11). The term *iconic* is perhaps best explicated by the word *imagic*. I use iconic here to denote the concept of a static image lacking the dynamics of development and change. To the extent that an icon may also be understood as symbolic and hence allude precisely to the multilayered connotations inherent in any one particular image, I have also appended the term imagic. I am grateful to Professor Harvey Hix (Kansas City Art Institute) for his comments on the potential complexity denoted by the term iconic.

12. The meaning of the dream appears to be so clear that the text records not one moment of conscious/directed interpretation: the brothers merely tax Joseph with the implications of what must be the dream's "obvious" import.

13. White, *Narration and Discourse*, 258.

14. The term used, "ba'al hahalomot," is itself modified by the derogatory identifying adjective "halozeh'" (Gen. 37:19).

15. The Book of Genesis recounts that after Joseph is forcibly thrown (by his brothers, particularly Simeon) into the pit, he is sold into slavery in Egypt to the highly placed Potiphar (Pharaoh's Chief Executioner). Joseph does well there and is eventually entrusted with running the entire household. Joseph's refusal to respond positively to the amorous advances of his master's wife, however, lands him again in prison, this time on the trumped-up charge of attempted rape. Joseph's accurate interpretation of the dreams of Pharaoh's Chief Butler and Chief Baker while in prison eventually brings him to the attention of Pharaoh himself, when that monarch is similarly puzzled by a dream that proves crucial to his own and Egypt's future well-being.

episode here from Joseph's first pair of dreams.[16] First, there is an intricacy in the structure of these new dreams: in the Butler's dream, he is busy doing his job; in the Baker's dream, the birds are busy undoing the fruits of his labors. Second, this complexity denotes a process: these dreams are not static repetitions of iconic images. Instead, things develop and consequently change. Third, as a result of these alterations, tangible implications are attached to these dreams: they announce important life transformations for their protagonists. Finally, unlike the situation with his brothers, Joseph does not have to beg his audience to listen to him.[17] Instead, the Butler and Baker willingly recite their mysterious dreams.

But this point is not as simple as it might appear. Perhaps intuitively sensing the importance of the feelings of others for improving his own personal welfare, Joseph carefully prepares the ground to facilitate the opening up to him of these strangers, upper servants in the royal court whose prejudices against slaves and Israelites were well known.[18] The text records that Joseph carefully observes their moods as reflected in their facial expressions before asking them what the matter is. Unlike his manner with his brothers, Joseph does not immediately demand to express his personal understanding of things ("please hear my dream") but waits for them to express their own sense of the problem. Upon hearing what the matter is, Joseph additionally refrains from turning the spotlight on his own familiarity with dreams. Rather, Joseph invokes God as the possessor of all knowledge: his role, Joseph suggests, is to be merely the medium through which the correct interpretation may become known.[19] Unlike the first set of dreams, neither the dreams nor their interpretations ostensibly center on Joseph. The irony just below the surface of the text is that of course, these dreams—like all dreams in the Joseph narrative—are really all about Joseph.

In a roundabout way, it is this second set of dreams that eventually brings Joseph to the attention of Pharaoh. The story becomes a bit complex: the rehabilitated Butler does not, as promised, remember Joseph

16. Ackerman has noted the pattern of doubling in the Joseph story: Joseph dreams two dreams, he interprets two dreams in jail, and Pharaoh dreams doubly (or experiences a double dream). "Joseph, Judah, and Jacob," 85–86.

17. "Please listen/hear" (Gen. 37:6).

18. Cf. Gen. 43:32: "For the Egyptians could not eat with the Israelites because it was an abomination for them." In a similar vein is the Chief Butler's dismissive recollection of Joseph as "a young Israelite slave" (41:12).

19. "Does not God possess all interpretations/solutions? Please tell me" (Gen. 40:8).

and try to get him out of his (unjust) prison term. Instead, it is Pharaoh's unsolved riddle of a dream that jogs the Butler's memory regarding the unpleasant time when he himself was in prison, fearing for his life, and was subjected to a mysterious dream whose incomprehensibility further depressed him. The text emphasizes the repetitive quality of Pharaoh's dream right from the start. Grammatically, the term "miketz" (Gen. 41:1) denotes a continuous action taking place over a period of time: in this case, Pharaoh had been having this inexplicable dream for two years.[20] The point is further emphasized by the use of the present continuous ("holem") to depict the action of dreaming. The text unravels for us the content of the dream as Pharaoh dreams it:

> Pharaoh was dreaming a dream: and behold seven fine-looking cows go up from the river and pastured in the meadow/reed grass. And behold, seven other cows of bad appearance and lean flesh go up after them from the river, and stand next to the cows on the river bank. And the ill-looking, lean-fleshed cows ate the seven fine-looking, healthy cows, and Pharaoh awoke. And he slept and dreamt a second time, and behold seven good and plump ears of corn grow out of one stalk. And behold, seven ears of corn; thin and blasted by the east wind, sprang up after them. And the seven thin ears of corn swallowed the seven good and full ears of corn. Pharaoh awakened and behold, it is/has been a dream. (Gen. 41:1–7)

Although Pharaoh calls for both wise men and magicians to explicate his dream, nobody makes use of their talents in a way that satisfies Pharaoh's own sense of the dream.[21] Sensitive to the subtle nuances of the language utilized by the text, the Midrash points out that in fact Pharaoh's advisors and magicians do proffer their own interpretations of these dreams. Explaining each dream on its own, they proclaim that the seven healthy cows represent seven daughters that will be born to Pharaoh, while the seven emaciated cows represent the ultimate demise of those daughters.[22] Similarly, the seven full stalks of grain represent seven kingdoms that Pharaoh

---

20. Cf. Ohr haHayim on Gen. 41:2: "And Pharaoh is dreaming/*u'Phar'o holem.*"

21. "*V'ein poter otam l'Phar'o*/and no one could explain them [the dreams] *to Pharaoh*" (Gen. 41:8; emphasis mine).

22. How disconcerting to remark that the bovine imagery of womankind has its roots so far back in the ancient world!

will conquer, while the seven shriveled stalks represent his loss of those same seven kingdoms (Bereshit Rabbah 89:6, on Gen. 41:1).

Why does this interpretation not satisfy Pharaoh? For one thing, while the advisors' and magicians' explanations retain a superficial connection to Pharaoh's original dream (particularly in terms of the number seven), they do not explain its dynamics at all. Pharaoh's dream describes a process where things change: the cows move and the stalks grow; in addition, the situation of both is then materially altered. The advisors and magicians, on the other hand, reduce the dream to flat images: daughters are born and subsequently die, kingdoms come and kingdoms go. The court sorcerers' simplistic reduction of the elements of Pharaoh's dream—the strange transformations of cows and grains—to events that could be easily anticipated either in the personal or in the political life cycle, where both progeny and colonies are subject to loss, leads them to interpret the dreams superficially. Their error in logic—they advocate differences without distinctions—leads them to neglect Pharaoh's real concerns, as expressed in his dream. As a result, Pharaoh rejects their official explanation.

But images and the numbers connected with them do not form the substance of Pharaoh's distress: "Pharaoh was standing on the *y'or* [lit. river]."[23] Joseph's sensitivity to Pharaoh's self-awareness in the dream is precisely where Joseph distinguishes himself both from the other would-be interpreters and, significantly, from the more youthful version of himself as dreamer/interpreter. Joseph understands that Pharaoh's perception of himself in the dream will not only color his own perception of that dream, but it will also materially indicate the major theme of the dream and thus its accurate and accepted interpretation. Pharaoh's location near the river in his dream indicates not just Pharaoh's physical placement, but also his political preoccupation. The "y'or" as delineated in the dream is not just any river: its use in the Bible refers specifically to the Nile (Bereshit Rabbah 89:3, on Gen. 41:1). Moreover, in Egypt, the Nile embodies not just any waterway: it is *the* principal and dominant river, the source of

23. It is important to note that the issue of dominance (which, as revealed in his location, is so central for Pharaoh) is craftily hidden from Joseph as Pharaoh (with certain small but crucial changes) recounts his dream. In the version recited for Joseph, Pharaoh notes his location as being "on the banks of the river" (Gen. 41:17). Joseph, however, is aware of the physical situation of the dream and is able to express it as a function of Pharaoh's real query. For that reason, Pharaoh will characterize him not only as wise ("hakham," 41:39) but also as understanding ("navon," ibid.), which in traditional parlance indicates "deriving one thing from another/*meivin davar mitokh davar.*" Cf. Rashi on Exod. 31:50 [Ki Tisa]. Also cf. TB Hagiga 14a, Sanhedrin 93b.

Egypt's economic wealth and hence political power. Underlining this point, the ancient Egyptians worshipped the Nile as a Divinity. All of these concerns dominate Pharaoh's mind in his dream, where he is standing on/over ("'al") the Nile. For Pharaoh, the major question to be answered concerns the stability and the extent of his own power: "Will I be dominant over the Nile—Egypt's economic and religious life-force—or, alternatively, will the Nile dominate me?"[24]

Joseph's highly calibrated sensitivity to the intellectual questions of other people as developed in his prison encounters with the Chief Butler and the Chief Baker stands him here in good stead. Joseph takes his cue from Pharaoh (41:25), who always insists that his dream is a unified whole (the noun he consistently uses is in the singular; see 41:7). He thus deliberately rejects the sorcerers' insistence that he had dreamed two separate dreams, with which concept they justify their doubled reductive explanation of bad tidings. Like Pharaoh, Joseph agrees that the images of the one dream contain a unified message. But unlike the official court interpreters, Joseph is not paralyzed by the iconic imagery of the dream. He is able to integrate the process depicted by the dream into his interpretation. Instead of viewing the dream just as a series of images to be manipulated by its interpreter, Joseph understands the dream as a key to a greater comprehension of life's challenges. In other words, Joseph has progressed from seeing a dream as a simple repetition of one idea, or image, to a subtler notion of the dream as metaphorical text—that is, something that incorporates multiple levels of meaning and signification.

The results of this crucial development of Joseph's are seen first on the theoretical level, then on the moral. This explains why Joseph proffers his own (seemingly unrequested) solution to the problematic situation (the upcoming seven years of plenty and seven years of famine) foreshadowed by the dream. After all, reasons Joseph, if Pharaoh's concern is with his own political power, and if this dream represents not (just) one uniform image but (also) a metaphorical text to be deciphered on several levels, then he (Joseph) is obligated to furnish not just an explanation for a dream, but also a solution to a problem. This motivates Joseph's suggestion of food

24. This point also explains why Joseph's recommendation of centralized state economic power was "pleasing to Pharaoh and all his servants" (Gen. 41:37), even though, as Wildavsky points out, by this suggestion Joseph may well have prepared the way for a more diabolical Pharaoh to organize state-sponsored oppression of the Israelites. Aaron Wildavsky, "What Is to Be Done so That This People May Survive: Joseph the Administrator," *PS* (December 1989): 779–99.

storage and centralized economic planning. The vocabulary used by the text supports just this understanding of dreams as problem texts to be deciphered: in Biblical Hebrew, the term for explanation is *bi'ur*, which is not used here in connection with dream interpretation.[25] Rather, in interpreting Pharaoh's dream, the Biblical text utilizes the term "pitaron," which actually means solution to a problem. This choice of word also explains why Pharaoh is sensitive to Joseph's intellectual gifts, in particular his inferential ability ("navon"; see 41:39).

(En)visioning a Nation

This understanding of Joseph and the dreams that he interprets signals that Joseph undergoes a process of intellectual and moral growth throughout the years of dream interpretation. But how is this related to the larger enterprise within Genesis: the formation of a nation? The answer begins to become apparent in the masked encounters that Joseph stages with his brothers.

It is easy to assume that Joseph's elaborate deception of his brothers at the Egyptian court is part of a well-planned revenge for their previous ill-treatment of him.[26] But this alone cannot explain Joseph's desire to see his younger full brother Benjamin and his concomitant wish to discover whether the family dynamics regarding the sons of the favorite wife (Rachel) had positively altered.[27] Joseph has a dual aim in setting up the stylized

25. The root "b'a'r" is in fact utilized in the Pentateuch to depict a full interpretation, as in Deut. 1:5, when Moses is described as "clearly explaining this Torah."

26. Sternberg, *The Poetics of Biblical Narrative*, 288.

27. To this end, Joseph keeps only one brother in prison (Simeon, who in Midrashic tradition is identified as the brother who had actually pushed Joseph into the pit; cf. Rashi on Gen. 42:24 and Mizrahi gloss) so as to enable most of the brothers to go home bearing enough food to feed their extended families (this larger point is made by Sternberg, *The Poetics of Biblical Narrative*, 290). The Midrashic understanding of why Simeon was singled out by Joseph prefigures Joseph's later stance in reinterpreting the communal events of the relationship between him and his brothers, with its consequent life-transforming implications. That is to say, in both cases reinterpretation goes on in order to endow present, seemingly arbitrary, circumstances with a semblance of comprehensibility. Thus, for the Midrash, the need to explain why it is Simeon and not any other brother who is put in chains leads to the recognition that in fact this is not an arbitrary choice on Joseph's part. The singling out of Simeon is deliberately orchestrated to trigger the brothers' realization that the captivity of a brother— any brother—is not something to "get beyond," but rather should stimulate (as it eventually does) a collective sense of communal responsibility to redress the situation. In this sense, Joseph offers to his brothers the opportunity to demonstrate that they have indeed gone

encounters with his brothers. First, he wishes to discover whether the conditions for true resolution with his family can exist, because in his opinion a true reconciliation with his family becomes possible only if all family members have managed to overcome the hatred and jealousy that had up till now divided them.[28] Furthermore, Joseph wishes to ascertain whether the sons of Jacob could fulfill their national destiny of becoming the Children of Israel. In that context, it is crucial to overcome the hatred that had characterized the internal relations of this family, because the future existence of the Children of Israel as a nation would be assured only if these sons of Jacob could learn to overcome their past and act in concert to create a dynamic context for their future communal existence.[29]

To find out whether this national goal is at all feasible, Joseph must act on two levels. On the psychological level, Joseph must clarify the emotional forces that motivate his family. To do this, he recreates the situation of twenty-two years before that had resulted in his being "thrown into the pit."[30] Joseph fabricates a false accusation against his brothers, which forcibly recalls to them their own resentment of Joseph as an in-house spy when he bore tales of their bad behavior to their father, Jacob.[31] Joseph further insists on Benjamin's presence to see whether this youngest remaining son of their father—and hence the acknowledged favorite of a man who

---

beyond their former situation of internecine quarrelling and enmity. He offers them the chance literally to reexperience their past by recalibrating their previous responses. In much the same manner, Joseph's insistence that all of their past history, even those actions motivated by hatred on the part of the brothers, was actually engineered by God to provide for the greater common good similarly partakes of the idea that ultimate meaning depends less on "facts" as they are experienced than on experiences as they are (re)interpreted. Put another way, the human drive to interpret—the vagaries of life, the actions of other people—can be understood not (just) as the fetishization of the concrete aspects of life into an overarching text, but also as integral to the human quest for meaning, which Joseph and the Midrash, each in their own time, choose to interpret as a purposive aspect of the Divine. This approach is consonant with the Midrashic interpretation of the entire creation process, which understands the very first word of the Bible ("Bereshit") as signifying the purpose for which God engineers the creation (cf. Bereshit Rabbah 1:4). I am grateful to Professor Leslie Brisman (Yale University) for pointing out to me the connection between the interpretations of history offered respectively by Joseph and the Midrash.

28. Cf. Abarbanel on Gen. 42–43. Robert Alter expresses a similar sense in *The Art of Biblical Narrative:* "It is really the first of three climactic dialogues . . . about their shared past and the nature of their fraternal bond" (164).

29. Cf. in this regard White's comments in *Narration and Discourse*, 268–69.

30. Cf. Gen. 37:24: "And they threw him into the pit/*va'yashlikhu oto habora*"; and Gen. 40:15: "That they have placed me in the pit/*ki samu oti babor.*"

31. Sternberg, *The Poetics of Biblical Narrative*, 288. The verse referred to is Gen. 37:1, in which he brought to their father "bad tales/*et dibatam ra'ah.*"

himself had occupied the position of younger son in his family of origin—is likewise the object of murderous hatred. Finally, Joseph arranges for Benjamin to be accused of stealing Joseph's silver "divination" goblet, and thus apparently be destined to spend the rest of his life as a slave to the enigmatic vizier of Egypt. In all of these trials, particularly the last two, Joseph's aim is to ascertain whether the brothers still resent the (current) favorite son enough to leave him to his fate at their first opportunity.[32]

By the time that the brothers return to purchase food again in Egypt, Joseph has already seen that the brothers are capable of living amicably with one another and that they are not divided, as they once were, by internal hatred and jealousy. This is proved by the fact that it is Judah, the brother who had instigated the process of Joseph's sale into slavery, who now offers himself up as a slave in place of the current favorite son, Benjamin.[33]

But now Joseph is faced with another question: can his brothers fulfill their national destiny? To answer this question, Joseph functions on a second, historical level. This operation, however, does not concentrate on physical activities. Rather, it emphasizes discourse—the way that people establish a common set of meanings in order to engage in dialogue with each other. In a basic sense, however, this formulation merely begs the question: how does one go about establishing a conversation between the very individuals whose enmity has led them to plot against each other? How can individuals whose present circumstances testify to their past murderous feelings plan a common future? The continued presence of the destructive emotions of the past seems to pose an insuperable obstacle to Joseph's desire to recalibrate their communal existence. At first glance, using the powers of speech—which is to say, conversation and interpretation—to achieve unity among Jacob's sons seems to exacerbate the problem. Joseph's work as an interpreter has always been a solitary enterprise, both strange and estranging, highlighting the divide between the two worlds—the worlds of the dream and of the audience whom he must inform of the dream's meaning—instead of cementing the link connecting them.[34]

32. In putting forth this understanding of Joseph's testing of his brothers, Sternberg argues that Joseph's return of the purchase price of the food to the brothers has precisely this goal in mind: to see whether the brothers will take the opportunity to argue that they are helpless to prevent their unfortunate brother's fate and wind up both getting rid of the unwanted sibling and, as in Joseph's case, keeping their ill-gotten gains. *The Poetics of Biblical Narrative*, 293.

33. Ibid., 308.

34. Hugo C. White describes Joseph as a "solitary hermeneut existing between alienated worlds of discourse." *Narration and Discourse*, 240.

Now, however, Joseph's use of his interpretational powers is motivated by a different goal. Instead of using his abilities to emphasize his own view of the world, Joseph now utilizes his powers of explication to build a communal bridge of understanding. Joseph comes to realize that the very means of his alienation from his brothers—his ability to bestow meaning on seemingly insignificant items—may also serve as the instrument of their reconciliation. Ironically enough, he perceives this at the very moment that an old dream of his appears to be fulfilled: his brothers' bowing down before him. Instead of adhering to the conventional view of this moment, which understands this scene as the impetus for Joseph's well-planned revenge against his brothers, we may posit that the sight of his brothers bowing before him inspires Joseph to remember the dreams he had recounted to them—not as a model for vengeance, but rather as a *negative* example *to be avoided*, an example of how *not* to communicate to others his own sense of truth.[35] In other words, when Joseph remembers his dreams, it is not with self-satisfied elation at their purported fulfillment (the brothers are, after all, bowing down to him), but rather with a sense of regret at the extent of destructive feelings that were unleashed as a result of the manner of their recitation.[36] Joseph further capitalizes on this insight by learning from this negative example how to create, instead, a model of a positive, shared discourse.

Joseph understands that his task is not easy: he must create the possibility of discourse among people who have not only been isolated from one another, but whose only shared memories are mutually destructive. Joseph must therefore reconstruct his family's shattered past. But he is faced with a dilemma: how is it possible to change the actual facts of the past? Joseph's experience with dream interpretation has taught him that events themselves cannot be altered. What can change, however, is the way that this past functions in the present and thereby affects the future. In other words, the *meaning* of past events can be fundamentally revised. What is called for is not the negation of past events, but their reinterpretation.

35. Sternberg, *The Poetics of Biblical Narrative*, 290–91, 294. "And Joseph remembered the dreams that he had dreamed about them/recounted to them/*asher halam lahem*" (Gen. 42:9). Following the Hebrew text, we may understand the preposition "lahem" as alluding to not simply the dreams that Joseph had dreamt about them *'aleihem*—that is, regarding his brothers, as Rashi's commentary on this verse has it. Rather, this can be understood as indicating the dreams that he had dreamt *bishvilam*—that is, for them, with them as the subject, or even the beneficiaries, of the dream. For this relational and future-oriented approach to the dreams, cf. Ohr HaHayim on Gen. 37:51: "And Joseph dreamt a dream/*vayahalom Yosef halom*."

36. "And Joseph remembered the dreams that he had dreamt (about them)" (Gen. 42:9).

By reinterpreting past events, attributing to them meanings other than those apparent to the eyes even of those who had also lived through them, Joseph succeeds in making the past function in unexpected and creative ways. "Do not be saddened and angered that you sold me," Joseph tells his brothers. "For *God* sent me before you for the purposes of ensuring life/providing foodstuffs" (Gen. 45:5; emphasis mine). Joseph's repeated invocation of God is not (just) a pious declaration of fealty to the Divine, although the text makes clear that, from the time of his enforced captivity in Egypt, Joseph is careful to attribute to God all of his success in dream interpretation.[37] Rather, this also represents Joseph's re-visioning of past history. Significantly, this new look at the past is not a whitewash of earlier events: it neither excuses the bad intentions of the brothers nor pretends that these did not ever take place. Instead, Joseph makes the implicit argument that despite the felt motives for particular human actions at specific moments in time, the actual implications of these acts play out on another scale. In other words, Joseph utilizes history not for the purpose of allocating blame to specific individuals/events, but in order to emphasize that the larger implications of history are not (only) a function of individual motivation.[38] Joseph's reworking/rejudging of history underscores the fact that badly intentioned acts may yield good outcomes, and it is these positive elements that are critical to the construction of the national identity of the Children of Israel.

Joseph undertakes a revision of the past—he changes it—by re-visioning it, by looking at it anew. He thus succeeds in liberating the past from its superficially iconic state, which attributes to actions and events only one meaning. This attitude is paralyzing, because it assumes that all relationships and outcomes are predestined.[39] According to Joseph's new interpretation,

37. Cf. Rashi on Gen. 39:5. See also 39:9, 40:8, 41:16.

38. This point is validated in the text through the particular nomenclature of God invoked by Joseph as the ultimate authority and guide over all the events that have occurred to him and to his brothers. Joseph consistently uses the term "Elohim" (Gen. 45:5, 7–9), which, in the Biblical text, also connotes "judge" (as utilized, for example, in Exod. 21:6; 22:7).

39. Cf. the discussion in Susan Handelman's *The Slayers of Moses* regarding the divide between Greek and Rabbinic thought, particularly as these differentiate between seeing (an image, for example, as in Greek thought) and hearing (a discourse/text, as in Rabbinic thought). See particularly the chapters on "Greek Philosophy and the Overcoming of the Word," especially 10–21, and "Rabbinic Thought: The Divinity of the Text," especially 34–50; see also 51–82. In Handelman's words, "Rabbinic thought developed the doctrine of *polysemy* as opposed to *polytheism:* the multiple meanings that may be heard or read within the Word, rather than the many gods which may be seen. . . . The revelation was . . . a voice, not an image. . . . Revelation is not appearance" (34).

however, the past embodies a living instrument of understanding rather than the dead weight of inescapable fate. This rethinking, or re-cognition, of the *image* of the past as being instead a dynamic *text* allows the past to be constantly reimagined and reinterpreted. In essence, rethinking—re-cognition—of the past is necessary in order to fully achieve understanding—recognition—of it. In this way, the counterintuitive strangeness of Joseph's interpretations may now be viewed as promoting unity and coherence instead of division and discord.

But this re-cognition of the past must be a mutual effort if it is to succeed. Significantly, Joseph undertakes his proclamation of re-visioning the past only some time after he has heard his brothers openly re-consider their own actions of the past and subsequently condemn them.[40] By refashioning the memory of the past, Joseph enables his family to deal positively with the ghosts of their own history and thereby creates the possibility for a dynamic shared future.[41]

Thus, Joseph introduces the beginnings of discourse in what the Biblical text presents as a proto-society: the band of brothers.[42] Not unremarkably, this nascent political discourse focuses on the reconstitution of history, which progresses from denying any possibility for comity to enabling a sense of positive shared purpose and destiny. In effect, Joseph's "creation" of discourse is that he enables discourse to be born. Part of how that happens is through the medium of dreams; in effect, Joseph interprets them again so that the discrepancies in power between him and his brothers are seen not as threatening, but rather as granting them a new (surviving the famine) and extended (becoming a nation) lease on life.

In this connection, it is important to note that in the greater enterprise of forging a new understanding of the past, even deliberate lies may reveal the ease with which past events are in fact liable to many types of misunderstandings (even if their meaning appears to be clear).[43] In the staged

40. The reference is to Gen. 42:21–22. This connection is alluded to in Avivah Zornberg, *Genesis: The Beginning of Desire* (Philadelphia: Jewish Publication Society, 1995), 306.

41. In *Dancing in Chains* (Palo Alto: Stanford University Press, 1997), Joshua Foa Dienstag expresses Nietzsche's understanding of history and its effect on the human psyche in this way: "We can remake the past even as it is making us" (212; see also 206).

42. The anticipation of Freud can obscure the fact that these brothers want to eliminate not just their father, but also the brother with whom the father most identifies (and, as cited by traditional commentaries, most resembles).

43. Thus, in *Emet L'Ya'akov*, Rabbi Kaminetzky understands the false accusations to have precisely this cognitive/pedagogical function: to demonstrate the ease with which signs and texts may be strongly misread (shades of Harold Bloom?).

confrontations with his brothers, Joseph himself utilizes lies (the false accusations) in order to forcibly bring into the open the deeper falsehood at the center of the brothers' existence.[44] At the point when Joseph is making his case for re-visioning the past, this technique is instrumental in demonstrating metaphorically to the brothers the ease with which ostensibly "straightforward" evidence can be misinterpreted (as the brothers had done in the past). Therefore, Joseph emphasizes the necessity of utilizing subtle analysis in order to reveal the truth of any narrative (and to be able to construct a dynamic community in the future).[45]

Thus, we see that the reconstitution of the past is itself strewn with pitfalls and ambiguities. In *The Book and the Text*, Regina Schwartz points out that remembering the past ensures the future.[46] At the same time, remembering also implies putting together anew, or re-membering. This evokes the contradictory movements of both discontinuity and continuity.[47] Similarly, Avivah Zornberg notes that the names of Joseph's two children allude to the contrary movements of "forgetting" (Menashe) and "fruitfulness" (Ephraim).[48] Zornberg writes that fruitfulness (surviving well) often requires forgetting, because survival often entails both reconstruction and therapeutic "forgetting." In Joseph's life, personal fruitfulness is accomplished by acts of deliberate "forgetfulness." We may extend this insight to note that on the national level, survival is marked by acts of deliberate reconstruction—that is to say, eliminating some aspects and emphasizing others—of the past. In either case, creativity is achieved through assiduous pruning, not mindless hoarding.

As readers of the text, we are aware that every case of forgetting is also an instance of remembering. To the extent that, as Freud has shown us, reinterpretation is necessary for us to navigate our own lives, it is important to credit Joseph with the dedication to reconstruct the past as a metaphorical text.[49] Joseph emphasizes the multivalent interpretations to which the past may be subject in order to ensure the existence not (just) of a unified

44. White, *Narration and Discourse*, 261.

45. Cf. Rabbi Y. Kaminetzky, *Emet L'Ya'akov* on Gen. 42:9, pp. 212–13.

46. Regina Schwartz, "Joseph's Bones and the Resurrection of the Text," in *The Book and the Text: The Bible and Literary Theory* (New York: Blackwell, 1990).

47. Ibid., 55.

48. Zornberg, *Genesis*, 286–90; Gen. 41:51, 52.

49. See Sigmund Freud, *The Interpretation of Dreams*, trans. James Strachey (1899; New York: Basic, 1965), especially chap. 2, "The Method of Interpreting Dreams," and chap. 3, "A Dream Is the Fulfillment of a Wish."

sense of his own self and family, but also of a vigorous concept of a nation whose concrete existence he could as yet barely imagine.

In envisioning the creation of a common discourse as fundamental to the construction of national identity, Joseph is doing more than repairing the failed social structure of his family, and he is going beyond advocating yet another conventional (power-based) concept of national existence. Joseph is promoting a concept of nationhood that contradicts the idea of national identity prevalent in his own day. Although Joseph is the vizier of a country where power is centralized and institution building is the supreme badge of power, he does not identify nationhood with just the building of social institutions.[50] More than the concrete construction of monumental buildings, the promulgation of tax codes, or the enforcement of road regulations, Joseph appreciates that the essence of nationhood consists primarily as a set of common tropes, or ways of thinking. That is to say, the core of dynamic national existence is based not (just) on physical structure; rather, it is the expression of a common universe of shared meanings leading to the creation of a national spirit and identity.

The emphasis on common action and practice in constituting a discourse explains why this discourse, in order to be successful, cannot be compelled from above: Jacob cannot transmit a ready-made discourse to his children because the very idea of a shared conversation presupposes a commonality of thinking and feeling among the parties to that conversation, which cannot be strictly imposed. In many ways, Joseph anticipates what Benedict Anderson has characterized as the essence of the modern (post-Enlightenment) understanding of a nation, calling it an "imagined community."[51] This idea of nation as imagined community is subsequently

50. Cf. in this regard Joseph's centralization of state economic power in the matter of food distribution, and eventually in the matter of ownership and even residential locations for the newly enserfed Egyptian population (Gen. 47:13–23). Joseph's hermeneutical approach to nation-building is encapsulated in Hugo C. White's description of Joseph, cited above, as a "solitary hermeneut existing between alienated worlds of discourse" (*Narration and Discourse*, 240).

51. With this phrase, Benedict Anderson defines the commonality of a nation less as a function of tangibles than as the realization of a unity of thinking about the polity. In Anderson's words, "The nation . . . is an imagined political community—and imagined as both inherently limited and sovereign. It is imagined because the members of even the smallest nation will never know most of their fellow-members. . . . Yet in the minds of each lives the image of their communion. . . . Communities are to be distinguished . . . by the style in which they are imagined." Anderson, *Imagined Communities*, 8. For further development of these themes, see especially the chapters entitled "Introduction" (1–8) and "Cultural Roots" (9–36). In *The Nation as a Local Metaphor* (Chapel Hill: University of North Carolina Press, 1997),

borne out in the Biblical text.[52] Significantly, the first pronouncement of God regarding the first consciously communal act of the Israelites does not concern tangible items (although this—the preparation of the Paschal Lamb—follows in short order). Rather, God's first directive to the Children of Israel conceived as an autonomous nation (at least in theory, if not completely in terms of their work requirements vis-à-vis the Egyptians taskmasters) concerns a change in the way that they will henceforth imagine time: from now on, the springtime month of Nisan will be counted as the first month (and not the more traditional Tishrei, or some other as-yet-undesignated month of the year). In other words, it is the ability to imagine a major concept, like time, in a new way that marks the Children of Israel as an autonomous nation even while they are still physically mired in the slave state of Egypt. At this point, however, Joseph is not in a position to enact new laws for his family in preparation for their future existence as an autonomous nation; the continued presence of the past as a negative influence over their present interaction still prevents them from anticipating fully their future role of nationhood.

Closing the Book

One question remains to be answered: does Joseph succeed in his enterprise? Utilizing Sternberg's view that the Bible is characterized by a "poetics of ambiguity," we must conclude that Joseph's success is only partial.[53] On one level—the personal—Joseph seems to fail: the Biblical text recounts that upon returning from Jacob's interment in Canaan, Joseph's brothers send him a message purporting to be from Jacob (speaking before his death), urging Joseph to forgive his brothers. The brothers subsequently offer to be Joseph's slaves in perpetuity (Gen. 50:17–18). In view of his previous efforts to reconstruct the past so as to enable all of Jacob's sons

---

Alon Confino expands on the theme of "imagined community" to depict the development of nationalist feeling in modern Germany (1871–1918) as an extension of the people's (particularly the middle class's) material quotidian experience. See particularly "Thinking Germany" (3–23, especially 4); "A National Lexicon" (125–57); and "The Nation in the Mind" (158–89, especially 158–60).

52. This incident reports God's command that Moses and Aaron speak to *all* the Israelites, who are designated for the first time in their communal identity as "the *entire* congregation of the Children of Israel" (Exod. 12:3; emphasis mine).

53. Sternberg, *The Poetics of Biblical Narrative*, 166.

to move forcefully into a common future, Joseph realizes now that the brothers' inability to break free completely of the structure of the past arises out of their alienation from this new understanding of past events. Thus, Joseph reacts in the only way possible (for him): he cries (Gen. 50:17).

Why is Joseph's success only partial? Sternberg's answer is that both for characters in and readers of the Bible, liberty is provided for the process of experiencing/interpreting the events of the narrative, but nothing is guaranteed in terms of actual results.[54] This both establishes moral choice and highlights the paradox of the human condition.[55] As readers of the Biblical text, we, like the characters in the narrative, also puzzle out the connections, and thus participate actively in the Biblical process of discovery.[56] In matters of both hermeneutical and legal understanding, the Bible is ripe for human interpretation.[57] How we choose to interpret—divisively or dynamically, looking backward or forward—is a matter with decisive implications for the existence of a common future.

On the personal level, Joseph's life may point to the absence of perfect achievement of his goals. But on the national level, Joseph rises to the higher challenge of reinterpreting the past and succeeds beyond his wildest dreams. The complex implications of Joseph's interpretative project are fulfilled after his death when his bones are brought up from Egypt. The importance of this action is more than symbolic. It points to the ongoing national awareness that the political future of the Israelites is realized because of Joseph's actions. The re-visioning of the text that Joseph valorizes enables the Children of Israel to become the People of the Book.[58] In that sense, it is not just the bones—the "atzamot"—of Joseph that go up to the Promised Land, but his "atzmut"—his very essence—that helps define the unique identity of the Israelite nation.

Although the discourse that Joseph fosters is crucial for the establishment of a successful Israelite polity—only Joseph's bones, not those of his brothers, are brought up—the manner of the journey of these bones reveals

54. "The Bible guarantees us the greatest freedom in manipulating the journey, but the least freedom in establishing the terminus." Ibid., 179.

55. Alter, *The Art of Biblical Narrative*, 177.

56. Sternberg, *The Poetics of Biblical Narrative*, 326.

57. Cf. Susan Handelman's discussion of the "Oven of Achnai," a Talmudic incident that revolves precisely around this point. *The Slayers of Moses*, 40–42.

58. The implications of the development of the Children of Israel into the People of the Book is taken up later in the Book of Esther, when Esther establishes a new sense of community based on communal practice and the shared activity of textual interpretation. See Chapter 6.

that the realization of Joseph's dream is not the result of the actions of Joseph alone. Significantly, the Biblical text notes that Joseph's bones are taken up by Moses (Exod. 13:19), himself a member of the Levite tribe, the name of whose progenitor signifies union and cooperation.[59] Despite Joseph's central role in formulating the common discourse that defines the Israelite nation, the Biblical text points out that other tribes make crucial contributions in their own right. Specifically, it is the tribe of Judah who is given the mandate of actual political power, which is ratified in the valedictory blessings of Jacob to his sons, and of Moses to the Children of Israel, before their respective deaths (Gen. 49:10; Deut. 32:7).

Politics as a Hermeneutical Field

After the protracted emphasis on Joseph's power position as depicted in Genesis, this attribution of actual political power within the Israelite polity appears puzzling. It is possible, of course, to ascribe this equivocation to the Biblical penchant for moral ambiguity, or as a reflection of the internal contradictions of the human experience. [60] Alternatively, we may consider the ambiguity of Joseph's position in the constellation of Israelite power structures to foreshadow/reflect the tragic nature of the events that will overtake the embryonic Israelite nation in Egypt. But there is another way of reading the ambiguity of Joseph's very partial success in trying to maintain an open discourse with his family on the personal level and in failing to consolidate his own (tribe's) power position among the tribes in the national context: Joseph's own contribution to Israelite national life finds its most complete realization precisely in the open-ended nature of the location of power and of the structure of political discourse.

The paradoxical notion of power and its realization is manifest in what appears to be Jacob's deliberate passing over of Joseph when entrusting the

59. This is made clear when Leah names her third son Levi in the hope that her estranged husband, Jacob, will now be her companion (Gen. 29:34).

60. See Sternberg, *The Poetics of Biblical Narrative*, 166, regarding the "poetics of ambiguity." On contradictions, see Alter, *The Art of Biblical Narrative*, 177: "The biblical outlook is informed . . . by a sense of stubborn contradiction, of a profound and ineradicable untidiness in the nature of things." Despite Alter's attempt to accommodate contradiction within the Biblical text, his comments reveal his concern with the univalent approach to textual meaning evinced by the Documentary Approach. (Briefly and simplistically, the Documentary Approach understands the Biblical text as a compendium of different sources and historical periods.) Cf. in this regard particularly his comments on 20 and 132–34.

role of national leadership to the tribe of Judah (Gen. 49:10). Just why he does this is never completely explained in the Biblical text, although Jacob does note that Judah's brothers acknowledge his leadership (49:8, 10). At one level, however, this rationale seems to be little more than a functional recognition of reality, rather than a moral justification of a particular set of power arrangements. In this context, the Midrashic commentary on the respective personalities of Judah and Joseph can help us understand a text that appears stubbornly circular in its reasoning. The Midrash (Tanhuma Yashan Vayigash 2) portrays Judah as a rope, in contradistinction to Joseph, who is depicted as a pit. This imagery is based on the Biblical narrative, which describes the incident when Joseph thrown into the pit by his brothers. Sometime later, according to the Biblical text (presumably it is the same day, because the brothers are described as eating a meal together after disposing of Joseph), Judah suggests that the brothers avoid (direct) guilt for Joseph's demise and "rid" themselves of any (potential) problem(s) by selling Joseph into slavery. While this incident may not strike the (modern) reader as delineating the (moral) justification for leadership, the episode demonstrates Judah's functional talent to diffuse immediate crisis while delaying moral accounting to a time when perhaps cooler heads might prevail. Following the Midrashic imagery, only Judah the "rope" was capable of drawing out the hidden depths of the enigmatic "pit" that was Joseph.[61] The implication is that a man with Judah's practical abilities will be the most effective ruler of the nation. This is the leadership that Jacob remarks as acknowledged by the brothers, and which he confirms with this choice.

In effect, though, Jacob does elliptically offer another reason to justify his singling out of (the tribe of) Judah as the leader of the (future) Israelites. This alludes to another incident that the Biblical text records right after the sale of Joseph, centering on Judah's relationship with Tamar, whom he at first repudiates as a whore until he recognizes the staff and seal that he had left with her after their sexual encounter. As the Biblical text narrates the incident, Judah's reaction upon seeing the proof of his own behavior is to acknowledge that Tamar is right: "She is more righteous than I am."[62] Jacob alludes to this admission (*hoda'a* in Hebrew, deriving from the root *h'd'h*) on Judah's part to justify his confirmation of Judah's acknowledged

---

61. Zornberg, *Genesis*, 322–24.
62. Gen. 38:26. See Rashi on Gen. 49:8; Bereshit Rabbah (new version) 2:19 on Gen. 49.

(deriving from the same root of *h'd'h*) position of leadership. In this reading, Judah is given the responsibility of ruling the (future) nation because he has the psychological/moral ability to acknowledge when he is wrong. This interpretation identifies the essence of leadership as focused primarily not on the desires of the ruler, but, in the final analysis, on a certain elemental level of justice that is due to the people in general, including those in a position of (relative) powerlessness. A leader capable of acknowledging his own mistakes can provide justice for his people. This approach credits Judah with the personal sympathy needed to make the vision of Joseph, expressed in the creation of a common discourse, a lived reality. In this reading, Judah is given the role of leadership because of his strong personal sense of justice, which in turn makes him the more sympathetic, and thereby unifying, leader.

But the complexity of the Biblical text does not admit just one interpretation, either of the Joseph saga or of the implications and responsibilities of political leadership. There is another way of understanding the ultimate denial of sovereign leadership to Joseph and its bestowal instead on Judah. This alternate reading takes into account the open-ended nature of the political discourse that Joseph fashions for the Israelite nation. While it is true that Jacob identifies Judah as the future bearer of political authority, Judah—like Joseph before him—does not take on that mantle by himself.

Indeed, it is possible to argue that it is only by fully engaging in Joseph's national discourse that Judah is able to accede to the position of political power. This idea is first alluded to in the Biblical verse that portrays the revelation of Joseph to his brothers and their subsequent (personal, if only partial) reconciliation. With its simplicity of structure and economy of words, it is easy to overlook the cataclysm of opposing ideas at which this verse hints. Dramatically, this verse marks the climax of the almost unbearable tension that has been building up throughout Joseph's purposeful masquerade and false accusations against his brothers: "And Judah approached him [i.e., Joseph]" (Gen. 44:18). The wording of this verse is significant, telling us that the ability to free oneself from the constraints of past history can come about only when two separate individuals—even two opposite entities—are forced to approach, to take each other's full measure, and together construct a dialogue that renders their encounter interactive instead of repetitively static. Traditional commentaries emphasize both aspects of the implications of this verse, allowing that the very oppositional nature of the essences represented by Joseph and Judah, respectively, can in their best sense encourage each other's most dynamic aspect.[63]

This latter point is likewise signaled in the Midrashic reading, which, in comparing Joseph to a pit and Judah to the rope that alone is capable of drawing out the treasure concealed in the depths, implies that it is in the dialectical confrontation of opposing forces that hidden possibilities and solutions are made possible. In this image, the benefits of the confrontation are not limited to the personification of the pit. That is to say, it is not only Joseph who benefits (spiritually or politically) from this encounter. As much as the rope is necessary for the revelation of the treasures that are secreted in the depths of the pit, it is also the presence of the pit itself that allows the untapped capabilities of the rope to manifest themselves. Thus, it is the very existence of the anxiety created and fostered by Joseph—the obvious strangeness that he injects into every encounter with his brothers—that enables the leadership qualities of Judah to come forcefully to the fore. Neither Joseph nor Judah could fully realize his own potential without the other.

The tension-filled situation that is the background to the (finally) positive confrontation between Judah and Joseph hints at another historical truth of these encounters. These relationships are never easy, and their final implications remain always in flux. In this, the (political) development of the Israelite nation is remarkably different from the development of other nations depicted in the Bible. In the laconic portraits offered by the Pentateuchal text, ancient nations are generally portrayed as fixed in character—often they are little more than reflections of their absolute rulers.[64]

---

63. Thus, in *Ohr Gedalyahu*, Rabbi Gedaliah Schor characterizes the basic characters of Joseph and Judah as opposite, with the latter exemplifying heart and feeling, while the former emphasizes the rational processes of the brain (134). While this imagery may be understood as delineating mutually contradictory and oppositional forces, opposing forces can also be viewed as complementary, bringing out the best possibilities in each other. This is the point of the Midrash Tanhuma Yashan 2 (cited in Zornberg, *Genesis*), which compares Joseph to the pit and Judah to the rope.

64. Strictly speaking, Prophetic texts contain more about the political systems and development of the gentile nations in contradistinction to that of the Israelites than does the Pentateuchal text. Many reasons might be adduced for this—not the least of which may be that the Pentateuchal text seems to be written from a more internal point of view, concentrating on Israelite political development rather than on comparative national evolution. The prophecy of Amos, for example, contains instances in which he specifically holds up the Israelite pattern of behavior to that of the surrounding nations; as the similarity in literary style and rhythm of these examples seems to attest, he apparently finds little to distinguish them morally (Amos 1:6–2:6; 9:7). Despite this, however, the basic distinction between the Israelites and the other ancient nations in terms of their political development still holds.

In the case of the Israelite nation, however, the Biblical text allows us to witness an almost constant encounter between the people and their rulers, with the tone of this national discourse ever shifting. As we will see, it is the extent to which and the ability with which the Israelite leader participates in this dialogue that in effect determines his/her success in both the political and moral arenas.

Linking open discourse to both political and moral success reflects Joseph's contribution to the redefinition of the scope and goal of politics. As we have seen, Joseph does not merely catalogue the rules for attaining and maintaining political authority, which explains why the Joseph narrative does not terminate merely with the recitation of Joseph's own power and status. The textual emphasis on Joseph's efforts to reinterpret the past and recalibrate his relationship with his family, oriented as they are toward the future of territorial possession and nation founding, do not derive their moral coherence only from this forward drive. To establish this new understanding and direction with his interlocutors, Joseph must also appeal to a common standard of what constitutes present (moral) meaning. This Joseph finds in his evocation of the Divine (Gen. 45:5), which he understands in

---

The context of Amos's prophecy centers not on the relationship between the leader and the nation (which, in its presentation in connection with the Israelites beginning in Exodus, is always portrayed as complex, almost never following expected patterns of behavior) but rather on the moral consequences that derive from patterns of sinning against God. In the Biblical text, God makes it repeatedly clear that these sins will never go unpunished, regardless of their national provenance. Interestingly, the distinctive syntactical structure of Amos's prophetic style ("Did I not bring Israel up from Egypt and the Philistines from Caftor and Aram from Kir?" 9:7) can result in this verse's question being understood not as a rhetorical device equalizing all three nations, but as a method comparing the Bible's presentation of what it considers to be an undisputable historical fact (Israel's Divine deliverance from Egypt) with counterexamples of other nations who have not had such Divine attention bestowed upon them. In that reading, the implied question would be answered with a rhetorical negative (cf. Kimhi and Malbim). In the context of comparing (and perhaps equalizing) the Israelite nation with the other nations, cf. also Robert Polzin, *Moses and the Deuteronomist* (Bloomington: Indiana University Press, 1980), especially 51–55; see also Polzin's (attempted) resolution, 68–72. I am grateful to Professor Marshall Berman (CUNY) for having raised the issue of the political comparison between Israel and the other contemporaneous nations cited in the Biblical text, with the important caveat that this comparison is too complex to be ranged simply as "simple/bad" and "complex/good."

The most obvious example of a leader's characteristics being absorbed by the nation is the case of the evil Pharaoh in Exodus, who is portrayed as the sole determiner of the Egyptian response to the repeated Israelite demands. It is important to note that this statement holds true not just for the manifestly evil rulers presented in the Bible, but for the "good" rulers as well. Even the "good" Pharaoh of Joseph's time is portrayed as governing the most minute details of his subjects' lives. Pharaoh's elevation of Joseph is expressed in terms of the absoluteness of power that Pharaoh is capable of bestowing on him (Gen. 41:40, 44).

the context of the moral and intellectual challenges presented to the human players on the historical scene. Thus, the Biblical account of political development underscores the causal link between the realization of politics as incorporating a transcendental moral (God-centered) standard and its resultant political success.[65] According to this context, Joseph's acknowledgement of God and God's role in politics emphasizes the consciousness of the Divine in the full realization of the human self. In the Biblical text, Joseph understands that possession of personal/political power cannot be considered a morally positive achievement if that power is viewed only as a function of the expression of the self. Rather, politics must always be measured in terms of the relationship between the human and the Divine. Realization of the self achieves positive force to the extent that it grapples with the challenges and standards presented by God.

Still, just the symbolic awareness of moral transcendence and its place in political life is itself no guarantee of material, political permanence: the presence of diversified and open dialogue regarding politics and leadership does not mean that the establishment of political power will be everlasting. The ephemeral nature of political power is depicted historically in the Hebrew Bible: the dissolution of the Israelite monarchy in the days of Solomon's son Rehoboam is portrayed as the breakup of the kingdom precisely along the ancient fault lines of the Joseph/Judah divide. In an ironic inversion of the discourse established by Joseph, in which human dynamism is predicated on the constant awareness of the Divine, the Biblical text portrays the political life that Jeroboam recreates in the northern Ephraimite kingdom of Israel as reducing the Divine element to no more than a fig leaf for the new political understanding and structures of power.[66] Consequently, it is not surprising that national life and discourse in the north is depicted as losing the dimension of meaning that would render its existence morally transcendent. The northern kingdom is shown to be the first Israelite kingdom to go into an exile where it (unlike the later exile of the Judean kingdom) loses its identity as an individual nation.

65. In this connection, it is possible to understand the rationale for the strictures in Leviticus against "tale-bearing" (19:16) and "hating your brother in your heart" (19:17) as prohibitions not only against destroying the relationship between the people and the Divine, but also countering the undermining of the social relations among people themselves, alluding directly to the themes in the Joseph story.

66. 1 Kings 12:26–33. The text there presents Jeroboam's construction of the two Golden Calves (in Bethel and Dan) as motivated by his fear of losing his kingdom to Rehoboam once the northern Israelites travel on pilgrimage to the Temple in Jerusalem. See also 12:26–28.

But it would be a mistake to conclude that the Biblical text consequently comes down in favor of a purely Judahite version of rule/political community.[67] Read in this limited perspective, the nature of political engagement is reduced to a matter of personal style (although, as reflected in later historical developments, these elements of style often can translate into issues of moral and political substance).[68] Rather, the Biblical text itself may be read more fruitfully as promoting the continuation of the encounter between the Judah and the Joseph versions of political discourse. From the Biblical perspective, the maintenance of this confrontation between different understandings of political discourse and national community is the best (although imperfect) guarantee of political dynamism and moral coherence.[69]

In many ways, the complex nature of human encounters echoes the dreams furnishing the template for the development of Israelite political discourse. To be sure, this template is fraught with controversy: in their Biblical presentation, dreams also provoke dissonance and consternation because they force their interlocutors to reexamine the conventionally accepted notion of what constitutes "reality" and to reassess the forces that actually provoke change. Indeed, at the time that the dream occurs, the dreamer may not be entirely certain of where reality lies (i.e., whether the dreamer is asleep or awake). Further complicating matters, as already

67. This conventional approach conforms to Marc Brettler's understanding of the Deuteronomic narrative (comprising Deuteronomy, Joshua, and Judges) as valorizing the "southern," Judahite monarchy against its "northern," Ephraimite (Josephite) counterpart; however, this approach does not capture the diverse nature of the Biblical narrative of the Israelite political sphere.

68. Thus, to give just one example, Joseph's proclivity to behave as a "solitary hermeneut" (White, *Narration and Discourse*, 240) is reflected in the pre- and post-Judahite monarchs (Saul, from the tribe of Benjamin, is directly related to Joseph, as a descendant of Joseph's only full brother, while Jeroboam is an Ephraimite, and thus a direct descendant of one of Joseph's sons). In contrast to David, Saul is portrayed as lacking a consistent sense of communication with the people of Israel (cf. 1 Sam. 10:27; 13:11; 15:24), resulting in his eventual loss of the kingdom. Moreover, Jeroboam's "new" hermeneutics and interpretation of the commandments are directly implicated in the loss of royal power from his house (cf. 1 Kings 14:7–11; 15:25–30).

69. This is reflected in the words of Later Prophets. Ezekiel, for example, does not portray the era of ultimate human liberation as one of stasis. Rather, he envisions it as a dynamic union between both Josephite and Judahite concepts of political community. Ezekiel's identification of the ruling tribes of Judah and Joseph with trees (Ezekiel 31:19–22) underlines the fact that both approaches to politics represent a force of nature that, although altering its appearance over time, carries with it the hallmark of permanence. With this imagery, the Biblical text suggests that difference be seen as the source not of altercation, but of a more richly fulfilling life for everyone.

noted, dreams, strange as they are, may evoke the essence of reality more exactly than the routine occurrences of everyday life. This explains why Joseph's brothers evince such anger after he recounts his dreams to them: after all, if dreams are merely empty arrangements of images, the resentment that they provoke remains inexplicable.

The explosive—and even revolutionary—nature of dreams affects more than the onset (albeit intermittent in nature) of Israelite political discourse. Importantly, dreams become crucial to the development of community and freedom later on during the Israelite sojourn in Egypt. This time, however, these are the dreams not of a single man, but of a group of women.

Community Dreams

At first glance, it appears counterintuitive to attribute nation-building powers to the dreams of the Israelite women in Egypt, particularly in the context of the Biblical description of this period. Most obviously, there is no evidence within the confines of the Biblical text of the occurrence of those dreams, let alone an appreciation of their supposed influence. In fact, these dreams are presented as an artifact of the Midrashic text. But this Midrashic text may be viewed as crucial to understanding an otherwise enigmatic chain of events in the Biblical account of the enslavement of the Israelites in Egypt.

The Biblical description of the details of Israelite servitude in Egypt avoids the painfully obvious question of the mechanics of the humanly experienced process of liberation. For modern readers of the text, it is difficult to understand how it may be possible for an enslaved population, bereft of any allies within the local (or international) communities, to manage to become free. To be sure, one can always adduce the figure of Moses and his perceived/demonstrated powers. Crucially, however, the Bible records that the enslaved Israelites do not attach the aura of savior to Moses at all: when Moses comes to liberate the Israelites, they respond by ignoring him and even blaming him for the official Egyptian reactions to his request, which results in increased labor quotas for the Israelite slaves (Exod. 4:20–23; 5:9). In the context of Israelite experience, then, from where does salvation come?

In the absence of a readily accepted figure of deliverance, Israelite emancipation must (logically) emanate from another location. Showing us this provenance is the task fulfilled by the Midrashic depiction of the

Israelite women in Egypt. Consonant with the "hermeneutic indeterminacy" of the Biblical text, however, the Midrash does not portray these women as directly manufacturing salvation.[70] Instead, the Midrashic text describes the Israelite women in Egypt as enabling others to imagine deliverance along with them, and thus, eventually, to impel their own liberation.

This is the Midrashic text:

> Pharaoh decreed that the Israelites [men] not sleep in their homes [and thereby not propagate]. . . . What did the Israelite women do? They drew water . . . and cooked . . . and went to the fields to feed their husbands. . . . Once they ate, they would take their mirrors and look at them with their husbands, and [she] would say, "I am better looking than you" and [he] would reply, "I am better looking than you." And from this, they would accustom themselves to desire, and were fruitful and multiplied. (Midrash Tanhuma Pekudei 9)

The seemingly arbitrary Midrashic joining of awakened desire with fecundity through the agency of the Israelite women points to the portion of the Biblical narrative where the Egyptians—in particular, the (new) Pharaoh—express their sense of political discord: "Behold, the Israelite nation are more numerous and stronger than us" (Exod. 1:8). This concern of the Egyptians appears directly after the Biblical text's notation of Israelite fruitfulness (Exod. 1:7). Subsequently, Israelite fecundity becomes the pretext for their enslavement.

For the modern reader, however, even this Midrashic narrative does not seem like much of a dream; certainly it bears little resemblance to the transformative epics recounted by Joseph. Unlike many of the protagonists of the Joseph story, the women of this Midrashic narrative remain anonymous. Unlike Pharaoh, or even the Chief Butler or the Chief Baker of the Joseph narrative, these women do not have the luxury of sleeping/dreaming at night in special places dedicated to their nocturnal comfort. Instead, the women actively work by themselves to create a dream world. Trapped in an existence of unyielding stone, the women foster a haven, if only for a few hours, where they can eat and communicate with their spouses.[71]

---

70. Cf. Sternberg's "poetics of ambiguity" (*The Poetics of Biblical Narrative*, 166) and Alter's "untidiness and contradiction" in the Biblical text (note 60 above).

71. Avivah Zornberg makes a similar point when she characterizes the period of slavery in Egypt as one of total blockage: the Israelites do not hear, their Egyptian taskmasters

The Midrashic text amplifies the seemingly disjointed Biblical verses, focusing on the Israelite women who radically reimagine the circumstances of their enslavement. As the alienating Egyptian gaze problematizes Israelite fecundity and therefore enslaves the Israelite people, the Israelite women invert this look to suggest that fecundity may become the key to Israelite freedom. But this transformation is neither easy nor obvious. In the Midrashic narrative, Egyptian slavery so oppresses the Israelites that, even after having enjoyed a meal together, the awakening of sexual desire on the part of the Israelite men and women is not at all assured. They have to "accustom themselves to desire," which is accomplished only after the play with mirrors. In this interaction, the Israelite women encourage their husbands to gaze upon themselves with admiration ("I am better looking"), thus negating the deadening, alienating looks directed at them by their Egyptian taskmasters (Exod. 1:11–12).

But this gaze does not remain purely narcissistic: importantly, the look of self-validation extends itself to admiring and therefore desiring the other member of the dyad. Ostensibly a contest of vanity—"I am better looking than you"; "No, I am better looking than you"—the act of gazing at their own reflections allows the women to inspire their husbands to reflect on the possibilities of a new reality. In this dream space, having children represents not an offering to the insatiable Egyptian appetite for Israelite destruction, but rather a hopeful belief in a better future. The confluence of the love of themselves and the love of each other—the fascination with their own images—leads them together to create the next generation in their own images, thus enshrining this multifaceted love in the embodiment of their personal and national/communal future.

In effect, the Israelite women present their husbands with a dreamworld of domesticity that combines intimations of normalcy with hints of radical strangeness. Although the intimacy in the fields is presented by the Midrash as an aspect of the Israelites' enslaved and hence degraded existence (they do not even have the privilege of privacy for their conjugal relations), it is also possible to view—and the Israelite women in the Midrashic depiction do so view—the changed venue as a fillip for the mutual expression of love between husband and wife. The Israelite women utilize this

---

mechanically torture them and enforce work quotas, and the Israelites are forced to build structures of sturdy brick. At the highest level of political power, Pharaoh hardens his heart and remains obdurately closed to Moses's pleas and demonstrations to send forth the Israelites from Egypt. *The Particulars of Rapture* (New York: Doubleday, 2001), 37–41.

opportunity to project a completely new way of looking toward the future. Out of an enslaved existence that perforce constructs the Israelites as degraded Other, the Israelite women introduce an element of strangeness, of disjunction, into their quotidian reality in order to transcend it. The Israelite women use their dreams to imagine life differently. In their dreams, evoked within an oppressive slave state, domesticity, normally portrayed as routine and even boring, becomes strange, unattainable, even exotic.

And their ephemeral dreams have tangible consequences; the continued propagation of the Israelites through the worsening conditions of Egyptian slavery provides the material basis for their future liberation. Contrary to their expected decimation and eventual absorption into the Egyptian population, the Israelites prove a potent force to be reckoned with, even when oppressed. This method of concrete resistance is itself the product of a reverie—a vision of life as it could be—nurtured by the Israelite women. In this context, the Midrash suggests that it is the dreams of the women that help keep the yearning for freedom alive within the Israelite slaves. In the right hands, dreams become revolutionary, and narratives alter lives.

In *Dancing in Chains*, Joshua Foa Dienstag draws the connection, as expressed by Nietzsche, between dreams and the evocation of memory.[72] Precisely because dreams have a complex connection to reality—they evoke reality but they are not quite "real" in and of themselves—they are capable of employing reality not (only) as a construct to be suffered, but rather (also) as an artifact conducive to reflection and therefore change.[73] Thus, dreams may be understood as a prelude to revolution. In this connection, the Midrashic understanding of the Biblical leitmotif of the promise of God's remembering[74]—encoded in the hazy mists of Israelite memory as the mantra transmitted from their forefathers[75]—is energized by the structured dreaming of these anonymous Israelite women. In an act of willful determination, these women raise up the memory of the Divinely encoded

72. "Memory stands at the boundary of dreaming and wakefulness" (101).

73. This relationship to reality itself anticipates Derrida's analysis of writing; cf. *Of Grammatology*, trans. Gayatri Chakravorty Spivak (1974; Baltimore: Johns Hopkins University Press, 1976), especially 141–64.

74. This expression is styled as "*pakod pakadeti*/I have surely remembered" (Shmot Rabbah 3:8).

75. "And Joseph said to his brothers, 'Behold I will die, but God will surely remember [*pakod yifdod*] you, and will bring you up from this land to the land which he promised to Abraham, to Isaac, and to Jacob" (Gen. 50:24).

promise to launch their own liberation.[76] As Dienstag points out, memory and creativity may be seen not only as rigidly deterministic, but also as standing in complex and fruitful tension with each other. The Israelite women use their fruitfulness as a way to engender the positive potentialities of history to carry forward the destinies of their people. Like Joseph, these women recognize that dreams connect past and future, and thereby empower both.[77] These women can go beyond Joseph's *belief* that positive utilization of the past heralds a dynamic future; they plan for their actual freedom. Through their dreams, the women fashion the material for their eventual freedom and the embodiment of their own futures.

The centrality of the women's imagining and nurturing of Israelite fecundity into the instrument of liberation, foregrounded by the Midrash, is further supported by the narrative structure of the Biblical text. The second narrative dialogue in the Book of Exodus, cited shortly after the presentation of the Egyptian plan to enslave the Israelites, is reported as an order from Pharaoh, the embodiment of political power, to the Hebrew midwives, who personify the facilitation of Israelite fecundity. The aim of this conversation is to encourage the midwives to commit infanticide on Israelite male babies, thereby preventing the Israelite community from reaching the critical mass that would identify them as a national grouping with some claim to rights or power. (The Biblical text leaves indeterminate the precise nature of the Egyptian concern, but the words of the text link it directly to their perception of untrammeled Israelite population growth.)[78] By refusing to obey this command, the midwives continue physically to enable the dreams of the Israelite women as depicted in the Midrash (Exod. 1:17–20). Together, these groups of women literally birth the Israelite nation.

Unlike the conventional tropes of liberation, which often depict the process of freedom as a military victory achieved by designated heroes from above, the onset of liberty, as presented here in the Bible and as elaborated by the Midrash, is powered by the ephemeral dreams of ordinary people and announced by the risky labor of birth. The Bible figures not just the sign, but also the essence of Israelite national formation, as a birth process,

76. But see "The Paradox of Redemption" in Zornberg, *The Particulars of Rapture*, 65–66. In this section, Zornberg emphasizes the "inadequacy" of the "Exodus couple" to effect their own liberation.

77. Dienstag, *Dancing in Chains*, 210.

78. Exod. 1:15–16. See also Exod. 1:8–9; and Malbim ad loc.

thus highlighting the central position of women in generating both the dream and the realization of freedom.[79] This point is emphasized by the early modern Biblical commentary of Rabbi Judah Loew (Maharal).[80] By highlighting the exile/Exodus movement as a birth process, Loew emphasizes the complex and doubly dissonant relationship between the maternal body and the fetus, which the body both nurtures and expels. By extension, the fetus is at once part of and strange to the maternal host: it is both the center of and alien to its existence. Israelite liberation from Egypt is thus portrayed as doubly strange: it is (improbably) engendered from below, and it is also figured as both a product of and alienated from the Egyptian host that had guarded/oppressed the Israelites since the advent of Joseph and the rest of his family into Egypt many years before.

Psychically and culturally, this birth image explicates the conflicted relationship in which the Israelites are commanded to engage with the Egyptians: on the one hand, they are forbidden to abhor them;[81] at the same time, however, any future Israelite king is forbidden to engage in practices that will result in the Israelites' return to Egypt (Deut. 17:16). The birth image with which Maharal depicts the primal national Israelite-Egyptian connection points out that Egypt is an inextricable part of Israelite *history*, but also, importantly, that this association is not an inevitable part of the Israelite *legacy*. This is consonant with the message of the dream of the Israelite women, as it is first presented through the dream education of Joseph: the past shapes the present, but it does not unilaterally determine it. The multivalent nature of reality—as it is lived, as it is interpreted—leaves the protagonists of the present free to fashion their own future. The Biblical framing of the Israelite slave narrative in Egypt with images of fecundity and of birthing intensifies the central message of the text: the liberation and realization of Israelite nationhood are fashioned (even if not solely) by the women as they literally and figuratively give life to the Israelite nation.

79. This point is important, because the standard Biblical image of the Israelite Exodus depicts Egypt as a cauldron of steel, in which the Israelites, portrayed as a nugget of gold, are purified and thereafter (Divinely) delivered. This image of the cauldron is repeated in Deut. 4:20, 1 Kings 8:51, and Jer. 11:4, among others. With this imagery, liberation takes on a technical, if not technological, cast.

80. In his commentary on the Israelite Exodus from Egypt (*Gevurat Hashem*, chap. 3), Rabbi Judah Loew (1525–1609) insists on the birth image as central to the Exodus movement. The actual words are narrated in Deut. 4:34, retelling the events of the year of the Exodus.

81. "Do not despise/hate an Egyptian, for you were a stranger in his land" (Deut. 23:8).

As presented in the Bible, dreams interrogate the nature of conventional reality, while enabling the creation of an alternate and even revolutionary truth. In the process, however, the situation of the dreamer may be compromised or even, as depicted in the Joseph narrative, alienated. The tension faced by the dreamer encapsulates the Biblical understanding of the leader's dilemma.

2

MOSES: THE POLITICS OF ALIENATION

Most Biblical portraits of political leaders are laconic in nature: these leaders are described (mainly) with reference to their acts of political strength or military might.[1] When the Pharaoh of Genesis is introduced, for instance, his function in the narrative is to explain Joseph's rise in Egyptian politics; otherwise, little revealing personal detail about this Pharaoh is offered by the text (except to underline his absolute power).[2] The less benign but equally autocratic Pharaoh of Exodus is likewise presented only in terms of his exercise of power, which he utilizes for diverse purposes: to enslave the Israelites, to deny the existence of any deity that he cannot control,[3] and finally, according to the Biblical text, to pursue the Israelites into the sea, where he and his army are drowned (Exod. 14:27–29).

In this context, the introduction of Moses as the leader of the nascent Israelite nation strikes a different note. In presenting Moses, the Bible introduces a consciously new way of analyzing power. Instead of adopting the view of the absolute monarchs heretofore described in the Biblical text, who consider the exercise of power to be their right and privilege, the story of Moses introduces the understanding of power as something alienating. In this view, power is morally problematic not only because its incorrect implementation can lead to injustice (one way of reading both Pharaoh

---

1. Cf. in this regard the account of Nimrod's extended political power (Gen. 10:9).
2. The Biblical text records Pharaoh's declaration to Joseph regarding his own political power as exceeding that of Joseph in named rank only (Gen. 41:40).
3. "Who is God that I should obey him?" (Exod. 5:2).

sagas of the Bible).[4] In addition, the story of Moses demonstrates that power, even if discharged in the most scrupulous way, is inherently distancing and destabilizing. In other words, the very presence of power represents an ethical difficulty. Thus, the central question of the Israelite political order is not (just) the (efficient) arrangement of power, but rather (also) the minimization of power's estranging elements. For the Bible, the dilemma of the leader is how to deal with this strangeness, which defines the extent of the his/her moral and political success.

The Alienated Leader

The Biblical text does not depict Moses as concerned with the intricacies of political power, although, as the leader of an as-yet unformed nation, this might well have been expected. In fact, the practical requirements of an orderly application of power do not appear to bother Moses at all. For example, the adjustments that are later made in the procedures of judicial administration, whose original structures threaten to overwhelm Moses, are mandated at the behest of Moses's father-in-law, not Moses himself (Exod. 18:14–24). By contrast, as the Bible embarks on the growing awareness and self-consciousness of the Israelites as a new nation, the Exodus narrative itself focuses on the account of Israelite servitude to the Egyptians,

4. In his commentary on the Bible, Malbim (1809–1879), a central European Biblical exegete known for his logically based and philologically sensitive commentary on the Biblical text, argues that the dictatorial power of the Pharaoh of the Exodus can be seen as a theoretical and practical consequence of Joseph's centralization of economic and planning authority in the hands of the king. The theoretical link is not hard to see: Joseph's Pharaoh eventually owns all the people (as serfs) and nearly all the land in exchange for feeding them during the famine years. The slavery of the Israelites enacted by the Pharaoh in Exodus may thus be viewed as an extension of this method. Malbim explains that the "storage cities" built by the Israelites in Egypt function to hold the one-fifth produce that, after Joseph, becomes the standard agricultural tax paid to the king (Malbim on Exod. 1:11). Particularly interesting here is Malbim's at least partial tracing of the structure of Egyptian slavery as described in Exodus to Joseph's ingenious solution years before, as recorded in Genesis. It would be simplistic to read this opinion as laying some of the blame for Egyptian slavery on Joseph: after all, this is an idea hatched by the Exodus Pharaoh of his own free will. It does point, however, to the law of unintended consequences, and the need always to scrutinize plans that, with the passage of time, can be transformed into instruments of contrary accomplishment.

On the other hand, the Bible also presents an example of a leader who, unlike the Pharaoh in Exodus, deliberately eschews utilizing his position of power for self-aggrandizement. This incident is presented in 1 Kings, when Solomon asks God to make him wise (not rich or powerful) in order better to judge the Israelites and so more completely fulfill his duties as king. In this narrative, God rewards Solomon with wealth and power as well because Solomon is selfless enough to understand that the essence of leadership is to attend to the welfare of the people, not his own glory as monarch (1 Kings 3:5–13).

followed by a seemingly unconnected incident relating the rescue by an Egyptian princess of an anonymous baby born to a nameless Israelite couple (Exod. 2:1–10).

It is only with the bestowal of an Egyptian name on this baby that the readers of the text are able retrospectively to identify this infant, survivor of the Egyptian decree to kill all Israelite newborn males, as the future liberator of the Israelites. In view of this crucial association, it is additionally strange that Moses does not identify with Israelite suffering from his childhood. This is explained in the text by Moses's physical location: Moses is raised in Pharaoh's palace, isolated from the common run of his people (Exod. 2:10). To be sure, Moses does not remain unaware of his people's predicament: the Biblical text notes a positive effort on his part to observe and even to ameliorate their plight (Exod. 2:11). But counterintuitively for a leader who becomes closely, even intimately, identified with the people that he guides, Moses starts out as a stranger to them.[5] That Moses is separated and even alienated from his people allows him to both maintain his individual moral perspective and act against injustice, even when this contravenes the power relations legally enacted by the dominant society.[6]

But this estrangement, however necessary it is to establish the independent framework intrinsic to dynamic leadership, comes at a considerable price. It sets the tone for the conflict that characterizes Moses's relationship with the people he leads. From the beginning, this association is fraught with tension and permeated by alienation. Moses is forced to flee for his

5. To be sure, traditional folklore also reflects a different model: that of the leader as foreigner, because the foreigner accomplishes what no native founder could achieve. Thus, for example, Oedipus solves the riddle of the Sphinx and consequently is proclaimed king of Thebes. (Technically, of course, Oedipus is a Theban, although, because he is raised in Corinth or, according to another version of the myth, Sicyon, he remains functionally a foreign founder.) In the Bible, however, rulers are closely associated with their people (Deuteronomy forbids a non-Israelite to be king over the Israelites), to the point that Moses reportedly asks to be erased from the Bible if God will, as He threatens, destroy the Israelites: "And if not, please erase me from the book that you wrote" (Exod. 32:3).

6. Exod. 2:12. On this verse, Malbim comments that Moses's sheltered upbringing in protected circumstances fits him for his future role of leader, because he does not need to overcome the cringing servile attitude that is forced on the slave. For a similar view, cf. Ibn Ezra on Exod. 2:3; and Shmot Rabbah 5:2. In *The Prince*, Machiavelli famously comments that the enslaved status of the Israelites in Egypt made them more likely to follow Moses' leadership and leave Egypt. Another view on the issue of Moses's alienation views his estrangement from Egyptian society as paralleling the national experience of the Israelites in Egypt, thus allowing Moses to empathize with the people from whom his early life (physically, at least) distances him. Caroline Peyser, "The Book of Exodus: A Search for Identity," in *Torah of the Mothers: Contemporary Jewish Women Read Classical Jewish Texts*, ed. Ora Wiskind Elper and Susan Handelman (Jerusalem: Urim, 2000), 379–97.

life as the result of saving a fellow Israelite from Egyptian violence.[7] Consequently, Moses seeks refuge in Midian, where he is again openly identified as a stranger.[8] There, Moses profiles himself in a way consistent with his previous actions that had set him apart in Egypt: he publicly remonstrates against injustice (in this case, he comes to the aid of the beleaguered daughters of Jethro, the priest of Midian). Still, as demonstrated by the previous incident in Egypt, Moses remains removed from the inner social circle: he does not receive the courtesy of a complimentary meal until the priest of Midian himself asks after the stranger (Exod. 2:17–19). Even after marrying Zipporah, a daughter of this priest, Moses still feels his foreign status keenly enough to enshrine it in the name of his firstborn, Gershom (*"ger sham*/a stranger there"), which Moses explicitly elucidates by saying, "For I was a stranger in a foreign land."[9] Tellingly, Moses's daily occupation at this juncture is precisely that which had marked the Israelites as strange and despised to the Egyptians when they had first entered Egypt: he shepherds his father-in-law's flock (Gen. 46:34).

Moses's first Biblically described encounter with God in the desert further elaborates on this theme of strangeness. This experience is heralded by a phenomenon that appears dissonant with all known natural facts: a bush that is not consumed by the fire that burns it (Exod. 3:2). In terms of Moses's own displaced status in Midian, the Divine mission that mandates him to return to Egypt actually represents a chance to return to the society with which he is most familiar. Interestingly enough, however, Moses does not jump at the opportunity offered by the Divine charge to leave his tentative status as a stranger in an alien society. Instead, he challenges God: Moses disputes his suitability to liberate the Israelites, cavils at how

7. Exod. 2:14. The implication is that Moses has been informed on by one of his own nation (Midrash Tanhuma Shmot 10).

8. Exod. 2:19. The fact that Jethro's daughters identify the stranger as an Egyptian indicates that his clothes or speech must have given him away (Shmot Rabbah 32:8). In this connection, it is important to note that in the Biblical world, where security adheres to the individual only to the extent that he is protected by or subservient to the local monarch, the status of the stranger—that is, the noncitizen—is tenuous. In that context, Moses's escape from Egypt takes on the character not of a lasting solution, but of a first step in a series of increasingly destabilizing circumstances.

9. Exodus 2:22. While this naming seems to recall Joseph's similar referencing of his strangeness upon the birth of his first son, an important difference exists: with the naming of Menashe, Joseph makes the claim that he has been able to forget his strangeness (although that point is highly ironic, as the real status of forgetting, once the oblivion is purposefully recalled, remains doubtful at best). Here, however, Moses openly embodies his strangeness in the name of his eldest son.

he should word his mission, and insists that the Israelites will not believe him anyway (Exod. 2:11, 13; 4:1). Moses's protests seem to elicit an alien behavior from God, who, in this conversation, becomes the representative of counterintuitive sources of Otherness. Instead of acting in a properly "Divine" manner, enunciating an ever-grander elaboration of His mission, God simply provides signs that actually foreshadow the necromancy later performed by the Egyptian astrologers.[10] This dialogue of increasing disaffection ends with Moses becoming physically estranged from himself: his hand turns leprous.[11] This event marks the point at which Moses begins to understand that estrangement is his lot, regardless of whether or not he chooses to accept the Divine challenge.

In truth, this understanding is only a beginning. Moses's acceptance of leadership does not betoken just the acquiescence to an inevitably rocky first period of adjustment in the face of a new development in the process of Israelite nation formation. Rather, Moses's entire leadership of the Israelites is marked by nearly perpetual estrangement from his people. Even during the process of liberation, Moses does not succeed in getting the Israelites to believe in his mission or even to listen to him.[12] Once the Israelites are delivered from Egypt, they still do not hesitate to excoriate Moses for the dangers that beset them: "Are there no graves in Egypt that you have taken us to die in the desert. . . . This is what we told you in Egypt saying, 'Leave us alone, and we will serve Egypt'" (Exod. 14:11–12). Like Winston in Orwell's *1984*, the Israelites' long period of servitude in Egypt has accustomed them to their erstwhile position as slaves. Raised

10. Exod. 7:11. In *Of Grammatology*, Jacques Derrida elaborates on the moral immediacy of speech as contrasted to the manipulable ambiguity of signs. See especially "The Violence of the Letter," 101–40, especially 136; and "That Dangerous Supplement," 141–64, especially 144–52.

11. Exod. 4:6–7. The estranging quality of leprosy is highlighted when Moses's skin regains its former healthy appearance; the words of the text are finely calibrated to draw attention to the aspect of alienation that leprosy represents: "And behold, it [Moses's skin] had reverted as *his own flesh*" (emphasis mine). In other words, the leprous skin is not perceived as Moses's own flesh.

12. Exod. 6:9. Quoting Sefath Emeth, Avivah Zornberg in *The Particulars of Rapture* notes the connection between free breathing and the unimpeded hearing necessary for liberation (110–12). In the passage in Exodus, the Israelites' inability to breathe naturally develops into their inability to listen to Moses and his words of freedom. The Israelites utilize the same image of breath and its odor when they accuse Moses of having made their situation worse insofar as their dealings with Pharaoh are concerned: "You have made our odor rotten to Pharaoh" (Exod. 5:21). In the slave state of Egypt, the Israelites, like Pharaoh, can imagine no other reality but the one in front of their eyes. It is not happenstance that the Israelites' first active choice as a nation is couched in the expansive imagery of hearing (Exod. 24:7).

in the depths of the ancient Egyptian empire, the Israelites fondly recall the particulars of their former diet when they were slaves: the cucumbers were so delicious! The watermelon tasted so good! And the fish was free! (Num. 11:5).

At this juncture of alimentary grumblings, however, the Israelites are actually receiving food: they collect manna every day. What seems to disturb the Israelites is the unfamiliar nature of the manna. In this connection, their purported nostalgia for Egypt (which is actually perverse in terms of the horrors of the slavery that they had just experienced there) is really an expressed preference for the familiar. Ironically, the Israelites, who have just undergone the experience of being oppressed as strangers themselves, find that they prefer not to encounter the challenge of the unfamiliar. In effect, the Israelites prefer the known security of slavery to the strangeness and perils of freedom. In so doing, they enact the message of Dostoevsky's Grand Inquisitor: human beings will gladly trade their freedom for the bread that they know.[13] By their words, the Israelites acknowledge that freedom can be frightening, while bread—any bread, even the bread of affliction, which had been their lot in Egypt—embodies the safety of survival, albeit at a minimal level. Moses's contrary insistence that the Israelites actively choose their portion in life—that they structure even their quotidian practices with performative ritual that demands conscious decision-making on their part—strikes the former slaves as troublesome and even perverse. Thus, the Israelites charge Moses with conspiring to kill them; later on, they propose to counteract his leadership by returning to Egypt.[14]

After several such rebellions on the part of the people whom he is supposed to lead, Moses has a question of his own for God: "Have I conceived this people? Have I begotten them, that You should say to me, Carry them in your bosom, like a nursing father?" (Num. 11:12). Moses is disturbed by the contradictory and hence alienating demands of leadership: to be both strong and nurturing; to insist on the forward march of the people to its

13. "In the end, they will lay their freedom at our feet and say to us, 'Make us your slaves, but feed us.'" Fyodor Dostoevsky, *The Grand Inquisitor*, ed. and trans. Ralph E. Matlaw (New York: Penguin, 1991), 127.

14. Num. 13:4. Importantly, this suggestion takes place after the reported ill-fated mission of the spies to scout out the Promised Land. Its ultimate expression is found in the words of Dathan and Abiram, who participate in a rebellion against Moses shortly after the spies' abortive mission. In this later charge against Moses, Dathan and Abiram invert the larger meaning of "the land flowing with milk and honey," deliberately using it to refer to Egypt, the land of slavery (Num. 16:13), in defiance of its traditional, Divine ascription uniquely to the Promised Land (Exod. 3:17).

ultimate goal, while still demonstrating the psychic energy necessary to deal with their negative reactions and the ensuing challenges, which at times must have appeared to Moses to be on the order of communal temper tantrums. The answer to Moses's question is located in the image of carrying/weight-bearing that he himself utilizes. Implicitly, the Bible states that a leader must carry the people, incorporating the determination to see the responsibility of leadership through, even if that entails physically constraining the people; all this must be coupled with the concern with which a parent takes on the burden of a young child who cannot yet walk.[15] Moses, however, seems to exhibit some difficulty with this concept of leadership. It is not that Moses refuses to understand that leadership cannot employ a uniform formula at all times: circumstances, he realizes, can change, thus requiring different reactions from the leader. This is modeled by the different Divine reactions to the diverse Israelite requests for meat, one of which is answered without much comment (Exod. 16), and one of which provokes a deadly plague (Num. 11:33). Rather, Moses's difficulty with this dual-model answer arises from the fact that the people themselves are perennially changing, altering their outlook on both the world and their own conception of their national identity. Two models, Moses begins to realize, may not be enough.[16]

How does one lead a nation that persists in unmaking its identity? How can one guide a people who reject their destiny, the fulfillment of which motivates their deliverance from slavery? Following the trajectory of this logic, what can prevent a nation, once estranged, from re-estranging, or reinventing, itself? This question becomes perplexing because it is not clear that the Bible argues against a periodic reinvention of self, an episodic rendering of accounts, as it were. This is precisely what happens much later in Biblical history, when Ezra reestablishes the Jewish commonwealth after the Babylonian exile, although he is careful to justify his reforms by ascribing them to the fundamental practices and principles of traditional Israelite belief.[17] In an earlier context, however, an opportunity to question the very basis of Israelite political structure occurs soon after this nation's first self-conscious incarnation: when Korah rebels against the leadership of

15. Wildavsky's response to this question—"Exactly"—reflects the answer to this query but not the complexities inherent in it. *Moses as Political Leader* (1984; Jerusalem: Shalem, 2005).

16. The Biblical text may be read as valorizing Moses's reaction: in the context of Moses's questioning of God in this chapter, he is given seventy elders to assist him. In other words, many different models of (auxiliary) leadership are provided.

17. "And send portions of food to one who has none ready" (Neh. 5:10).

Moses and Aaron. Korah frames his mutiny in terms of what he perceives as Moses's politically calculated self-estrangement from the Israelite community as a whole: "All the covenanters are holy. . . . Why do you elevate yourselves above the congregation of the Lord?" (Num. 16:13). Korah's confrontation has long held the appeal of a democratic challenge to the tendencies of monarchical exclusivity. But the attraction of Korah's argument rests on the uncritical acceptance of his contention that Moses and Aaron deliberately "elevated [them]selves above the congregation of the Lord," implying that they reserve for themselves privileges to which all Israelites are equally entitled. No hint of this is evident in the Biblical account, however, which insists, to the contrary, that Moses persistently defers the question of leadership until he is finally coerced (by God) to accept his mission. (That same text does not hesitate to attach Divine displeasure to Moses's reactions—hence Moses's momentary bout with leprosy.)[18]

To be sure, it is possible to understand Korah's resistance to the separation entailed in leadership, based on the presentiment that this deliberately imposed distance may presage the slide into estrangement (and, Korah would argue, into alienation as well). The Biblical text itself may be read as tacitly supporting (at least part of) this reading by its notation of Moses's successive physical and perceptual alienations from the Israelite community: Moses pitches his tent at a distance from the Israelite camp so that he may be perpetually ready to receive Divine prophecy, and the radiance of Moses's visage after receiving the Ten Commandments actually frightens

---

18. The Bible records several episode of the contraction of leprosy by the Israelite leadership, including the cases of Moses (Exodus) and Miriam (Numbers). As these incidents are both preceded by speech that is critical of its subject matter, the Midrash opines that Moses (like Miriam; see further note 19) was punished for baseless slander: in Moses's case, it is the Israelites who are the object of his implied criticism, as he doubts the likelihood of their meriting redemption (Sifrei Ki Tetze 141:9). On this occasion, the Midrash presents God as speaking harshly to Moses: "I appeared several times to Abraham, Isaac, and Jacob . . . and they did not question My conduct . . . [By contrast] you at the beginning of your mission [asked Me], 'What is Your name?'"; "Since I have come to Pharaoh to speak in Your name it has become worse for your servants [i.e., the Israelites]"; "Therefore, you will see what I will do to Pharaoh . . . but not [to] the 31 [Canaanite] kings. . . . From here you learn that Moses received the judgment not to enter the Promised Land" (Tahuma Va'Era 1). For another version of this Midrash, which places the emphasis on the relative righteousness of the Israelites in the midst of all their travail, see Shmot Rabbah 4: "And on this it [the verse] says, 'And I will uphold my covenant' that was given to them [the patriarchs] that I will give them [the Israelites] the Land [of Israel], and they [the Israelites] did not question Me, and even though the Israelites of that generation did not behave properly, I heard their groans because of the covenant that I established with their forefathers [patriarchs] as it is written, 'and I remembered My covenant.'"

the Israelites, so that Moses feels obliged to cover his face with a veil (Exod. 33:7; 34:33–35). In fact, members of his own family perceive Moses's progressive distancing as off-putting: his sister, Miriam, protests against the separatism, which she perceives as needlessly estranging.[19]

In the larger arena of national life, however, one can argue that the separation mandated by leadership has a useful goal: in a complex society/enterprise, separation of function allows for greater efficiency and efficacy in the performance of specific tasks. This logic will later be adduced precisely in the realm of leadership by the Israelites themselves in the days of Samuel, when they request a king for his perceived skill in leading the nation in battle (1 Sam. 8:4–22). In the political context, then, Korah's argument promoting sameness of function loses much of its putative salience.

While the Korahide rebellion ends in the textually described extraordinary death of the insurgents, the concerns raised about the politically dangerous consequences of estrangement do not disappear from the Biblical text. These fears may be read as influencing the Deuteronomic strictures regarding the selection of the Israelite king. Primary in the order of the textual parameters is that the king not be a stranger: "From the midst of your brethren shall you set a king upon you" (Deut. 17:14–20). Additionally, the king may not become so enmeshed in his own personal or pecuniary acquisitions that his heart "rises above his brothers," such that he, in effect, becomes estranged from them. Finally, the king must performatively commemorate his fiduciary responsibilities to the people by inscribing all of these rules on a scroll, which he is mandated to proclaim for the rest of his life.[20] Many years later, in his peroration to the Israelites urging them not to establish a monarchy, Samuel elaborates on the alienating tendencies of power: the king, he warns, will take the Israelites' sons and daughters for runners (emphasizing the king's personal glory) and cooks (personal servants). Samuel predicts the devolution of power from estrangement to exploitation. Monarchy, says Samuel, will precipitate the degeneration of politics into enslavement.[21] Unlike the Deuteronomic text, Samuel

19. Num. 12:1. Miriam's complaint against Moses centers on what she considers his excessive "strangeness," the emphasis of which is revealed in the careful wording of the Biblical text. The Bible reports that Miriam comments on "the Cushite woman that he [Moses] took"—that is, the theme of her statement is the foreignness of Moses's actions. It is well to note that the country of Cush abuts Midian, Zipporah's land of origin.

20. "So that his heart may not raise itself above its brothers" (Deut. 17:20).

21. This is a point adduced by political philosophers in ancient Greece; cf. the argument in Plato's *The Republic*, books 8–9, on the moral weakening of society as expressed in the decline of governmental forms.

expresses little fear that the monarch might return the Israelites to Egypt. The absence of this parallelism is perhaps the most trenchant criticism of all. By the very fact of establishing the monarchy, the king will already have enshrined the spirit of Egypt within the Israelite community.

In the actual process of establishing the Israelite nation in the Promised Land after the death of Moses, the Bible depicts the era of the judges as one concerned with the question of establishing a leadership that maintains enough distance ("estrangement") from the people to be able to enunciate a solution to current problems of power without resorting to alienating exploitation. Although the period of the judges appears maddeningly circular in its narrative, evincing little or no moral progress, the Biblical portrayal of distinct leaders during this period yields important clues about the possibilities and pitfalls of political power (Judg. 2:10–19).

Judges as Estranged Leaders

Although the judges are portrayed, at least from the structural point of view, as possessing great dominance within their respective ambits, their actual exercise of power does not support the existence of an authoritarian type of rule. In the Biblical text, judges are as likely to be ignored as obeyed, possibly because they often seem to lack the means or the temperament physically (i.e., violently) to enforce their commands.[22] In addition, their sway generally encompasses no more than several tribes at best. These apparent limitations circumscribing the judges' political exercise of power, however, may also be viewed as an attempt to bring about a permanent amelioration to the dilemma of power: how to prevent the centralization/efficiency of power from degenerating into exploitation.

In this context, one way that the Biblical text reveals its concerns with the perplexities of power is its presentation of the Israelite judges. Each of the judges whose tenure is described in narrative form is depicted as fundamentally weak, lacking an integral component of what is culturally accepted as (political) strength. For example, Ehud, an early judge, is presented as a person with a hampered right hand.[23] This unexpected frailty in a part

22. Judg. 5:15–17. Deborah complains that her call for troops is ignored, and she particularly singles out the tribes of Reuben and Dan.

23. While the colloquial translation of this verse, "iteir yad yimino," is normally translated as "left-handed," the actual import of the words is that "his right hand was hampered/weakened" (Judg. 3:15).

of the body normally associated with military might bodes ill for a leader charged with liberating his people from the harsh rule of Moab.[24] In effect, the Bible portrays Ehud as a leader who does not appear very much in command. At the same time, however, this dissonance paradoxically gives him hidden powers: specifically, the weapon of astonishment. Ehud capitalizes on his ability to catch people unawares by strapping a double-edged sword on his right thigh, where its location and thus its eventual utilization would give him the advantage of surprise. The text's humorous wordplay on the verbal identity between Ehud's tribal roots and his physical weaknesses—the text describes him as *"ben hayimini; ish iteir yad yimino*/a Benjaminite with a hampered right hand"—nearly obscures a more serious source of potential weakness in Ehud's leadership: his tribal provenance. Ehud hails from the youngest tribe of the Israelite nation, whose progenitor is heard to utter not one syllable during the entire drama in Genesis that centers around his welfare and survival.[25] True to his roots, Ehud speaks only four words in his encounter with the king of Moab, and he kills his enemy by capitalizing on his dexterity utilizing a left-handed weapon. Subsequently, Ehud's flight takes place in virtual silence, and his battle plan centers on the surprise trapping of the Moabite forces (Judg. 3:26–30).

The victory of the next judge cited by the Biblical text over the enemy of the Israelites appears even less probable than that of Ehud, if due only to that particular judge's gender. To be sure, Deborah does not depart from the traditional sphere of feminine activity by leading the Israelite troops

24. Regarding military might, cf. "Your right hand, O God, splinters the enemy" (Exod. 15:6). Regarding Moab, see Judg. 3:14–15. To argue that physical strength is not a necessary component of leadership is irrelevant in this context: conventional expectations argue for a physically strong, as opposed to a disabled, leader, particularly in that era, when a major function of a leader was to lead the nation into battle. To be sure, it is true that some (highly successful) leaders have been disabled: Franklin Delano Roosevelt comes to mind as just one example. But the salience of that point is quite limited: FDR occupied the presidency at a time when a great deal of the necessary work was sedentary rather than ambulatory; and, more significantly, he went to great lengths not to acquaint the American public with the full nature and extent of his disability. (Most Americans at the time of FDR's presidency were not aware that he was largely confined to a wheelchair.)

25. See Chapter 1 of this volume. The Midrashic reading of Benjamin's character connects his personal traits with his tribal stone on the breastplate of the high priest: "This teaches us that ... Benjamin ... derived the quality of silence [the Midrash goes on to detail the familial provenance of this characteristic]. . . . His stone on the Priestly Breastplate was jasper [*yashpeh*]; that is to say, he knew about Joseph's sale and remained quiet: *yashpeh=yesh peh* [the Midrashic wordplay on the Hebrew word for the jasper stone is reminiscent of the Hebrew word for mouth; i.e., the organ of speech]" (Midrash Esther Rabbah 6:12).

into battle herself, nor does she personally decapitate the Canaanite general Sisera: these feats are accomplished by Barak and Yael, respectively. Still, the narrative appears discombobulated, if only because the heroic function is displaced onto three people. This complexity in narrative is extended to a multifaceted appreciation of the causes of the Israelite victory: during the narrative, and during Deborah's Song of Thanksgiving, triumph is variously attributed to Divine causes and to human machinations (in particular, those of Yael).[26] To be sure, these different understandings of the foundations of victory are not mutually contradictory: rather, they consciously invoke a more nuanced acquaintance with the complexities of the political scene, which itself is depicted as a mediating layer in the universal order.

With the Gideon narrative, the Biblical text's focus on the weaknesses of the leaders centers on their putative social deficiencies. This is more than a nicety of etiquette, however: social weakness/strength is an important marker of the level of skill with which the leader is able to function in the society that s/he is supposed to guide. Thus, the fact that Gideon is the youngest son of the smallest tribe does not augur well for his ability to unshackle the Israelites (Judg. 6:15). Still later in the period of the judges, Jotham, reciting a parable intended to inspire the Israelites to take political responsibility for their fate, appears an even less-likely liberator. As the lone survivor of a massacre that he escapes only because of his easily hidden small stature, Jotham does not seem to embody the courage normally deemed necessary for leadership (Judg. 9:4). The background of the next

---

26. Judg. 4:15, 23; 5:20–21, 24–26. Classical source-critical literature attributes the differences in the versions of events of Deborah's victory over Sisera's forces in the Book of Judges (chap. 4) and Deborah's victory song itself (chap. 5) to the different historical eras in which these texts are said to have arisen. The victory song is judged to be of more ancient vintage; cf. the nuanced treatment of the various issues raised by source- and form-critical literature in Marc Zvi Brettler, *The Book of Judges* (New York: Routledge, 2002), especially chap. 5. In the Biblical text itself, Deborah does not take credit for her winning tactics on the battlefield; that is to say, she does not attribute her victory to any particular strategy of forcing the Canaanite enemy to fight the battle on Israelite terrain (which was perhaps unfamiliar to them). Certainly the hilly country of the battlefield is not conducive to flexible movements on the part of a chariot-laden Canaanite army. Deborah recognizes, however, that this tactic alone does not explain her victory. After all, many battles in the Book of Judges are fought on Israelite territory, not all of which are won by the Israelites. Neither does the (seemingly) ever-present mud always cooperate by ruining the enemy chariots; consequently, Deborah attributes her victory to God. On the other hand, Deborah's praise of Yael's killing of Sisera is not just appreciation for a trivial action: the loss of a charismatic military leader can often mean a public relations victory that solidifies the triumph for the winning side (cf. in that regard David's victory over Goliath, 1 Sam. 17:51).

Israelite chief similarly gives little cause for rejoicing: Jephtah is the son of a prostitute and is banished by his own brothers (Judg. 11:1–2).

Despite their differences in character, all of these Israelite leaders appear to be unlikely guides. Fundamentally, what unites all of these disparate leaders is their materially grounded estranged status. This estranged position is double in nature: these leaders are alienated from the culturally accepted image of the successful leader, and perhaps partly in consequence of this, they are also distanced from the people whom they lead. Their respective reactions to these circumstances, however, differ. Not all of these leaders accept their position of power with equanimity: Gideon, like Moses, protests against his accession to leadership, while Jephtah, by his active participation in the pronounced negotiations that precede his agreement to lead the Israelites, acknowledges his own awareness of the distance that separates him from the respected social position that, in the Bible, normally accompanies and is a condition of leadership (Judg. 11:6–10). Deborah's alienated status as leader is marked by the dubious distinction of being the only chief in the Book of Judges to be ignored openly by her own people: Deborah's gender seems to elicit a pronounced (if anachronistic) democratic tendency among the Israelites, who tend to accept her as a judge (Judg. 4:1) but not as a military/political leader (Judg. 5:15–17).

At first glance, the one chief whose personal description might seem not to adhere to this narrative of physical estrangement is Samson. Unlike the other Israelite judges, Samson is distinguished by his physical prowess, which disturbs even the Philistines (Judg. 15:10; 16:5). Certain textual dissonances, however, reveal the inherently alienating aspects of Samson's leadership. First, Samson's Nazirite status marks him as different from both his Israelite community of origin as well as his Philistine opponents, who are complicatedly linked to Samson by his (ultimately abortive) marriage to the Timnite woman. Paradoxically, Samson's long, flowing locks, which are visually the most obvious sign of his estranged Nazirite standing, symbolize both the ascetic marginality of his position as well as the full-blown hedonism in which he seems to engage. Furthermore, Samson's riddling technique, which he utilizes in order to engage—but also alienate—his Philistine adversaries, points up the dissonance between his obvious intelligence and the traditionally imagined stupidity of the strongman. Finally, Samson is both an estranged and estranging figure because, alone of all the judges, he questions the very possibility of applying a neat political solution to the complicated travails of the Israelites. By his conscious use of political violence, which mirrors the ferocity with which the Philistines interact with the Israelites, Samson interrogates the ability of politics alone to solve all problems of national and international relations. The alienation that exists at the center of Samson's being reflects the destabilizing effect that he has both on his family and the political communities around him. Samson challenges us to understand the exercise of political power not only as a constitutive element of nation building, but also as a force that can lead to a nation's decay. (This point is echoed centuries later in the split of the Solomonic Israelite kingdom into the northern kingdom of Ephraim and the southern kingdom of Judah.)

In summarizing all the estranging and estranged characteristics of the Israelite judges—weakness (Ehud), mediocre social status (Gideon), dispossession (Jotham), banishment (Jephtah), destabilization/difference (Samson)—the common picture that emerges is crystallized around the image of woman. In effect, the Biblical text figures all of these judges as women. Reflecting the culturally accepted image of women, these leaders are weak; they are marginalized; they possess little or no social status. Moreover, like women, these judges are identified largely by their physical attributes: they are frail (like Ehud, with a weak right hand); they are small (Jotham; although technically, Jotham is not presented specifically as a judge but more generally as a model leader); they have long flowing hair (Samson).[27]

Estranged Models of Power

But leaders in the Bible are not just physically presented as women. More strangely still, many of these leaders (consciously or not) are influenced by the example of women central to Israelite history. Thus, just as these leaders embody strangeness in their displaced relationships to power, they further increase their own sense of alienation by modeling their understanding of power—of what it consists, what it can accomplish—on the public example of women who are themselves perceived as Other in the contemporary structure of (Israelite) communal existence. Thus, for example, Moses's unique approach to his leadership duties may be understood as deriving largely from the leadership that his sister, Miriam, enacts throughout her life.

27. Picking up on these textual clues, the Midrash also portrays the young Joseph as paying conscious attention to his looks, "fiddling with his hair," and so forth (Bereshit Rabbah 84:7).

This is evident from Miriam's first appearance in the Biblical text. Her steady observation of her baby brother as he drifts among the bulrushes of the Nile expresses her confidence that despite the death decree against Israelite male babies, the fate of her brother would be different; that is why she can bear to watch what will happen to him.[28] Aside from this demonstration of certainty on Miriam's part, her seemingly quiescent act of waiting is in fact a move of philosophical activism, staking out an approach entirely different from that espoused by the conventional wisdom of the period.[29] Throughout her life, Miriam, in her theoretical understanding of the circumstances that surround her, expands on this difference, thus embodying a voice entirely her own. In this way, even as a young girl, Miriam is able to understand that the medium of Israelite suffering—the waters of the Nile—can potentially be transformed into the vehicle of their salvation. Miriam's ability to see reality as nuanced, instead of dualistic and exclusionary, leads her to interpret sensitively, uncovering multiple layers of meaning.[30] Consonant with her actions early on in the Exodus narrative, Miriam continues to model the act of interpretation by actively promoting the creative reframing of events that lies at the heart of innovative leadership. Her example proves crucial, for her brother in particular and for the Israelites in general.

Many years later, Miriam expresses her own individual opinion on the (to her mind, unnecessary) isolation that Moses's leadership brings in its train. Although the Biblical text records that she is punished for her words, Miriam does not lose her position of leadership as a result (Num. 12:1–10). The Israelites do not journey onward as long as Miriam is isolated outside the Israelite camp, and when her enforced separation is over, she returns

28. This point is derived by way of a negative contrast. Gen. 21:15–16 recounts the dilemma of Hagar, who, convinced that her son is about to die, can no longer bear to watch him. When a person is convinced that something bad is bound to occur, she can't bear to look. Miriam, however, is different—she is not convinced that something bad would happen.

29. This point is made by BT Sotah 12a, which records that when Pharaoh decreed that all male babies be put to death, Amram and Yokheved decided to separate, believing that it was useless to bring children into the world just to feed Pharaoh's killing machine. It is Miriam who persuades them to get back together, reasoning that her father, by this action, was preventing the birth of both male and female Israelites.

30. The Talmud makes the connection between Miriam's ability to interpret and her thematic connection with water (TB Ta'anit 9a). Traditionally, the Israelites' source of water in the desert is called the well of Miriam. Importantly, the (Biblical) term for "well" in Hebrew derives from the same root as the word for interpretation: *b'a'r.* Consonant with her actions early on in the Exodus narrative, Miriam models the act of interpretation (multiple meanings, polysemy).

to her accustomed place in the Israelite directorate.[31] The centrality of Miriam's example to Moses's continued success comes to the fore when the text records his ultimate sin. As a direct result of Miriam's death, Moses hits the rock instead of speaking to it,[32] which prevents him from entering the Promised Land (Num. 20:1). With his model of leadership gone, Moses (fatefully) stumbles.

Concepts of leadership modeled on the example generated by women also characterize the style of Samson, the last major Israelite judge depicted in the Biblical text. Samson, as will be discussed later on, is distinguished by his deliberate use of riddling to challenge the Philistine rule of his day. A little-noticed aspect of this riddle is that its images not only refer to contemporary events (whose identity forms the central conundrum of the riddle), but also connect directly to a previous Israelite leader of that era. This connection lies at the center of Samson's paradigmatic riddle, "From the strong came forth sweet." Although Samson's ostensible reference is to the honey that he had found several days before in the carcass of a lion, Samson's image may also be seen as alluding to Deborah, whose name translates as "bee," the actual source of the honey in Samson's riddle. Surprisingly, in view of Samson's strongman image, the model to whom Samson refers is the one major female Israelite judge. More than a coded allusion to a bizarre occurrence, Samson's riddle may be understood more fundamentally as presenting a phenomenon even stranger than the one he had encountered on the way back from planning his wedding festivities. In the context of the harsh domination of the Israelites by the Philistines, Samson promotes a different model of leadership, identifying its essence with a sweetness that nevertheless does not belie its inner strength. The image of the bee underlines power's complicated connotations: even as the sting of the bee yields the luxurious sweetness of honey, the political implications of power may prove troublesome and even hurtful, although its results may ultimately be positive.[33] With the implied source of the riddle's central figure being a prominent female judge, Samson's words suggest that leadership may be epitomized in the combined strength and sweetness of a woman. Still, an important question remains for the contemporary reader: why does

31. See, for example, the description of all three as leaders of the Israelites in Mic. 6:4 and 1 Chron. 5:29.

32. Numbers 20:8–12; and see Rashi ad loc.

33. For a similar reference, cf. Socrates' allusion to himself as a gadfly. "Crito," in *The Republic and Other Works*, ed. Benjamin Jowett (New York: Anchor, 1973), 460.

the Biblical text choose to style its portrayal of leaders in this way at this juncture of Israelite history?

The Politics of Estrangement

One way of answering this question is to point to the marginalization of women's position within contemporary society at that time.[34] In that context, women's estranged position provides the template for the destabilizing nature of power, together with its accompanying and alienating consequences. The act of rendering something strange makes its character unknown (perhaps unknowable) and hence potentially threatening to the established political order. When this occurs in the context of a leadership that is portrayed as weakened, the consequent feeling of alienation on the part of the leaders—the fact that their position of authority is not automatically accepted—may well cause them to rethink their relation to the people whom they lead. With this frame of reference, leaders might now emphasize the fulfillment of their responsibility to the people as opposed to the evocation of privilege that the leaders (traditionally) demand from the people. Leaders that are estranged in this way may likely be solicitous of the people's welfare (minimally), seeing in the people's well-being the source for the security and the permanence of their own political position.[35] Paradoxically, the instability evoked by estrangement may yield steadying countermoves by the leadership, resulting in political stability and at least a minimal level of equity for all society.

Estrangement, then, can have a salutary effect on an elite group of leaders, to the extent that it may allow them to appreciate the people's welfare

34. See Carol Meyers, *Discovering Eve: Ancient Israelite Women in Context* (New York: Oxford University Press, 1988), especially chap. 6, "Eve's World: The Family Household," 122–38; and chap. 7, "Household Functions and Female Roles," 139–64.

35. This point is repeated throughout chap. 19 of Machiavelli's *The Prince*: "The prince should try to avoid anything which makes him hateful. . . . One of the strongest counters that a prince has against conspiracies is not to be hated by the mass of the people. . . . A prince should . . . not let himself be hated by the people." Niccolò Machiavelli, *The Prince*, ed. and trans. Robert M. Adams (New York: Norton, 1977), 151–54. For a Biblical counterexample to this approach, cf. Rehoboam's spurning of the more sage advice of the elderly counselors when he informs the Israelites, soon after the death of his father Solomon: "My father worked you hard, and I will increase your burdens" (1 Kings 12:14). The inevitable result is the split of the United Israelite Kingdom: "The [Israelite] nation answered the king saying, 'What portion do we have in David [i.e., in the Davidic monarchy]. . . . To your tents, Israel!' And Israel went to their tents" (1 Kings 12:16).

enough to advocate a certain measure of justice for them. But what occurs when estrangement colors community interaction? What if one part of the national community is forcibly estranged by and from the other? What effect does that have on the ability of the community to cohere politically and socially? A narrative centering on this topic, known as the concubine in Gibeah episode, occurs at the end of the Book of Judges. This text recounts the story of a Levite, domiciled in the northern portion of the ancient Land of Israel (which was allocated to the tribe of Ephraim; the Levites, dedicated to Divine service from Biblical times, received no contiguous landholding among the territories of the other Israelite tribes), who journeys to his father-in-law's home in Beth-Lehem to persuade his concubine (a form of common-law wife with secondary legal rights) to return with him to his home up north. On their journey, they are forced due to the lateness of the hour to turn aside for the night in the village of Gibeah, where they seek hospitality. None is forthcoming, and so the party (the Levite, his concubine, and his manservant) prepares to camp out in the street for the night. Upon seeing them, an old man, himself originally a native of Ephraim, offers to take them in for the night. Later that evening, the old man's house is surrounded by certain townsmen of Gibeah who demand to "get to know" the Levite (the implication is that this would be a homosexual group encounter).[36] The old man offers them his unmarried (virgin) daughter and the Levite's concubine instead, but the townsmen refuse. Finally, the Levite forcibly thrusts his concubine outdoors, whereupon the Gibeahites torture and rape the concubine the whole night long. At daybreak, the concubine crawls to the door of the old man's house; the Levite, ready to leave, requests that she get up and accompany him back home. Upon receiving no answer—it is not clear from the text itself when precisely the concubine finally dies—he places her on the mule.[37] Once he reaches his home in the landholding of Ephraim, the Levite cuts her body—by now, certainly dead—into twelve pieces, which he sends to the

36. This traditional reading identifies "knowledge" with sexual intercourse. The textual basis for this conclusion is the utilization of the verb "y'd'," which, in Biblical Hebrew, connotes sexual relations. The proof text for this reading is Gen. 4:1: "And Adam knew [y'd'] Eve his wife, and she conceived and bore Cain"; the causal connection between the first and second parts of the verse attributes a sexual overtone to the otherwise cognitive concept inherent in "knowing/y'd'." In order to transmit the sense of "knowledge" as friendly acquaintance, the proper verb to use is "h'c'r."

37. This ambiguity in the text is one source of the apologetics that have been offered on behalf of the Levite: after all, could it be that it appeared to him that his concubine died not of sexual violence but simply of exposure to the cold?

other Israelite tribes, requesting that they take action in response to what has occurred.

The nature and effects of this response constitute the last two chapters of the Book of Judges. The offending town of Gibeah is in Benjaminite territory, and the other tribes vow to punish the tribe if they do not hand over the malefactors. The Benjaminites do so refuse, and a war subsequently erupts, yielding at first terrible losses for the United Tribes (the Bible's statistics report that the first two days of battle result in forty thousand dead).[38] The tide turns on the third day of battle (the Biblical text notes this as the result of direct Divine intervention).[39] After their victory, the United Tribes vow never to allow their daughters to marry any surviving Benjaminite man. Because tribal affiliations traditionally adopt the father's origins, this implies the eventual planned disappearance of the Benjaminite tribe. Subsequently, the United Tribes regret this rash vow, because it would result in the permanent alteration of the makeup of the Israelite community. But the United Tribes are now faced with a dilemma: they want to respect what they perceive as the Divine will in establishing the Israelite people with its full complement of tribes; on the other hand, they are religiously enjoined from breaking the terms of their vow.

To avoid either outcome, which in their eyes would mean disrespecting the Divine order, they come up with a plan, which as far as they are concerned carries with it the added advantage of underlining the moral imperative of full participation in the just-concluded fight against the tribe of Benjamin. The United Tribes discover that of all the localities in the ancient Land of Israel, only the people of Jabesh-Gilead had failed to send soldiers into battle against the Benjaminites. In retaliation, they kill all the inhabitants of that city, with the exception of four hundred (virgin) maidens, who are then assigned in marriage to the remaining Benjaminites. As

38. It is not clear from the text whether this refusal on the part of the Benjaminites is based on a sense of tribal privacy or, alternatively, is a manifestation of "tribal rights" (much in the manner of the American political doctrine of "states' rights"). In terms of the structure of the Book of Judges, an ironic distance separates the actions of various Benjaminites at the beginning and end of this book. At the beginning of the narrative presentation of specific judges, the tribe of Benjamin is presented as the tribal background of a judge whose weak appearance masks the cunning that helps him liberate the Israelites from their oppressors. By the book's end, the tribe of Benjamin has become the direct source of oppression for an integral part of the Israelite community: first, in the perpetration of the outrage against the concubine at Gibeah; second, in the manner of their repatriation into the Israelite community.

39. According to the Bible, over twenty-five thousand Benjaminite soldiers are killed, with additional civilian casualties.

it happens, however, there are still two hundred Benjaminites (males) for whom wives are not provided. The Israelite elders suggest that at the next religious festival near Shiloh (the location of the Tabernacle at that time), these Benjaminites should lie in wait near the fields, where it was customary for the young maidens to dance on festival days, and kidnap wives for themselves. This they do, and everybody returns to their landholdings. It is worth noting the Biblical text's last remark on what might at first glance appear to be a "satisfactory" ending to this episode; these words end this story, as well as the entire Book of Judges: "In those days, there was no king in Israel; each man would do what was right in his eyes" (Judg. 21:25).

Modern sensibilities do not take kindly to the ease with which the old man in Gibeah is ready to turn over his daughter—and the Levite's concubine—for the pleasure of the townspeople, just in order to save his guest from the "unnatural horror" of the proposed encounter.[40] In terms of the preoccupation with strangeness, however, the text implicitly justifies the negative categorization of the proposed act by referring to it as "to'evah," meaning "unnatural" or "abomination"—that is, *estranged* from the norm. At the same time, however, the Levite's own subsequent actions toward the body of his concubine—systematically carving her body into twelve pieces—are no less estranged from the standards of common decency than the feared actions of the Gibeahites.[41] It is worth realizing, too, that while the war against the Bejaminites unites most of the Israelite tribes, the final outcome of the battle renders the Benjaminites so (e)strange(d) that they are effectively placed outside the Israelite community.[42]

The "resolution" of this episode as depicted in the Biblical text, "reuniting" the Israelite community, makes full use of the irony of the Israelites' inner estrangement from one another, which, tellingly, also marks the

40. It is worth noting that the Midrashic reading of the Genesis narrative harshly critiques Lot for offering up his own daughters in order to save his own guests from what was then considered a "fate worse than death" (Midrash Tanhuma VaYera 12). The Midrash accuses Lot of a lack of moral imagination and of faintheartedness, asking why he does not risk his own life to fight both for the safety of his guests and the moral virtue of his daughters. In that regard, the irony of the next chapter, in which Lot is the object of sexual activity on the part of his own daughters, is morally telling.

41. The Levite, in recounting his tale to the other tribes, reports that the Gibeahites had planned to kill him (Judg. 20:5).

42. For an ironic gloss on the Book of Judges that contrasts this war (perceived as emblematic of national barrenness) to the first wars of this book (read as more positive in origin and implication), see Lillian R. Klein, *The Triumph of Irony in the Book of Judges* (Sheffield: Almond, 1988), especially 191–92, 195–200, 211.

opening of the Book of Judges.[43] The final price of the Benjaminites' re-inscription into the Israelite community is capture and constraint for the enablers of this re-inclusion: the group of kidnapped Shilohite women. The position of the women, existing both inside and outside the community, highlights the paradox of state founding by pointing out that the Other is originally always located within the community itself. The very women who are indispensable for the physical creation of community and the transmission of its culture are treated like foreign prisoners of war, forced to perform activities whose essence, in normal circumstances (i.e., marriage and cultural transmission), are portrayed as quotidian activities with allowances for discretionary choice. An additional layer of complexity is added by the fact that this whole process is provoked by the estranged (legal) status of the Levite's concubine, whose standing is alienated even in death. In contradistinction to the general run of Biblical texts describing the lives and deaths of members of a married couple, the text records no private mourning ritual for the concubine's death: her hacked body is used functionally as a public call for action, and she is denied even the common repatriation to the earth, emblematic of the close of human life (Gen. 3:19; 4:9–11).[44] As a result, the moral efficacy and practical durability of what is supposedly accomplished on the political scene is highly questionable.

The paradox of state founding highlighted by the Biblical text, under-lining the role of the stranger in establishing the polis, also forms an important theme in recent critical writing. In *Democracy and the Foreigner*, Bonnie Honig notes the thematic identity of the state founder with the stranger.[45] She offers valuable insights not only regarding the function that the foreign founder fulfills specifically in democratic theory, but also concerning the action of political founding in general. According to Honig, the stranger in effect performs two contradictory roles, which both complicate and simplify the process of state founding.[46] On the complicating side, the stranger makes the process of state founding "undecidable"; that

---

43. See the tribally based (and not nationally executed) battles for the individual territories of each tribe described in chap. 1 of the Book of Judges, which counterpoints Moses's original admonition that all Israelites fight together in the battles to conquer Canaan (Num. 31:20–42).

44. In marriage narratives typical of the founders of the Israelite nation, the marriage partner remains a matter of individual choice. See, by contrast, the Bible's lengthy recounting of Abraham's grief at the death of his wife Sarah (Gen. 23:1–20).

45. Bonnie Honig, *Democracy and the Foreigner* (Princeton: Princeton University Press, 2001).

46. Ibid., 32.

is to say, it is not always clear to the regular citizens of the polity that all the change incurred in the process of the (new/re-) founding of the state is a good thing. At the same time, however, the fact that the founder of the state is a foreigner, "outside" the community, makes this undecidability easy to deal with: the citizens can always decide to expel the foreigner, returning the state founder to his origins outside the polis.[47]

In *Speaking the Unspeakable*, Diane Jonte-Pace further develops the idea of strangeness and its alienating functions within society by identifying it specifically with the feminine.[48] Jonte-Pace structures this identity on the Freudian notion of strangeness, which is explicated in Freud's 1919 essay "The Uncanny." According to Freud, the origin of strangeness, or the "uncanny," is located within the very person who names a particular object/person as "foreign" or "different." Jonte-Pace expands on this identification by arguing that the notion of the uncanny perforce refers to the feminine—more specifically, to the body of the mother.[49] The body of the mother, says Jonte-Pace, is the ultimate embodiment of the uncanny, because it contains within itself the fundamental contradictions of Eros (the forbidden eroticism attributed by Freud to the child-mother relationship) and Thanatos (the temporary absence that the child feels because he is not the sole possessor of the mother) that impel human development and interaction. Taking seriously Freud's naming of the inexplicable dream by the (ostensibly metaphorical) term "navel," Jonte-Pace points to the actual navel in the body, containing the permanent marking of this individual antenatal connection to the maternal source, as the root of Freud's description of the uninterpretable/"uncanny" aspects of dreams that defy analysis.[50]

Working on a similar trajectory, Julia Kristeva clarifies the political implications of the connection between difference and violence. Kristeva

47. Honig expresses it in this way: the strange origins of the founder also provide a (prudent) scapegoat in case things do not work out (ibid., 32, 33–40).

48. Diane Jonte-Pace, *Speaking the Unspeakable* (Berkeley and Los Angeles: University of California Press, 2001).

49. Jonte-Pace puts forth her thesis to counteract the notion that there is only one narrative in the Freudian text (i.e., the Oedipal paradigm). Jonte-Pace contends that there are many points in Freud's theory where a counter-thesis to the dominant "master plot" emerges—instances when Freud (curiously) does not continue his interpretation along the standard (Oedipal) path. Typically, these cases are replete with references to the mother's body, which, following Freud, Jonte-Pace identifies with the "uncanny."

50. In *Speaking the Unspeakable*, Jonte-Pace remarks, "The navel of the dream . . . evokes the human navel, the scar that marks the site of the connection to and separation from the mother. It is the site of connection to and separation from the mother that Freud cannot interpret" (30).

focuses on Freud's explication of the dialectic of the "homely (familiar)/ uncanny (strange)" ("heimlich/unheimlich"). Freud argues that the "uncanny" is really not "strange" at all; rather, it is the psyche's way of disguising the presence of unwanted, dark aspects of one's own character. According to Freud, we then proceed to reify these "uncanny/*unheimlich*" aspects as Other and therefore evil. Subsequently, we expel them.[51] In *Strangers to Ourselves*, Kristeva posits that the uncanniness/strangeness of those aspects of ourselves that we want to reject reflects itself in the identity of those whom we construe as "strangers" in our society (and whom we therefore often fantasize about banishing). In other words, for Kristeva, the stranger/ foreigner/immigrant in our society is actually a reification of the strange/ uncanny within our own selves. She therefore concludes that rejecting the stranger is in effect refusing the uncanny aspect of ourselves. The result, while comforting (to the individual) at the present moment, yields a doubly negative effect: it not only retards psychoanalytic closure (which prevents individual development), but also thwarts the possibility of establishing a dynamically peaceful and productive society.[52]

While much has been written in modern times about the respective links between strangeness and violence on the one hand, and between violence and women on the other, it is important to recognize that the complex interaction of all of these themes is already raised in the texts of the Hebrew Bible. The Bible contributes decisively to the discussion about the political implications of difference by locating the roots of this difficulty in the way that women are viewed by society. In this connection, the concubine in Gibeah episode is most fruitfully read as exposing the personification of difference in the body of women, whose "strangeness" is then used to justify the violence perpetrated against them. Ironically, this violence is committed against the very women who are themselves part of the community. Therefore, violence is seen as an inextricable part of establishing the polity.[53]

51. Julia Kristeva, *Strangers to Ourselves*, trans. Leon Roudiez (New York: Columbia University Press, 1991), 182–88.

52. Ibid., 192; see also 187, 191. For Kristeva, however, the identity between the uncanny/ *unheimlich* within ourselves and the stranger/foreigner in our society does not mean that our politics must inevitably remain impaled on the horns of alienation and division. On the contrary, the acceptance of this identity and the integration of difference is indispensable for the establishment of an authentically democratic society in the modern world.

53. These themes are also developed in Rousseau's *Le Lévite d'Ephraïm*, where he replays and enlarges on the violence perpetrated on the women/strangers who are themselves an integral part of the community. This violence is then justified as an inevitable consequence of community founding.

This equation of strangeness and violence that plays out against the backdrop (and on the backs) of women is asserted both at the beginning and at the end of this Biblical narrative. The onset of the story's political implications occurs when the death of the heretofore-existing Israelite community is symbolically inscribed on the inert body of the Levite's concubine.[54] In a similarly violent denouement, the political and personal survival of the remaining Benjaminites is achieved through the bodily subjection of the maidens of Jabesh-Gilead and Shiloh.[55, 56] Thus, the Israelite men compel the women to ratify the male sense of community: the women validate "le nom du père"—the essence of the fathers' identity—by acceding to the proscriptions of their fathers: "le non du père."[57] This is evident in the textual representation of women as collectivities of absence: while nominally alive, the women consistently lack status, voice, and name. Even their materiality, as incarnated in their bodies, does not exist in its own right, but merely as an instrument for the inscription of the will of others (i.e., men).[58] In either incarnation, it seems to follow that personal and political survival for men is predicated on the annihilation of women.

At one level, it may appear convenient to use violence against the stranger to bolster a community's sense of unity and, hence, political stability. But as the identity of the "troublesome" stranger becomes increasingly

54. Alice Bach, "Rereading the Body Politic," in *Judges: A Feminist Companion to the Bible*, ed. Athalya Brenner (Sheffield: Sheffield University Press, 1999), 146.

55. In this connection, it is telling that Benjamin's personal and tribal survival is always predicated on the physical travail of women. For an account of Benjamin's birth resulting in his mother's death, cf. Gen. 35:17–18.

56. Bach, "Rereading the Body Politic," 146.

57. The connection between "le non du père" and "le nom du père" is treated by Tony Tanner in "Julie and 'La Maison Paternelle,'" in *The Family in Political Thought*, ed. Jean Bethke Elshtain (Amherst: University of Massachusetts Press, 1982); it is based on the affiliation adduced by Foucault in his article "Le non du père," *Critique* (March 1962): 195–209. According to Foucault, the Father's ability to maintain the "non" hinges on his identification with the Law, which he both names and which names/designates him as its authority. The Father proclaims the Law that separates, that forbids: "*Le père est alors celui qui sépare . . . prononçant la Loi . . . la Parole dont la forme première est celle de la contrainte*/The father is he who separates . . . pronouncing the Law . . . the Word whose first form is that of constraint" (205). Cf. Luce Irigaray: "The man (father) will persevere in develop his individualization by *assimilating* the external into and for the self. . . . Blood is burned to cinders in the writing of the text of law whereby man produces (himself) at the same time (as) the double—differently in him, in his son, and in his wife." *Speculum of the Other Woman* (Ithaca: Cornell University Press, 1974), 221, emphasis in the original; cf. also 308–10.

58. In other words, the women are recognized only in their capacity to give birth and perpetuate the line of the men who legislate the community's rules: thus, through their birthing abilities, the women physically and literally perpetuate "le nom du père."

obscure, and the preferred strategy for dealing with this issue becomes progressively murky, uncomfortable questions arise. In the context of the Biblical narrative, who is the "stranger" that must be forthwith expelled: is it the immoral and unwelcoming Gibeahites? The Benjaminites certainly don't think so, and, consequently, a civil war develops. Within this framework of hostilities, it is the Benjaminites who are "estranged" by the United Tribes to the point of near annihilation. When the United Tribes collectively realize that this potentially irrevocable alteration of the their tribal structure would in effect render the Israelites strangers to themselves, they target a new group from their own midst to be estranged and be treated as Other: the women of Jabesh-Gilead and Shiloh, who are given forcibly in marriage to the remaining Benjaminites. Superficially, this final act of estrangement might appear to ensure the stability of Israelite society. In actuality, however, the Israelite social structure remains fundamentally unsteady: the Biblical text relates that Israelite history after this incident includes yet more internecine warfare. The result is further division, ending in the eventual defeat of the Israelite community, which is then consigned to live as strangers, first in their own land, and then on foreign soil. Ultimately, the text demonstrates that the progressive estrangement of others leads not to a stable social and political nucleus, but instead to a society that devours its own members and inevitably disintegrates.

But the overriding point of the Biblical text is that it does not have to be this way. Strangeness/difference need not automatically yield violence. Emphasizing this point, the Bible specifically highlights the estranged figures of women to demonstrate that beyond the technical problematics of integrating strangers/strangeness, strangeness itself can actually provide as yet unimagined solutions to the complex issues raised by politics. For the Bible, difference has a transcendent role to play in the construction of community. If all members of the community can be made to feel "different," then difference becomes not an alienating stigma, but a tool that allows everyone to enter into and expand both their own humanity and that of their interlocutors. Paradoxically, suspending all citizens in the category of "strangeness" keeps the humanity of all of them alive, as no one can arrogate to themselves a status of greater importance or meaning. In this way, difference can enable politics to reach its ultimate ethical expression. Thus, it turns out that in not accepting and not integrating the stranger both within and without, we doom ourselves to eternal estrangement from our own personal and political fulfillment. As the Biblical text progresses in dealing with this issue, the integration of difference becomes the yard-stick by which to measure both the establishment of (philosophical) justice as well as the (practical) establishment of a dynamic political community whose constitution can withstand the test of time.[59]

The integral role of difference in establishing a just polity is highlighted in Leviticus, when God remarks to the Israelites, "You are strangers and settlers with Me" (25:23). Curiously, the role of difference is connected here to God's point of view, a seeming anomaly in a narrative detailing the allocation of land portions in the Promised Land. Furthermore, in the con-text of a narrative centering on a nation that is eagerly anticipating the pos-session of its Promised Land, it seems strange to insist that the quality of Israelite nationhood is based on maintaining an aura of dissonance between a nation and their land. This seems to negate the durability of connection, which conventionally expresses the material, and hence, from the human perspective, permanent, aspect of nationhood.[60]

For the Bible, this restructuring of the political arena, anchored by the location of strangeness at its center, can also by extension justify the theo-retical broadening of the political sphere beyond the strictly human—it can include the Divine. From the Biblical perspective, this invocation of the Divine goes beyond Joseph's recognition that politics has a human func-tion to fulfill beyond the selfish desire for power consolidation on the part of an individual (ruler). To be sure, the active inclusion of the Divine may still seem counterintuitive in the context of (theorizing) nation formation, because politics traditionally (according to ancient Greek and Roman polit-ical thought) is viewed as a realm of purely human action. In that context,

59. This refers specifically to verses that some (adherents of the Documentarian approach) see as part of a later evolution of the Biblical text: "And you shall love the stranger" (Deut. 10:19). For the most part, however, references to the "stranger" in all parts of the Bible, whether in Exodus or Leviticus, whether styled as the legal code or the priestly code, empha-size the equality and responsibility of all residents (thus, Exod. 22:20, 23:9; Lev. 19:33, 25:35, etc.). Regardless of what critics may ascribe to the historical evolution of different parts of the Biblical text, the entire corps of this text itself foregrounds a concept of citizenship under-girded by the notion of strangeness.

60. It is easy to insist that this verse in Leviticus perforce refers only to the allocation of land, pointing to the periodic return of the ancestral portion to its original family of heritage. Retaining that exclusivist focus, however, insistently disregards the additional element intro-duced in the verse, highlighting the relationship of God to the Israelite citizens of the land. In the context of the cycle of land ownership alone, the mention of God, strictly speaking, has no place: the issue of social fairness, to name just one theme, might be more appropriate. Intertwining the Divine with the cycle of land possession makes sense only in the context of the generalized and specific Otherness that the Biblical text valorizes as an integral part of citizenship.

to the extent that politics is defined as the highest and quintessentially most human activity, it seems counterproductive for Divine constraints to manifest themselves here, and thus seemingly to limit the human potential for self-expression and -actualization.

The Biblical response to this point of view does not negate the centrality and moral imperative of human liberty, but it defines the essence of humanity differently from the traditional models projected by classical Greek political thought or modern political theory. For the Bible, humanity is characterized not wholly in terms of its own self and desires, but also in relation to something greater than and outside itself. The Bible identifies this other source of moral value as the Divine. This understanding of the relationship between the Divine and the human does not view the acknowledgement of the Divine as inherently constraining human achievement. On the contrary, the Biblical appreciation of the Divine source of humanity serves to expand the horizons of human value and influence, because the finite world alone no longer defines the extent of the human experience.

Thus, for the Bible, the deepest expression of humanity is evident when one permits God to enter the picture. As expressed by the Biblical text, both God and other people are, to differing qualities and degrees, manifestations of Otherness.[61] In this way, the incorporation of God-centered moral standards promotes the human dimensions of politics, because the inclusion of

61. Biblical examples of the role of this expanded concept of Otherness in the constitution of shared political discourse include, most obviously, the story of Joseph, where his representation of history specifically evokes the central role of the Deity, invoked in His character as judge (cf. above, Chapter 1). By implication, intimations of this are also evident in the Biblical summary to the concubine in Gibeah episode (Judg. 21:25; see the discussion in this chapter and, further, in Chapter 6), as well as in the personality of Gideon (see further, Chapter 4, this volume). Emmanuel Levinas elaborates philosophically on the rationale of the identification of various types of Otherness: "The absolute other is the Other. . . . God rises to his supreme and ultimate presence as the correlative of justice rendered unto men." *Totality and Infinity*, trans. Alphonso Lingis (1961; Pittsburgh: Duquesne University Press, 1969), 39, 78. To be sure, one may ascribe this awareness of two realms, the secular and the divine, and the justification of the former by values promoted by the latter, to the developments of the "Axial Age." S. N. Eisenstadt, "The Axial Age Breakthroughs—Their Characteristics and Origins" and "The Axial Age Breakthrough in Ancient Israel," in *The Origins and Diversity of Axial Age Civilizations* (Albany: SUNY Press, 1986). The primarily historical and historicist point of this theoretical understanding, however, omits the unique contribution of the (Hebrew) Biblical text: namely, that the (human) category of self is morally justified and most fruitfully develops precisely through interaction with and recognition of the multiplicity (and not the single manifestation) of other identities, all of which also point to the absolute Divine Other. The clear difference in this regard with New Testament theology is also noted by implication in Steven Grosby, *Biblical Ideas of Nationality: Ancient and Modern* (Winona Lake, Ind.: Eisenbrauns, 2002), 115–16.

the Divine prevents human life from being limited merely to its own self-referentiality and, hence, potentially depreciated.[62] The Otherness inherent in the Biblical understanding of power, and its inclusion of marginalized people in its portrayal of legitimate political power, both reflects and impels the (later) Kantian definition of the human as an end-in-itself rather than a selfishly directed "means."[63] Consequently, in the Biblical view, politics has the potential to become truly redemptive in the social, individual, and spiritual arenas. For the Bible, politics is a dialectic in the most open sense of the word: a perennially moral confrontation between self and Other at every level.[64]

The persistence of the theme of strangeness in Israelite history and development, as well as its encapsulation in the Leviticus verse defining Israelite national existence cited above, imply that dissonance and nonconventional thinking are the hallmarks of Israelite nationhood. Instead of viewing nationhood as a convenient method of organizing power relations within (one's corner of) the world, the Bible introduces another possible understanding of national definition, with nationhood representing the opportunity to interrogate empirical power relations and their accompanying moral implications.[65] As the story of Joseph emphasizes, the Biblical text demonstrates that the integration of strangeness has a constitutive role

62. As the Bible expresses it, it is the inclusion, not the exclusion, of God in the conduct of national discourse that enables the political enterprise to expand to include all of the inhabitants within its borders. Otherwise, it is all too easy to find a perfectly rational and even "humane" reason to withhold the epithet of personhood, and thus survival, from any weak or disrespected group.

63. In *Perpetual Peace*, Kant writes, "Since, like a tree, each nation has its own roots, to incorporate it into another nation as a graft, denies its existence as a moral person, turns it into a thing, and thus contradicts the concept of the individual contract." *Perpetual Peace and Other Essays*, trans. with introduction by Ted Humphrey (Indianapolis: Hackett, 1983), 108. Kant continues: "The sole established constitution that follows from the idea of an original contract, the one on which all of a nation's just legislation must be based, is republican. For first, it accords with the principles of the *freedom* of the members of a society (as men), second, it accords with the principles of the *dependence* of everyone on a single, common [source of] legislation (as subjects), and third, it accords with the law of the equality of them all (as citizens)" (112).

64. For more on the connection between allowing for both human and transcendental others in one's life as a condition for the further development of the self, see my "A Life of Faith and a Life of the Mind," in *Still Believing: Muslim, Christian, and Jewish Women Affirm Their Faith*, edited by Victoria Lee Erikson and Susan A. Farrell (Maryknoll, N.Y.: Orbis, 2005).

65. This traditional view of politics comes to the fore with the personage of Nimrod, who is described as an autocratic ruler. He is, in fact, the first of the emperors (Gen. 10:8–12). By extension, the narrative in Judges often depicts fealty to God as propelling/accompanying political deliverance from foreign domination.

to play in the material establishment of dynamic political community. This has implications not only for the moral inferences of the political sphere, but also, and perhaps more immediately, for the practical realization of the energetic polity whose identity continues to develop throughout time. As we have seen, the Bible specifically highlights women, traditionally associated with the troublesome problematics of the stranger/Other, to point out the transcendent possibilities of this connection. The link between strangeness and the establishment of the dynamic national identity crucial to the founding of a vibrant polity is evident already during the period of the judges, and it forms the central theme of the Book of Ruth.

3

RUTH: THE POLITICS OF DIFFERENCE

At first glance, the Book of Ruth seems to say little about either politics or the exercise of political power: no sustained strife is recorded in this book either between specific clans or among different groups of nations. The text of this book appears to be essentially positive, conforming to conventional standards of what is right and possible within a world where personal circumstances change rapidly and without warning; the tale adheres closely enough to traditional standards of happy endings in order to deflect critical, or even revolutionary, responses.

In essence, the Book of Ruth presents the contemporary reader with the paradox of familiarity: the text that we think we know can surprise us when we least expect it. The essence of the paradox should perhaps not astonish: the danger with well-known stories is that we read the narrative we have come to expect instead of what is actually written in the text. So it is with the Book of Ruth: we are all familiar with the story of the widowed stranger who loyally follows her bereft mother-in-law to find fulfillment and (a measure of) acceptance in a new land, becoming in her turn the matriarch of the Davidic dynasty. In this traditional recapitulation, the Book of Ruth nicely fits the romantic "stranger at the gates" typology, whose happy ending harmonizes with the dominant notions of what is deemed correct by society at large. Alternatively, more contemporary approaches to Ruth focus on the traditional role of women in a patriarchal society, whose existences are validated only insofar as they strengthen the patrilineal links on which that society is founded.[1]

1. See, for example, Alicia Ostriker, "The Redeeming of Ruth"; Gail Twersky Reiner, "Her Mother's House"; Nehama Aschkenasy, "Language as Female Empowerment in Ruth";

In fact, both versions of this narrative can be found within the Book of Ruth. While on the surface these two accounts of Ruth seem to have little in common, their essential grasp of the subject matter is the same. Both of these versions of the Book of Ruth view work as bereft of any real crisis or tension, because the women in this book are portrayed as unquestioningly fulfilling a preordained role.[2] In addition, both of these approaches are alike in neglecting a major portion of this book, which centers on what seems to be a legalistic technicality. Far from reflecting a calm and conventional philosophy of life, the Book of Ruth is in fact filled with unsettling questions, most of which bear directly on the nature of national identity and the requirements of leadership.

The dissonances that exist in the Book of Ruth are not (just) a function of the dramatic tension regarding Ruth's achievement of personal and/or financial security. Rather, the disquiet in the Book of Ruth derives from the consideration of a philosophical issue: how to actualize a sense of self while living a religiously directed life. The text focuses on the sustained philosophical search by its protagonist for a coherent understanding of selfhood that can include both self-affirmation and other-directed giving. In the process, Ruth lays the foundation for a dynamic understanding of nationhood that will also pave the way for the institutionalization of its leadership and, hence, the stability of its political arrangements.

Importantly, the philosophical and political strands of the Ruth narrative do not take place in dislocated spheres. Instead, the philosophical and political themes of the text inform one another. The implications of Ruth's philosophical quest touch on both external (social/political) and internal (philosophical) aspects of contemporary Judean life. The text presents a trenchant critique of contemporary Judean society, which did not fulfill its mandated ethical responsibilities regarding the treatment of those of its own citizens considered to be of insufficient stature to deserve full social accommodation.[3] In addition, the Book of Ruth considers the role of difference in constructing national life and examines the coherence of national

---

and Mona DeKoven Fishbane, "Ruth: Dilemmas of Loyalty and Connection," all in *Reading Ruth: Contemporary Women Reclaim a Sacred Story*, ed. Judith A. Kates and Gail Twersky Reimer (New York: Ballantine, 1994).

2. In summarizing contemporary critical appreciations of Ruth, Avivah Zornberg notes that for the modern reader, "There doesn't seem to be a moment of crisis in the entire book." "The Concealed Alternative," in *Reading Ruth*, ed. Kates and Reimer, 66.

3. Thus, Naomi is ignored by her relatives and even by her erstwhile friends in Beth-Lehem (Ruth 1:19).

community as a function of its acceptance of difference. The Book of Ruth enacts the possibilities of strangeness in a world fixated on identifying and isolating the Other, whether of a different nation, gender, clan, or social class. Instead of being defeated by this marginalization, Ruth, the unlikely protagonist of a tale in which every other character remains centered in their origins, manages to utilize the contradictions of strangeness to organize the conflicting sides of the national dialectic in a dynamic balance. This enables her to establish the dynasty that embodies both political stability and national redemption.

As with the mutual referencing of political and philosophical themes, the individual and political implications of strangeness are also intercalated: dealing with strangeness on the personal level enables the dynamic participation of strangers in the national sphere.

Ruth as Social Critique

The first verse of the Book of Ruth appears merely to locate the story in a specific historical context: the era of the judges in the ancient Land of Israel. Two comments in other Biblical texts reveal that this is not considered to be morally the most auspicious moment in Israelite history. A brief remark at the beginning of 1 Samuel points to the corruption in the higher circles of religious leadership during the era of the judges.[4] In a similar vein, the Book of Judges ends on an ominous note: "Each man would do what was right in his own eyes" (21:25). As the context of this remark is the story of the multiply raped and murdered woman in Gibeah whose severed body provokes a bloody civil war, the sarcasm and irony of this phrase leads to the conclusion that moral chaos characterizes this epoch.

The moral clues given by the textual identification of the specific historical period are further expanded in a literary analysis of the first verse of Ruth offered by the Midrashic compilation Ruth Rabbah.[5] Focusing on the repetition of verbs[6] in a normally laconic text,[7] and attempting to link

4. "And the word of God was dear in those days; prophecy was not widespread" (1 Sam. 3:1).

5. It should be noted that Ruth Rabbah is one of the older extant Midrashim and, like the Midrash Tanhuma (itself one of the earlier Midrashim), compiled in the Land of Israel.

6. The reference here is to the repetition of the verb "to judge [sh'p't]," so that the normally laconic text reads "the time of the judging of the judges" instead of the more usual "the time of the judges."

7. See Auerbach, *Mimesis*, especially 10–12.

a set of seemingly disjunctive phrases in the first verse of the book,[8] the Midrash presents a negative evaluation of the Israelite judges of that time. According to the Midrash, Israelite judges of that era were themselves liable to be judged by the very people who came before them for judgment. In the Midrashic reading, these judges deserved to have their authority and dignity thus challenged, because they did not possess the moral rectitude demanded by their positions. The dominant theme in the Midrashic elaboration of these judicial failures is that the judges proclaimed laws to which they themselves did not adhere. Their hypocrisy extended to the perversion of the legal system. In the words of the Midrash, "A judge would sit and proclaim, 'You shall not pervert judgment'—and he himself would pervert judgment; 'You shall not judge with favoritism'—and he himself would render judgment with favoritism; 'You shall not take bribes'—and he himself would take bribes."[9] The consequences of this have a terrible logic of their own: the Israelites trivialized the importance of the legal process, to the point of visiting violence on a judge who did not render the expected verdict.[10]

The attitudes described here reveal a profound alienation between the people and their leaders. According to the Midrash, the leaders do not even pray for—or, presumably, care about—the people when they are in need.[11] To be sure, the leaders' attitudes do no more than reflect the self-centeredness of the people themselves. The Midrash locates the roots of the people's selfishness early in Israelite history, dating from the death of Joshua, as the settlement process of the ancient Land of Israel was drawing to a close. Despite his central role in the realization of the Israelites' agrarian dreams, the Midrash reports that the Israelites found no time to give their leader, Joshua, a proper burial, because they were too involved

8. At first glance, the litany presented by the text—of the "judges being judged," followed by the notation of a famine and the voluntary dislocation of a particular family—seems inappropriately juxtaposed. It is this seeming disconnection that the Midrashic reading tries to categorize and thereby rationalize within a system of larger understanding.

9. Ruth Rabbah Petihata 7.

10. "In the days of the Judges, an Israelite would worship idols, and [when] the judges would attempt to call him to task [lit.: render judgment on him], he [that is, the man being judged] would strike the judge" (Ruth Rabbah Petihata 7).

11. In Ruth Rabbah Petihata 9, we read a condemnation of this attitude. The Midrash unfavorably compares the leaders during the period of the judges to Moses, who was ever ready to defend his people, even against God. The words of the Midrash accuse the leaders of this period of "not jumping into the breach" to take the part of their people even against Divine accusations: "You [the Midrash portrays God as he speaks to the current Israelite leadership] did not jump into the breach like Moses."

in their agricultural pursuits.[12] Alienation worked both ways, and it left the people and their leaders estranged at all levels.

Following that indictment, the Midrash understands the second half of Ruth's introductory passage, recounting the famine that strikes the Land of Israel, as the outcome of the moral schizophrenia described in the first half of the verse. Significantly, the narrative relates the tangible realization of this moral inadequacy: consonant with the alienation of the people from their leaders, we read that one of these leaders leaves the famine-struck Land of Israel, taking himself and his family to the neighboring (and presumably more fruitful) fields of Moab. Even without the Midrashic indictment of judicial malfeasance, the text itself makes clear that the leadership of the time was morally insensitive: Elimelekh, designated by the text as an important man ("ish"), abandons his people to their fate.[13]

As reported via the Midrash on the Book of Ruth, Elimelekh's sin is not caring: he chooses to move his family to escape the worst of the famine, even though the very presence of the economic resources utilized to effect this household displacement reveals that he might have, had he so chosen, elected to stay and utilize (some of) his wealth to ameliorate the fate of his starving countrymen. Instead, Elimelekh rejects that responsibility and opts to focus only on his personal well-being. For the Biblical text, it is no accident that he winds up in the fields of Moab, whose founder is described in the Bible as the son of Abraham's nephew, Lot, conceived in an incestuous relationship after Lot's flight from the destruction of Sodom (Gen. 19:31–38). In the Biblical narrative, the very name of Sodom carries with it the additional connotation of a culture of inhospitality and moral indifference that degenerates into social oppression.[14] Although Lot himself continues, while in Sodom, to adhere to the Abrahamitic vision of kindness and openheartedness (even to strangers), his subsequent (incestuous) behavior indicates that his sojourn in Sodom left negative traces on his character.[15] Elimelekh's choice of Moab as the location to wait out Israel's famine

12. The Midrash puts this trenchantly: "This person was occupied with his fields, and this one was busy in his vineyard" (Ruth Rabbah Petihata 2).

13. See Ozick, "Ruth," 218–19. Also see Zornberg, "Concealed Alternative," 71.

14. Cf. Gen. 18:20: "The cry of Sodom and Gomorrah is great." Also, Lot's house is surrounded by enraged Sodomites when it is learned that he is harboring guests inside, and it is obvious that no good is intended either for Lot or his guests (Gen. 19:4–9).

15. The Midrashic judgment on Lot is harsher than the textual evidence at first glance would seem to demand. Commenting on Lot's move eastward toward Sodom, the Midrash Rabbah focuses on the use of the (relatively esoteric and) largely historical term "kedem" to signify the eastern direction. Comments the Midrash: "Lot removed himself from the

thus acquires an aura both of moral indifference and acquiescence to sin. This foreboding is borne out in the Biblical text by the fact that soon after his death, his own sons echo Elimelekh's virtual disengagement from the Israelite people by marrying Moabite women, who stand outside of this (normally) endogamous community.

The first four verses of the Book of Ruth thereby condemn the Israelite leaders of that time not only regarding the fulfillment of their professional roles, but also in terms of their personal choices. Not surprisingly, as exemplified by Elimelekh's family, these leaders prove incapable of transmitting the values and beliefs for which they stand—perhaps because indeed they do not really accept all the elements of their faith. In this context, the wide rift between the people and their leaders bodes ill for the future of the Israelites, particularly in terms of the ethical function of the nation as a unified moral force in the world at large. The opening verses of Ruth depict a world of stasis degenerating into moral chaos. The nihilism of this world is reflected on both the personal and artistic levels by the physical disintegration of the family that had entered the fields of Moab just a few short years before.

At this point, the Biblical text appears to abandon its wider critique of social estrangement. The focus narrows to just the personal plight of Ruth and Naomi, the two refugees returning to Beth-Lehem. Just below the surface of the story, however, the theme of strangeness manifests itself once again. When Naomi and Ruth return, they find that one of them is no longer recognized and the other is virtually ignored.[16] Although the Judeans themselves are no longer caught in the throes of famine, they have still not learned the lessons of kindness and consideration.[17]

In terms of absolute fairness, it must be noted that this lesson still had not been entirely absorbed by the Israelite leadership either. This is highlighted by Boaz's reaction—or rather, the complete lack thereof—to the news that his kinswoman Naomi had just come back from Moab in greatly

---

Originative force of the world. He said, 'I desire neither Abraham nor his God'" (Bereshit Rabbah 41:10). As the Midrash reads it, Lot's move was not only a change of venue, but also a change of moral compass: Lot was consciously separating himself both from Abraham and from his monotheism. In that respect, Elimelekh's move to Moab takes on even more of a negative moral coloration.

16. "Is this [really] Naomi?" (Ruth 1:19).

17. To say, as Rabbi Joshua Bachrach does in *Mother of Kings* [*Ima shel malkhut*] (Jerusalem: Yeshivat Ohr Etzion, 1984), 41, that the people were simply too busy with the harvest to bother greeting Ruth and Naomi does not excuse their behavior. Rather, it condemns them for maintaining the selfishness with which the Midrashic reading of the text already charges them at the time of Joshua's death (see above).

reduced circumstances.[18] The argument has been made that his aloofness is due less to a lack of sympathy for the plight of these women than to a prudent sense of (political) self-preservation. In order to appreciate this point, one may note that the acceptance of a Moabite person into Judean society at that time posed a particular problem in view of the Deuteronomic prohibition against accepting either Ammonites or Moabites into the Israelite community.[19] To be sure, the text in the Book of Ruth does *not* note that Boaz was concerned with that particular legal controversy. In any event, the legal issue regarding Ruth's Moabite identity was to prove irrelevant regarding her acceptability into the Israelite community: with his intellectual sophistication, Boaz would discern that the Deuteronomic precept did not bar female Moabites from entering the Israelite community.[20] Thus, one may still ascribe Boaz's neglect of his kinswoman Naomi not just to simple unawareness of her predicament, but rather to a deep desire on his part not to get involved in complex (legal or personal) issues that would be likely to generate social controversy. Boaz's silence at this juncture is noteworthy, especially when contrasted to his later involvement on both the economic and social levels.

For the Bible, however, (moral) aloofness is taken as a sign of moral cowardice, not moral leadership: in subsequent Israelite history, this stance of moral avoidance on the part of the first Israelite king justifies removing his mantle of sovereignty.[21] Excessive fear of public opinion may seem like deep reverence for the people, but it often actually masks a deep-seated lack of concern for their true welfare—the very same alienation that opens the Book of Ruth. Ironically, it is the triply disadvantaged Ruth—a Moabite in an Israelite community, a woman in a patriarchal society, and a poor person in a world structured by economic hierarchies—who demonstrates to the Judean community the centrality of kindness in personal interaction,

18. Rabbi Bachrach (again) tries to excuse Boaz's (lack of) reaction to his kinswoman and her plight by arguing that he, too, was busy with the harvest (*Mother of Kings*, 43).

19. Deut. 23:4. Cf. Bachrach, *Mother of Kings*, 43.

20. This point is based on the traditional reading of the Midrash, which attributes to Boaz and the Israelites (Judeans) of his time legal concerns that, properly speaking, are noted later on by the Mishnah; the Midrash views Israelite customs and laws of the Biblical period as transmitted orally in essentially the same or similar format as would be later inscribed in written form in legalistic texts like the Mishnah.

21. The reference here is to the conversation between Samuel and Saul after Saul has not obeyed the Divine command to destroy completely the Amalekites in battle. Significantly, it is only after Saul confesses that "I feared the [Israelite] nation and [therefore spared some of the Amalekite cattle]" that Samuel concludes that Saul's royal dynasty will not last beyond his own lifetime (1 Sam. 15:24–26).

with its attendant political and national implications. Importantly, the consideration that Ruth proffers is not destructive of either the object of kindness or the person who extends that benevolence. She demonstrates the ability to give to another person while retaining her own sense of moral vision. Ruth never confuses valorization of the Other with abnegation of the self: Ruth the foreigner is never alienated from her own identity.

Ruth, Kindness, and the Development of Self

It is particularly striking that the term most often used to describe Ruth is that of *hesed*, or loving-kindness/consideration.[22] This description appears at first to be inapposite, especially considering both Ruth's nation of origin and the actual behavior of the community to which she journeys. Historically, the city of Sodom, from where Ruth's Moabite ancestor hailed, is portrayed as inhospitable, to the point of severe intolerance for any sort of difference. This is highlighted in a vignette of Sodomite inhospitality cited by the Talmud, which relates the kind of Procrustean "welcome" offered to wayfarers unlucky enough to request lodging for the night: visitors deemed too tall for the chosen bed would have their legs cut off, while the limbs of shorter travelers would be forcibly stretched.[23]

To be sure, it is possible to argue that Lot's own behavior, as represented by the Biblical text, occupies a middle ground between his Sodomite surroundings and his Abrahamitic roots. Lot's conduct certainly does not mirror the actions of his Sodomite neighbors; by the same token, it does not stand in complete opposition to Ruth's own kindness and hospitality: after all, even in the city of Sodom, Lot does welcome the two mysterious strangers who come to his door. Nevertheless, the Biblical text also reveals how Lot's excessive solicitude for his guests collapses into moral disorder, as he unhesitatingly offers his own daughters to the townspeople of Sodom for their own pleasure, in return for allowing his guests to remain unmolested (Gen. 19:8). In so doing, Lot fetishizes the provision of hospitality toward his guests, valuing their comfort over the moral integrity of his own daughters.[24] Seen in that light, it is no wonder that in the caves outside

22. Thus, Ruth 2:12 (in essence, if not in exact citation), 3:10, 4:15 (by implication).

23. TB Sanhedrin 109b. I thank Rabbi Chaim Wasserman for this citation.

24. Abarbanel asks what kind of father gives up his daughters without fighting to the death for them (Abarbanel, *Commentary on Genesis*, question 26, 272). Also cf. Midrash Tanhuma VaYera 12.

of Zoar (Gen. 19:30), his daughters similarly do not allow their father to retain control of his own body and moral autonomy. Ultimately, the story of Lot proves that both extremes—the utter lack of loving-kindness, as well as the indiscriminate practice of generosity—lead to moral indifference. As we will see, Ruth's finely honed moral sensitivity avoids these philosophical traps, while offering more fully considered options that increase moral self-awareness in both the personal and national arenas.

Ruth's philosophical stance is different from that of both her community of origin as well as her newly chosen community of affiliation. But Ruth's "strange" viewpoint does not morally disadvantage both her implicit and her explicit critique of the Judean society of her time. On the contrary, her status as foreigner privileges her moral standpoint. Ruth's multiply estranged position in Judean society—she is a Moabite who has been married to a Jew, an intermarried person lacking a secure place in either society, and a widow in a "coupled" world—renders her temporarily mute but also, paradoxically, sharpens the acuity of her moral vision. Ruth's liminality, exemplified by her journey on the road, enables her to assess the deficiencies in both Moabite and Judean society.[25] Ruth does not, however, retreat to castigating all the social arrangements that she has experienced. Neither does she dualize these two very different societies, labeling one as entirely good and the other as entirely evil. Ruth takes the much-heralded and more complex "third way": in attempting to chart her path within a new society whose written rules are unfamiliar to her and whose unwritten cultural norms she has no way of instinctively "knowing," Ruth insists on pursuing her own moral direction. She resists blindly following the (well-meant) instructions of her mother-in-law, and instead she develops her own distinctive sense of moral rectitude. In so doing, Ruth formulates a new way of understanding the self in both its individual and social incarnations.

This last point about Ruth does not fit with the conventionally understood tone of the book, either in its traditional (Ruth as obedient daughter-in-law) or more modern (Ruth and Naomi as forging a united approach to deal with a patriarchal society) interpretations.[26] Careful reading of

25. Liminality, often seen as marginalizing, can also serve as a critical vantage point for analysis of the structure that one is prevented from joining. For more on this, see especially Robert Cohn, *The Shape of Sacred Space: Four Biblical Studies* (Chico, Calif.: Scholars Press, 1981), in which he elaborates on the concept of liminality. Avivah Zornberg makes a related point in *The Beginning of Desire*, 116; a similar approach is expressed in her lecture of March 1998.

26. See, for example, Roberta Apfel and Lise Gondahl, "Feminine Plurals," and Francine

the text, however, makes this more subtle approach amply evident. This complexity comes to the fore in the first extended speech that Ruth makes, attesting to both her undying personal devotion to Naomi and her religious fealty to Naomi's God. In those sentences, Ruth does not, as commonly supposed, promise that she will always do exactly as Naomi bids. This becomes clear when one considers the exact phraseology in the text. Ruth says, "I will go where you will go."[27] Significantly, Ruth does not say, "I will go in the path that you go" or "I will do exactly what you do." Instead, Ruth affirms that she will always do what is (ethically and religiously) demanded of her, but she will utilize methodologies consonant with her own judgment.

This point is more than a literary nicety, because it changes the practical outcome of the Ruth story. Throughout their relationship, Ruth takes it on herself to alter Naomi's instructions when her own good sense tells her that Naomi's advice does not represent the best available option. For example, upon their return to Judea, Naomi, sunk in bitterness, offers no advice to Ruth on how to go about the search for food. It is Ruth who takes the initiative and proposes to go out to the fields to glean. This suggestion requires a considerable imaginative leap on Ruth's part. The commandments regarding the harvesting of stalks (requiring the reservation of some for the poor) significantly differentiated Israelite agricultural practice at that time.[28] Surprisingly, Ruth, a new convert, is able to understand this new way of relating ownership to social responsibility and to apply it to her own situation, when her own mother-in-law, well-versed in the laws and customs of Israelite society, makes no such suggestion on her own. Moreover, Ruth goes about choosing the field in which to glean in a highly original way. The text highlights this by unleashing a plethora of action verbs denoting Ruth's quick and decisive activity.[29] Commenting on this, the Midrash reads into Ruth's actions a conscious decision on her

---

Klagsbrun, "Ruth and Naomi, Rachel and Leah: Sisters Under the Skin," both in *Reading Ruth*, ed. Kates and Reimer.

27. Ruth 1:17. In the Hebrew text, this point is signaled by the fact that Ruth says "el asher"—that is, "I will go *to* where you will go." In other words, Ruth agrees that her religious and moral aims are the same as those of Naomi. Significantly, Ruth does *not* say, "Ba'asher telkhi elekh"—that is, "I will go *in the way* that you go," which would have indicated that Ruth was binding herself to do everything in the exact manner in which Naomi instructed her.

28. See, for example, Lev. 19:9, 23:22; Deut. 24:19.

29. "And she went, and she arrived, and she gleaned [*vatelekh, vatavo, va'telaket*]" (2:3).

part to scout out the safest routes to the fields in which she would glean, being aware of her vulnerable status as an unaccompanied female of foreign origin.

This same sensitivity informs Ruth's response to Naomi's instructions after the harvesting season is over, when Naomi advises Ruth to go down to the threshing floor to make Boaz aware of her situation and of her interest in a proper marriage with children. Naomi's instructions to Ruth are for her to wash, anoint herself, and put on her best garments.[30] Ruth answers that she will do what she tells her, but Ruth inverts the order of operations. The text notes that she does down to the granary (3:6), and only once there does she perform all the other actions suggested by Naomi. Why does Ruth alter Naomi's instructions? In the Midrashic reading, Ruth makes these changes because she is sensitive to the possibilities of going out alone at night when she is all dressed up.

In addition to presenting Ruth's analytic and inferential abilities, this vignette also highlights the way in which Ruth's character remains distinctly "strange," differentiating her from the conventional expectations propounded by the surrounding society. Ruth possesses attributes that are normally considered contradictory to each other. In this case, Ruth's independent mind, coupled with the manifestation of the familiar "feminine" fears of going out at night and attracting the "wrong" kind of attention, seem to describe a person who is conflicted and even paralyzed by her new surroundings: indeed, at this point in the story, it is Naomi who urges Ruth to put herself forward in Boaz's granary. In truth, however, this unexpected combination of sentiments reflects precisely the pioneering spirit that leads the text to identify Ruth as the founding matriarch of the Judean royal dynasty. Ruth's moral autonomy allows her to choose a new nation and a new religion with which to affiliate without excising her own sense of moral choice. Practically and philosophically, Ruth charts her own course. In so doing, she also prepares the path for the (political) emergence of her adopted nation.

The Midrash notes that Ruth investigated ("vatelekh") the best paths to bring her to the fields so that she would not be beset by strangers who might take advantage of her lonely status on the way home (Ruth Rabbah 4:3; also Rashi on Ruth 2:3). In view of Ruth's provenance from a nation with roots in incestuous behavior, this sensitivity is particularly noteworthy.

30. Naomi instructs Ruth with this order of operations: "Wash, anoint yourself, put on your clothes and go down to the granary" (3:3).

Ruth and Redemption

In a short book that appears to concentrate improbably on the fate of one widowed convert uprooted from her native land, one entire chapter is devoted to what seems like an archaic legalism: the question of the redemption of the field belonging to Naomi, along with the concomitant responsibility of the redeemer to marry Ruth. Modern interpreters tend to see this portion of the text as a diversion from the central (romantic/personal) interest of the story line, which attests to the ingrained patriarchy of ancient Judean society.[31] Assessing what appears to be an extended example of levirate marriage,[32] modern commentators are quick to point out the Biblical relegation of the woman to exist just as the personification of her reproductive powers in order to ensure the ongoing familial memory of the deceased (which would occur through the bestowal of the dead husband's name on the anticipated progeny).[33]

A careful examination of the text, however, reveals that the required circumstances obligating levirate marriage do not obtain in the story. According to the Bible, the responsibility of levirate marriage exists only when there are male siblings of the childless deceased male who are in a position to marry the childless widowed sister-in-law (Deut. 25:5–9). In the case presented in the Book of Ruth, Naomi herself bitterly remarks that in that context, she has nothing more to offer.[34] Moreover, the ceremony undergone by "Ploni Almoni" (a designation similar to "John Doe" in American English) in the fourth chapter bears no resemblance to the *halitzah* ceremony mandated when the brother of the deceased refuses to accept the

31. See, for example, Reimer, "Her Mother's House," 103; Fishbane, "Ruth," 307; Judith A. Kates, "Women at the Center," 196, all in *Reading Ruth*, ed. Kates and Reimer.

32. According to the Biblical account, a childless widow was required to undergo a "levirate marriage" by her (erstwhile) brother-in-law so that the name of the dead husband would not be expunged from the tribal/national community (Deut. 25:5–10). Importantly, this same passage provides that if the said brother-in-law refuses to participate in this marriage (for one thing, fathering more children would result in smaller inheritance portions for his own children borne by his freely chosen spouse/s), he may undergo a ceremony known as *halitzah*, also described in that same passage.

33. Cf. Aschenasy, "Language as Female Empowerment in Ruth," 113–14, 121.

34. "Do I have any sons in my stomach that can be husbands for you?" (Ruth 1:11). This remark highlights the connection between the Ruth-Boaz and the Tamar-Judah stories. In both cases, it is the women who are concerned with the continuation of the family bloodlines. Tamar wants to have a child from Judah's family, and it is only when none of her marriages to Judah's sons yield children that she arranges to be with Judah; similarly, Ruth makes it clear to Boaz that she is interested in marriage and children with him. I am grateful to Professor Murray Baumgarten for pointing to this connection.

duty of levirate marriage.[35] Unnoticed for the most part is that the text does name the ceremony of transmission between Boaz and Ploni Almoni as "Ge'ulah." In fact, throughout the fourth chapter, the term "go'el," or redeemer, identifies Ploni Almoni. The reference is not fully explained within the Book of Ruth, but its relevance becomes clear when the eponymous law regarding "redemption" of land is consulted. This law mandates the (voluntary) acquisition by a wealthier relative of land forcibly sold by an impoverished (extended) family member. The consequence of this law is to prevent the diminution of the family landholding in the ancient Land of Israel (Lev. 25:25).

This recommended purchase of land on the part of the affluent relative is voluntary. Unlike the refusal to accede to levirate marriage—where denial is allowed but leaves a mark of shame on the recalcitrant brother-in-law[36]— the refusal to salvage a portion of family-owned property that would otherwise be sold to buyers outside of the clan is simply taken as a given of harsh economic reality. In any case, Biblical law provides for the return of all land to its original (tribal) owners during the Jubilee year (Lev. 25:28). No negative feeling accrues to the person who, for whatever reason, is unable to extend to his relative that additional (and optional) measure of economic help. Thus, Ploni Almoni's refusal to marry Ruth because he fears that any children born of his union would serve to dilute his land bequest to his original group of children is accepted without demur (in Biblical law, land bequests must be divided among *all* children, without selectivity in terms of the provenance of any particular child).[37] The book, and Judean society at that time, would seem to conclude that one can live a life of sufficient moral decency—the "good-enough life"—without engaging in acts of exemplary kindness. Apparently, it is acceptable to refuse to be a redeemer.

But Ruth is not interested in leading that kind of life. It is not happenstance that Boaz describes marriage to Ruth as redemptive (Ruth 4:4): by

35. In his analysis of the last chapter of Ruth, the early sixteenth-century exegete Isaac Abarbanel points out that the untying and removal of the recalcitrant brother-in-law's shoe by the childless, widowed sister-in-law is different from the shaking off ("shlifah") of the shoe, performed here as a sign of legally recognized transfer/acquisition ("kinyan"). Boaz says, "I have today acquired all that was Elimelekh's . . . and all that was Mahlon's . . . and also Ruth the Moabite" (Ruth 4:9–10). Furthermore, the son born to Ruth and Boaz was not called by the name of Ruth's dead husband, as would have been the case if this had been an instance of levirate marriage. Instead, Oved is given a name of his own.

36. Deut. 25:9–10 records that the brother-in-law is forever known by the mark of shame, "the house of him who has had his shoe loosened"—that he has undergone the ceremony of *halitzah* rather than participate in a levirate marriage with his childless sister-in-law.

37. For example, Deut. 21:15; cf. also Deut. 25:5–10, and Ruth Rabbah 7:10.

the end of the book, he has come to recognize in her the uplifting aspects of kindness and self that that he wants to incorporate into his own life. Boaz develops from a leader unwilling to disturb the status quo by involving himself in complex legal issues to a person willing to take on an extra measure of responsibility to achieve what he considers a morally worthwhile goal. By the end of the book, Boaz has fulfilled the potential inherent in his name and, as Ruth had instinctively surmised, within his character.[38] Boaz has the strength to change, to admit that Ruth's moral vision is the one to follow: "Your last kindness is greater than your first one," he tells her (Ruth 3:10).

This enigmatic phrase reveals extended moral growth on Boaz's part. He has become capable of admiring that kindness goes beyond merely doing inconsequential favors to other people in order to make one's own life easier. Boaz becomes able to admire the qualities of intellectual choice and moral discernment that Ruth brings to her acts of kindness. This is highlighted, strangely enough, in the encounter between Ruth and Boaz—more plainly, when Ruth throws herself at Boaz—in the granary at night. Ruth's deliberate utilization of sexually implicated actions and imagery stands completely outside what is normally accepted as pragmatically possible: after all, how likely is it for a poor gleaner to be welcomed by an acclaimed leader of society? It is precisely this encounter, however, deemed outside of the realm of the empirically feasible and the socially acceptable, that changes the parameters of concrete reality. In the granary at night, Boaz understands what really drives Ruth. It cannot just be the opportunity to marry, because, as Boaz notes, there are many younger men whom Ruth had already encountered (while gleaning in Boaz's fields), with whom Ruth could anticipate an easier and more fruitful married life.[39] Boaz now sees that Ruth's seemingly outré behavior on the granary floor is actually an act of kindness on her part: it represents Ruth's attempt to stabilize her own, and also her mother-in law's, economic and social survival. Boaz's counterintuitive realization is accompanied by the further recognition that this act of kindness exceeds Ruth's first act of kindness, which may be variously constructed as Ruth's accompaniment of her bereft mother-in-law

---

38. The verse's description of Boaz as a "man of valor"—literally, "*gibor hayil*/a man of strength"—alludes to the root of Boaz's name, which can be read as a compound of two words, "*bo 'oz*/in him there is strength."

39. Ruth Rabbah 6:2. Also see Aschkenasy, "Language as Female Empowerment in Ruth," 123.

back to a land that was strange to her, and/or Ruth's singular decision to go out to the fields to collect gleanings so that the two poor widows would have something to eat. Either way, Boaz is aware of the fact that Ruth is making her choice based on moral characteristics, not personal fancy.

For her part, Ruth has come to appreciate Boaz as a person willing to grow and live according to the best moral standard available, someone not content to limit himself to leading a life of bare ethical sufficiency. In understanding Ruth's real motivation, and the qualities of mind that she brings to bear on her own moral choices, Boaz proves himself worthy of helping to bring the Davidic ancestry into the world. Spurred by Ruth's example, Boaz's moral growth is reflected in the blessings heaped on him by the women of Beth-Lehem, who somewhat incongruously bless him with the wish that his marriage embody the union of Judah and Tamar.[40] Judah's mark of moral distinction in publicly admitting Tamar's ethical superiority to him comes about as a result of his sexual relationship with Tamar, a seemingly discredited outsider.[41] It is not happenstance that in both cases, the acknowledgment of the women's higher moral purposes in apparently risqué circumstances—by Judah in the case of Tamar disguised as a harlot, and by Boaz in the face of Ruth's solitary nocturnal encounter with him—leads to the justification of the future acquisition of power by their heirs. Judah's action is validated by Jacob on his deathbed, and the end of the Book of Ruth testifies to the establishment of the Davidic dynasty through the combined agency of Ruth and Boaz.[42]

Ruth's status as outsider heralds her ability to focus on a principle of moral activity of which even her mother-in-law is unaware. This is brought to the fore by a seemingly chance remark that Naomi makes at the beginning of the book. At that point, ready to depart the fields of Moab, she urges her daughters-in-law to remain in the land of their birth (Ruth 1:9). Naomi's wish for her daughters-in-law is that they find peace/repose (the term in the Bible is expressed as "menuha"). While Ruth accompanies Naomi and volunteers to convert to her religion, promising (in the qualified sense that we have elaborated above) to be guided by her mother-in-law, Ruth does not join Naomi in seeking the easy way out. In fact, the one constant in all of Ruth's choices is that she never seeks *menuha*. She

40. Ruth 4:12.
41. Gen. 38:26. Tamar had dressed up as a harlot to facilitate Judah's being with her; Naomi's comment about sons is echoed in the Tamar story.
42. Gen. 49:8–9; Rashi ad loc.; Ruth 4:18–22.

later chooses to marry Boaz, which, in terms of her own personal comfort, is a counterintuitive choice. Ruth understands that life's moral challenges require precisely the opposite of repose.[43] It is no accident that Ruth names her son Oved—a dynamic name emphasizing work, activity, and accomplishment. Ruth realizes that in order for a life to be well lived, one must search energetically for both meaningful experiences and actions that permit and demand growth. Ruth's life follows this pattern of action.[44]

Ruth and Difference

The generational information that constitutes the last verses of Ruth offers more than semantic closure—that is, ending the book with the historical/political type of statement with which it began, highlighting the nature of political society in the Land of Israel.[45] In addition, by presenting the genesis of the Davidic dynasty, the Book of Ruth points out the necessity of acknowledging and respecting difference in order to ensure moral and political dynamism in the life of the nation.

This is an important point, because "difference" is frequently only grudgingly acknowledged and accommodated. The stabilizing propensity of established societies often conspires to smooth over evidence of real differences, urging and even compelling assimilation into that society's accepted practices. In direct contrast to this model, Ruth the stranger does

43. In her juxtaposition of repose to a morally active life, Ruth's internal moral dynamic foreshadows Rousseau's remark on the likelihood of certain countries to achieve and maintain a democratic style of government. Writing in the mid-eighteenth century, a time of political flux in Europe not entirely dissimilar to the lack of political stability in ancient Israel during the time of the judges, Rousseau sees an exclusionary choice between repose (in the sense of economic ease and stability) on the one hand and freedom on the other. Rousseau insists that this choice is inescapable: "Repose and liberty seem to me incompatible; one must choose/*Le repos et la liberté me paroissent incompatibles; il faut opter.*" *Considerations on Poland,* in *Oeuvres complètes,* 3:955l. In her own era of political disquietude, Ruth similarly apprehends that moral choices cannot be easily avoided: the aim of life is not to live it peacefully, but to live it in full spiritual control of one's own moral liberty.

44. In casting its mark of approval of Ruth's conception of this moral imperative, the Midrash imputes to God a celebratory comment, describing God as so impressed by Ruth's morally conceived activities that He Himself decides to crown her efforts with success by speeding the process of Boaz's and Ruth's marriage. According to the Midrash, God says, "Ruth has made her efforts and Boaz has made his; I, too, will make Mine" (Ruth Rabbah 7:7).

45. The first verse of Ruth informs us that that the narrative of the book occurs during the time of the judges; the book ends with the birth line of King David, the first king of a united Israelite kingdom.

not return as a humble penitent to the society that had been voluntarily abandoned by her ancestor Lot (Gen. 13:11). Rather, she retains of her past what she deems useful, integrating it into the moral worldview of the Israelite nation that she longs to join. The Midrash takes cognizance of this complexity of origins in a pithy comment that highlights the dubious (Sodomite) provenance of the esteemed King David.[46] In valorizing the somewhat questionable roots of one of Israel's most accomplished monarchs, the Midrash asserts that the origins of a leader who can unify his/her nation should not be totally homogeneous; they must also partake of some outside cultural influence as well, if the leader is to accomplish his/her task.

For the modern reader, the question is, why does that have to be the case? In the Book of Ruth, Otherness is crucial to the dynamic expression of the individual on the personal level: as Ruth demonstrates in the conduct of her own life, moral sensitivity to others expands the boundaries of one's own self. The Biblical narrative also demonstrates that the estranged placement of the Other already serves a paradoxically central function at an early moment of Israelite history: thus, the narrative of Israelite liberation from Egypt is portrayed as occurring under the aegis of Moses, whose life history differs markedly from that of his enslaved people. Since a successful revolutionary leader is characterized by his negation of the status quo (in this case, the slave mentality).[47] It is precisely because Moses is familiar with Egyptian (cultural) strengths and weaknesses from early childhood onward, that he becomes the most effective combatant against its oppressive ideology.

The narrative of the Book of Ruth connects these two aspects—the personal and the political—and their relationship to difference in the constitution of a nation. The Book of Ruth demonstrates that human beings are too complex to be united successfully through a uniform manner of incorporation. The text utilizes the concept of difference to transform the potentially destructive tension that can exist between the individual and the surrounding social/political community into a relationship characterized by a dialectical understanding of the fruitful implications of contradiction and difference. Ruth insists that national life must be multifaceted: broad enough to be inclusive, but discerning enough to know where to place the moral limits. In the Midrashic discourse, God finds (the origins

---

46. The reference is to a verse in Ps. 89:21 where God proclaims, "I have found My servant, David." The Midrash's comment is incisive: "Where did I find him [i.e., David]? In Sodom" (Bereshit Rabbah 41:4, 50:10).

47. See Malbim on Exodus 2:10–11 ("And the lad grew up/*vayigdal haNa'ar*").

of) King David at Sodom. That is to say, the roots of the Davidic dynasty begin in moral chaos. But they do not remain there. They evolve over time to exemplify the highest synthesis of the moral center for the leadership of the Israelite nation. Contradiction lies at the core of all fruitful growth.

But contradiction can also prove to be troublesome. While the Book of Ruth acknowledges the political utility of difference, it also points out the practical difficulties in its actual incorporation. This allows a more tolerant assessment of the difficulties that the Beth-Lehemites evince in accepting Ruth. Difference is hard to integrate. It can even look like evil. It is not clear, at least at first, that accepting difference is the right path to follow. Thus, it is not obvious to the people of Beth-Lehem that accepting a Moabite woman into their society is within the bounds of Biblical code or custom.[48] Not every difference is automatically acceptable (as the Biblical prohibition against inclusion of the male Moabites testifies[49]), but not every difference is automatically excluded either. Difference alone is not an indicator of a discrete moral quantity to be applied unthinkingly to life's decisions, in the manner that one automatically plugs numbers into a mathematical formula.

The complexity of finding the correct moral standard for conducting one's life is treated by the Midrashic literature in the context of trying to establish the logical and moral justification for the creation of humankind. In the Midrashic retelling, this question is exemplified as the struggle between Kindness (Hesed) and Truth (Emet), with each side expressing reasons for and against the proposed creation of humanity. As the Midrash presents this dilemma, no completely convincing argument is presented by either side. At this point, God is depicted as interjecting Himself into the discussion: He "throws Truth to the ground," allowing for the creation of humanity (Bereshit Rabbah 8:5). For the Midrash, human and social relations can exist only insofar as they incorporate loving-kindness. Human life cannot survive only on rational calculation.

While this Midrash presents truth and kindness/love (Hesed) as two irreconcilable concepts, the Book of Ruth demonstrates that they are inextricably bound up with each other. Boaz clarifies the matter of the inclusion of Moabite women only after he has met Ruth. Ruth fulfills her personal

48. Deut. 23:4. See above.
49. The Biblical text grounds this prohibition on the unwelcoming stance of the (male) Moabites at the time that the Israelites were preparing to cross into their ancestral land of Canaan, refusing even to make bread and water available for them.

destiny, and that of her new nation, through the practice of discerning loving-kindness. Far from being polar opposites, truth and loving-kindness reveal themselves to be two sides of the same coin.[50]

This is demonstrated not only by the large-scale trajectory of events in the Book of Ruth, but also by the particulars of characters exemplified there. Ruth always maintains her own sense of ethical and moral hierarchy: she never loses her distinctive voice. The sense of self that Ruth retains has important implications on two levels. Morally, as we have noted, it enables her to define minimal and maximal notions regarding what entails a morally fulfilled life. This allows Ruth to serve as a critic of Judean society (the lack of welcome that she receives when she arrives in Beth-Lehem eerily recalls the antisocial Moabite society that she had just left) and also as its unifying moral force: she promotes a concept of nation that is not relentlessly uniform, but that expands to incorporate multiple levels of ethical achievement within it. By implication, this concept also incorporates the diversity of the human beings who perform these assorted actions.

As the events of the Book of Ruth demonstrate, this inclusive approach allows for progress. Thus, on the personal level, we see how Boaz's sense of moral responsibility expands under Ruth's influence. Politically, too, this inclusivity allows the Israelite nation to continue to develop as a dynamic entity, instead of choking off its life force from the inside by needlessly restricting its membership to people who are clones of one another. In that context, as we have noted, even less-than-perfect expressions of moral accomplishment still retain their place within the Israelite nation. Ploni Almoni is no less a member of Judean society for having refused to fulfill an expanded sense of his moral responsibilities. Even the accepted arbiters of Judean society—personified most obviously as the women of Beth-Lehem—are not ostracized because of their persistent failure to welcome a stranger into their midst. Tellingly, their disregard of the stranger is evident even at the end of the narrative: they never openly welcome Ruth, except as they bless Boaz on his forthcoming marriage and congratulate Naomi on her unanticipated progeny (4:11–12, 14–15). Still, they too remain part and parcel of Judean society. The Book of Ruth demonstrates that the hallmark of a vibrant nation is the ability to include all manner of people and all variations of accomplishment within its circle. It is this realization, engendered by the moral discernment of Ruth herself, that prepares

---

50. This is expressed trenchantly in Ps. 85:11: "Truth and Kindness met."

her to become the matriarch of the first national Israelite leadership: the Davidic dynasty.[51]

The relevance of the ancient Book of Ruth to the contemporary post-modern era of questioning and doubt becomes clear when considering the end of this narrative. Despite the conventional readings of its "fairy-tale" resolution with its simple and even childlike tone, the Book of Ruth is seriously misunderstood on both the narrative and ethical levels if it is read simply as a tale of goodness rewarded, with the consequent righting of all wrongs. At one level, of course, the conventional understanding of the narrative does hold true to the extent that Ruth does marry a prominent man and does become the "mother of kings." A closer look, however, reveals that the resolution of Ruth's personal story is not quite as simple as these narrative details imply. The historical identity of Boaz with Ivzan indicates that Boaz is quite old when he marries Ruth.[52] Indeed, the text's lack of further reference to him once the marriage is consummated leads the Midrash to opine that Boaz dies shortly after the ceremony.[53] In this reading, Ruth is not "rewarded" for her "goodness" in the way that such rewards are normally understood: as "tit-for-tat" exchanges with God, based on an economic model of social relations.[54] In the Midrashic interpretation, Ruth is left a widow once again. The Biblical text itself makes clear that she is

---

51. The philosophical complexity of Ruth's moral discernment has led certain commentators to read the text not just as a historical morality tale of personal and national development, but also as a handbook for spiritual redemption. Taking as its cue the verse in which Boaz promises to redeem the fields of Naomi and marry Ruth (3:13), this approach metaphorically reads the text as a guide to two methods of spiritual liberation: humanly engendered or Divinely led. The easiest method, of course, is the naturalistic one, exemplified by the anticipated fulfillment of the role of "Go'el/redeemer" on the part of Ploni Almoni. But if that possibility does not ensue (as exemplified in the Book of Ruth), then God Himself (signaled by Boaz's assertion of "I will liberate you") will step in to liberate His people. This is the approach taken by Bartenura, and similarly by the Ohr HaHayim, in their (respective) glosses on the Biblical requirement of the redemption of land (Lev. 25:25–28), which serves as the legal frame by which the story of Ruth is resolved. According to these exegetes, spiritual redemption usually comes about at the hands of the righteous (using as the proof text the verse in Lev. 10:2, "I will be sanctified by those near to Me"). But if the man (the impoverished holder of the familiar land plot in ancient Israel) cannot come by such redemption—and here, interestingly enough, the impoverished person is held to be a metaphorical reference to God, who is "impoverished" due to the moral irresponsibility of His people—that is, there are no righteous people to "lift" His fortunes, then "his hand will reach." That is, God Himself will exercise His own loving-kindness to redeem the spiritual impoverishment of His people.

52. Judg. 12:8–10; and Rashi, Radak ad loc.

53. Yalkut Shimoni 508; cited in Bachrach, Mother of Kings, 84; also Ruth Rabbah 6:4.

54. But see the contrary remark in Ruth Rabbah 2:14: "Why was the Book of Ruth written? To inform of the reward for people who perform acts of kindness."

never really personally accepted into Judean society; in fact, after the text's recording of Boaz's marriage to Ruth, Ruth herself is never mentioned again in the text and, in effect, drops out of the story. Certainly Ruth does not raise her social standing by joining this embattled nation.[55] Therefore, it is difficult to read the Book of Ruth as promoting a simplistic "happily ever after" narrative. In this context, it is similarly dissonant to argue that the text promotes relating to God as a kind of super accountant of the moral sphere. The story of Ruth demonstrates that moral comprehension must go beyond that simplistic understanding if full human potential is to be fulfilled. Living a fully realized moral life is best done not for any expected reward, but simply because it is the right thing to do.

On the ethical level as well, the moral discernment evinced by Ruth warns us against understanding her loving-kindness as simply another word for the self-abnegation traditionally expected of women in a patriarchal society.[56] Although Ruth herself functions within such a society, her actions clearly demonstrate that the highest form of kindness vis-à-vis other people is that which gives full expression to one's own sense of what is morally just. In other words, a "self" must exist before one can give *of* that self to other people.

Finally, the Book of Ruth underlines the political implications of the morally reflective life. The Bible acknowledges that the presence of fully realized moral selves, who accept substantial differences on the part of other people, is itself a sine qua non for the establishment of a vibrant national community. To be sure, there exists a fine line between a God-driven sense of self and a selfishly motivated concept of egoism. It is in straddling the potential fault line between the two—utilizing contradiction not as an excuse for paralysis, but as a method for impelling further growth—that the Book of Ruth continues to challenge accepted norms for the construction of both the individual self and national community.

---

55. Many commentators point out that Ruth herself was a Moabite princess, so becoming the matriarch of the Davidic dynasty does not really enhance but rather restores her social standing (cf. Judg. 3:20; Rashi ad loc.).

56. *Ethics of the Fathers*, an early Tanaitic compilation of ethical thought, tells us to abnegate ourselves before God (2:4) but not before other people. The difference is crucial: self-abnegation before other people ignores the Divine roots of all individuals, which exists irrespective of gender and, thus, cannot be the source of *Hesed* or any positive dynamic, whether political or personal.

4

JOTHAM: THE POLITICS OF PARABLE

Like a tree, each nation has its own roots.
—Kant

The ability to understand the Israelite polity as a product of both contradiction and inclusion sounds like a marvelous (if a bit anachronistic) democratic ideal. The fact that this goal (arguably) remains an unachieved ideal,
at least as this is portrayed within the Biblical text, strikes the modern
reader as less surprising than the fact that this idea is given expression at
all in the context of an ancient work. The astonishment at the presence
of this idea increases when the reader takes into account that the Israelite polity-in-becoming is described as being under physical siege from
various unfriendly neighbors bent on the conquest of the Israelite entity
in their midst.

The situation grows more complicated, however, as it becomes apparent that the forces desiring the unmaking of the Israelite polity, and the inclusive ideals that it entails, derive not only from external sources. As the
Biblical text describes the Israelites, their own self-conception is so weak
that it readily adapts to internal autocratic rule. These are the circumstances depicted in the central chapter in the Book of Judges, focusing
on the story of Jotham. The questions raised by this seemingly disjointed
and inconsequential narrative are crucial to the self-conscious awareness
of the Israelite polity: What happens to a community whose identity is so
weak that it readily accepts tyrannical rule? How can such a community
recognize politics not as the passive acceptance of the (realpolitik) status

quo, but as an arena demanding moral watchfulness and ethically driven political choice?

The story of Jotham takes place at a strange juncture of Israelite history: the previous judge, Gideon, has died, and one of his sons, Avimelekh, murders all of his siblings (except for Jotham, who escapes) and sets himself up as king in Shekhem. In the context of the development of Israelite political discourse, the narrative about the power struggle that Avimelekh generates seems alienated on many levels. First, this episode appears to bear no relation to the repeated cycles of crisis and salvation that characterize the Book of Judges as a whole. Instead of focusing on a hero who saves his people, this chapter highlights a ruler who oppresses them. By extension, the voice of truth is identified not with the military or community leader of the episode, but rather with Jotham, who appears to be a marginal character. In addition, the ending brings with it no obvious resolution: communication on the public level appears nonexistent; and politically, the best that can be said is that one tyrant is dead. Unlike the typical catastrophe-and-deliverance sagas of the Book of Judges, no resolution seems to emerge at the end of this episode. The concluding verse of the chapter (9:57) merely notes the fulfillment of Jotham's earlier curse (9:20).

Careful analysis of the text, however, reveals that this conventional reading does not adequately reflect the trajectory of the narrative. Rather than presenting Jotham as obviously "strange," the narrative itself actually challenges conventional perceptions of what constitutes strangeness. Jotham's presence and his message represent important counterweights to the dominant political discourse of power identified with Avimelekh. This is evident both in the events of Jotham's biography—Jotham is the only son of the previous Israelite judge, Gideon, who remains alive after Avimelekh's murderous rampage against his seventy siblings (9:5)—and in the content of Jotham's ideas. Negating the belief that possession of brute force alone makes political power inevitable, Jotham embodies the emergence of a different political choice. In his parable, Jotham questions both the conventional use of power and the traditional ascription of power (just) to certain groups. By implication, Jotham's challenge to the conventional locus of power contains the radical suggestion that power be relocated in people and places normally considered "improper" and even beyond the pale.

The central assertion of the Jotham narrative occurs when, in response to Avimelekh's attempt to solidify his power even further, Jotham delivers a parable whose overriding message questions the Israelites' acquiescence to Avimelekh's rule. The parable itself depicts a host of trees searching for a king. The olive tree, the grapevine, and the date tree all refuse the call to power, but the thornbush agrees to lord it over the other trees, with the stipulation that his rule be absolute and unquestioned:

> The trees did go to anoint a king over themselves. They said to the olive tree, "Reign over us!" But the olive tree said to them, "Should I leave my fatness, with which God and man are honored, and go to hold sway over the trees?" So the trees said to the fig tree, "Go you and reign over us!" But the fig tree said to them, "Shall I forsake my sweetness and my good yield [fruit] and go to hold sway over the trees?" So the trees said to the grapevine, "Go you and reign over us!" But the grapevine said to them, "Shall I stop my vintage that gladdens God and men, and go to hold sway over the trees?" So all the trees said to the thornbush, "Go you and reign over us." And the thornbush said to the trees, "If you truly anoint me to reign over you, come, take refuge in my shade; but if not, a fire will go forth from the thornbush and devour the cedars of Lebanon." (9:8–15)

Jotham's choice of the parable as his literary mode of communication is particularly apt. In Jotham's hands, the parable's potent imagery illustrates the performative power of words. Jotham uses the parable to attempt to persuade his fellow Shekhemites—and by extension, the other Israelites—to take action against the illegitimate power exercised by Avimelekh. Jotham believes that words can alter material reality. The parable accomplishes this by reframing even ordinary objects in what may be read as fantastical circumstances, thus forcing its audience to rethink their conventional methods of interpreting the world.

Discourse of the "Other," or, An "Other" Discourse

As both the political counterpart to and the physical contrary of the powerful and tyrannical Avimelekh, Jotham embodies the position of Other in this narrative. But he never accepts that this means that his message must be considered "alien" as well. Unlike most of the people arbitrarily designated as Other by Avimelekh and subsequently killed, Jotham utilizes his enforced marginalization to speak the truth about the perplexities and complexities of power to his fellow Israelites. In keeping with his situation as hunted prey, Jotham broaches his subject in an elliptical manner. Instead of openly proclaiming a discourse on power, Jotham styles his talk as a parable—that is, ostensibly a discussion about something else (in this case, trees). To be sure, the interlocutor/reader is aware that the parable about trees is not only, or really, about trees. By definition, then, this parable is an alienated discussion. Just as Aristotle's definition of metaphor emphasizes strangeness, the momentary alienation produced by the parable at the point of interpretation functions as a space in which the ostensibly immutable realities of politics may be interrogated and potentially changed.[1]

Through the recounting of his parable, Jotham succeeds in transforming his marginalization from its traditional insignificance to place his message within—and hopefully, even at the center of—Israelite political discourse. While ostensibly Other, Jotham argues that his words, rather than Avimelekh's brute military force, hold the key to Israelite political survival. Interestingly enough, these respectively contradictory approaches to power are evident in the very names of the two opponents. Avimelekh's name literally means "my father is king," as if to suggest that Avimelekh's right to political domination derives from the historical fact of his father's prior rule. By implication, this approach tends to belittle or even marginalize the importance of political discourse in legitimating power: within the narrow circumstances of accession to political power, political discourse is easily and even, in some circles, traditionally viewed as tangential to the establishment of political legitimacy. In that context, what counts primarily are the relevant bloodlines.

Ironically, this approach emphatically disregards the words of the progenitor of that bloodline (Gideon) on this very subject: he is described as steadfastly refusing to establish a political dynasty of his own during his lifetime, remarking, "Neither I nor my sons will rule over you; God shall reign over you" (Judg. 8:23). Avimelekh severely misreads[2] his father's political position of refusing to establish a dynasty; instead, he relies on the mere fact of his father's tenure to justify his own claim to power. In the end, it is Avimelekh's interpretation of power, rather than Jotham's, that is revealed

1. In the *Poetics*, Aristotle defines metaphor as "the application to a thing of a name that belongs to something else." Chap. 21, in *Aristotle on Poetry and Style*, trans. G. M. A. Grube (New York: Liberal Arts Press, 1958), 44. For more on this point, see Chapter 6, on the Book of Esther.

2. Bloom, *Anxiety of Influence*, especially the preface, xii–xlvii, and chapter 1, 19–45.

as peripheral. By ignoring Gideon's (and Jotham's) central point—that the exercise of power must be morally coherent—Avimelekh is himself relegated to moral and, eventually, political irrelevance. As if to emphasize that the justification of power is in no way related to specific parentage, Jotham's own name is an anagram of the Hebrew word for "orphan."[3] Implicitly, the text argues that parentage, in and of itself, is irrelevant to the moral justification of (political) power.

The Figuration of Trees

The meaning of any parabolic discourse is not merely a function of its literary form. In addition, the specific content of the particular parable helps to establish its import. The focus on trees may seem a strange choice for structuring a parable that refers to a *political* crisis: in such a situation, one may well have expected to be presented with a parable about animals, for example, which in their natural habitat do incorporate a hierarchy of power among themselves. One way of understanding Jotham's imagery is to situate the parable's figuration within the context of those Biblical verses that also present the tree as a metaphor, with both individual and national referents.

In these varying Biblical texts, trees take on differing allusive values. Often, trees are explicitly compared to the individual human being through simile.[4] In that context, the arc of biological development emphasizes the common motifs of growth, decay, and death that govern the life cycles of both humans and trees. Within the framework of this biological imagery, moral elements are elliptically designated as the factors promoting human flourishing.

The connection between trees and humans takes on a specifically liberatory cast, particularly when the Bible depicts trees as celebrants of freedom.[5] This angle becomes more acutely national in import when the general

3. Jotham's name in Hebrew, Yotam, may be read as an anagram of the Hebrew word for "orphan," *yatom*. The connection between the lack of (important) parentage and the suitable exercise of power forms an important theme in the Biblical consideration of power; it comes to the fore especially in the character of Esther, who, before being chosen as queen, is identified twice as an orphan: "She had no mother or father . . . and [when] her father and mother died" (Esther 2:7).

4. "And you will be like a tree planted on pools of water" (Ps. 1:3).

5. See, for example, Ps. 6:12: "And all the trees of the field will clap hands"; see also Isa. 55:12.

category of trees gives way in Biblical texts to the mention of specific trees: notably the grapevine, the olive tree, and the fig tree. This particular trio— or, at times, just two of these three types of trees—is often utilized to exemplify the fruitful nature of the Promised Land.[6] In addition, prophetic texts often cite single examples or multiple combinations of these types of trees to allude to the Israelite nation at various junctures in its history (Hosea 9:11), depicting the Israelites either as Divinely redeemed (Hosea 10:1) or as receiving just retribution (Joel 1:3–7). Consequently, punishment for the Israelites is often styled as a lack of fruitfulness, or, alternatively, with images of plant/crop destruction.[7] Correspondingly, redemption is often expressed as the miraculous flowering of these same trees (Hag. 2:19; Zech. 8:11; Mal. 3:11).

In one particular text, however, the passage appears to go one step further, directly equating human existence and plant life: "For man is a tree of the field" (Deut. 20:19).[8] The correspondence in this verse between plant and human life seems to underline the accompanying Biblical imperative not to destroy wantonly any and all plant life in the process of attaining a particular goal, no matter how important that goal may appear at the moment. Importantly, the heightened implication of this verse is manifestly political, as the context cited is one of war. Central to this verse's interpretation is the embedded nature of this text, as well as the increasingly fine distinctions demanded of the Israelites, who are commanded not to destroy trees even in the framework of battle. Even though a situation of war is more likely than quotidian peacetime surroundings to be accompanied by misreadings and errors, and despite the lack of ideal circumstances conducive to proper judgment, the Israelite soldiers are ordered not to destroy natural resources indiscriminately. In addition, lest this prohibition on the destruction of trees be read as a blanket statement, the text specifies that the soldiers are to differentiate between fruit-bearing and barren trees, because it is only the former whose *wholesale* destruction is outlawed.[9]

6. "A land of wheat and barley and grapes and figs and pomegranates; a land of olive oil and honey" (Deut. 8:8).

7. Cf. Hab. 3:12; Amos 4:9; Nah. 3:12; Ezek. 15:1–7, 17:6–24; Jer. 5:17, 8:12. In Jeremiah, the image of grass is used to portray the ephemeral quality of human existence (40:6–8). For more on the image of grass as a metaphor for human transience, see Robert Alter, *The Art of Biblical Poetry* (New York: Basic, 1985), especially 191–203.

8. Cf. Malbim on Judg. 9:8.

9. The Deuteronomic text states, "You shall not destroy its trees" (20:19), and then specifies, "Only that tree which you know is not for food may you . . . cut down (20:20). Cf. also Sifrei 127, 128, on Deut. 20:19; Malbim ad loc.

Jotham's utilization of trees in his parable is thus an immediate signal that the issue treated there is political, acute, and complex.[10]

The extremes of good and bad circumstances as encapsulated by these trees are further honed by Biblical images that focus on the intricacies embodied by their fruit products. Thus, Jeremiah wonders how it is that good grapes can degenerate into inedible ones (2:21); elsewhere, this complexity is figured as the "good" and the "bad" cluster of figs.[11] The moral choices symbolized by these trees and their fruit in turn hark back to the first mention of trees in the Biblical text: the Tree of Knowledge of Good and Evil, located in the primordial Garden of Eden. Like the trees of Jeremiah's prophecies, the Tree of Knowledge is linked to moral acts; as with the trees of Jotham's parable, these moral acts are presented as acts of persuasion. The logically seductive words of the snake are instrumental in encouraging Adam and Eve to eat the fruit of the Tree of Knowledge of Good and Evil, which leads God both to banish them from the Garden of Eden and to close the Garden itself.

Why does the Bible utilize the image of the tree in situations requiring moral choice? One possible answer is suggested by Avivah Zornberg's explication of the themes of horizontality and verticality in the Book of Genesis.[12] Zornberg utilizes these images to explain the moral tension within the human being, whose existence Zornberg defines by the oscillation between the demands of horizontality ("animal-like" drives) and verticality (the impulsion to embody the "higher" aspect of humanity, reflected in its Biblically depicted Divine origins). Further expanding on the implication of these ideas, a schematic model of this tension is present within the natural world itself: the tree towers high above plant and animal life while simultaneously being anchored in the earth through the horizontal broadening of its roots. Within this schema, the figuration of trees as the image around which issues of moral choice coalesce adheres to this commonly accepted duality.[13]

10. The situation described in Deuteronomy is one that can easily degenerate into all-out battle; in that sense, Jotham's metaphor may even be said to prefigure Hobbes's description of "the war of every man against every man." *Leviathan*, part I, chap. 13, ed. C. B. Macpherson (Harmondsworth: Penguin, 1968), 185.

11. Jer. 24:2; moral complexity is elliptically hinted at in Jer. 4:11–14.

12. *The Beginning of Desire*, especially 10–24.

13. As the story of Genesis makes clear, and as the parable of Jotham similarly underlines, issues of moral choice are realized as functions of knowledge: in effect, the moral nature of choice is contingent on the availability and use made of knowledge. But knowledge can be dangerous if put to (morally) incorrect use. This is one lesson traditionally imputed to the

The Tree and the Tower

But this neat, ordered view of the world is further complicated by the Bible's own use of horizontal and vertical imagery. In the Genesis text of the Tower of Babel episode, the narrative records that the construction of this tower so disturbs God that He disperses all of humanity by rendering their speech unintelligible to one another. In this story, the moral connotations of horizontality and verticality are reversed: while previous chapters of Genesis arguably may be read as portraying verticality as morally desirable and horizontality as morally base, here the project of building a high, vertical tower is presented as morally problematic. Consequently, horizontality—dispersing mankind over the face of the earth—is presented as a solution, even a human advance.

But the tower narrative does not just invert the moral resonances of horizontality and verticality. In addition, the account documents how the seemingly clear meanings of horizontality and verticality develop ambiguous implications. Thus, for example, it is not altogether apparent that the Babel episode presents an obvious wrongdoing deserving of Divine punishment. After all, there is nothing morally problematic about the construction of cities or towers as such. One might even argue that the cooperation involved in construction projects of such huge dimensions would encourage solid social relations among the inhabitants, boding well for the development of communal life.[14]

The ambiguity of the connotations of the Tower of Babel episode stands in ironic contradistinction to the figure of the tower itself, which, built of brick, can admit of no transformation in its structure. Consequently, interpretations of the tower episode that emphasize the indeterminacy of the tower's meaning do not limit themselves to interpreting just the physical structure of the tower, but decode also the words of the text that preface its construction. Thus, explaining some of the negative moral implications of the tower (and justifying Divine reaction toward it), traditional exegetes cite the specificity of the verse detailing the ultimate goal of the tower—"in the heavens"—as alluding to the desire to rebel against

---

Garden of Eden narrative in Genesis: the risk of the type of knowledge represented by the Tree of Knowledge of Good and Evil results from disobedience to the Divine decree that prohibits eating from this tree.

14. Cf. the Midrashic reading in Bereshit Rabbah 38:6: "Those people . . . loved one another . . . therefore a remnant of them remained."

God Himself.[15] On the other hand, more modern approaches to the narrative focus on the veil of hypocrisy that overlays the seemingly transparent structures of both speech and edifice.[16] One reading of the tower episode argues that the apparent conviviality highlighted by speech ("Come [havah], let us construct bricks," Gen. 11:3) actually indicates the manipulation and destructive competition at the tower's core. Significantly, the leading word (leitwort) of the inaugural speech act of the tower's construction ("havah") is the same word that introduces the primary Biblical example of social exploitation, utilized by the Egyptian Pharaoh to persuade his nation to connive in the oppression of the Israelites (Exod. 1:10). In both cases, the deliberate abandonment of equitable social relations is accomplished by words, which appear linguistically translucent, but which actually can conceal the corrupt purposes that eventually destroy the underlying web of social understanding.

Other readings of the text trace the roots of the social exploitation manifest in the tower episode to class-based (rather than just to individual) moral degeneration[17]—specifically the inability to recognize and uphold the interests of general sociability and equity in the face of untrammeled desires. According to this approach, the prior development of artificiality and luxury sets the stage for the building of the tower. This development also reflects and further encourages the human desire for self-aggrandizement and corruption.[18] In that vein, the putative reason given for building the city and the tower—"Let us make a name for ourselves" (Gen. 11:4)—may be understood not as the consensus of a united humanity, but rather as the concurrent wish, secretly expressed by all the different social classes and craftsmen, who were each trying to dominate the others.[19] For these

15. Cf. the Midrashic reading in Bereshit Rabbah 38:7, which traces the impulse of the tower builders to rid themselves of Divine morality (s.v. "VaYehi b'nas'am mikedem: mi'Kadmono shel 'olam").

16. This interpretation is offered by Don Isaac Abarbanel, a Biblical commentator whose life and political activity spanned late fifteenth-century Spain and early sixteenth-century Italy.

17. Cf. Abarbanel on Gen. 11:1–4.

18. The anticipation of Rousseau's eighteenth-century critique of modern society in just those terms, particularly in Lettre à d'Alembert sur les spectacles, is striking.

19. In a careful explication of the text, Ibn Ezra differentiates the diverse speakers in each verse of the tower narrative. (According to the rules of Biblical hermeneutics, each time the speech act is introduced by the term "va'yomru/and they said," one may infer that this portends a new speech act or speaker.) Thus, the speakers in Gen. 11:2 are the common people, who just want to construct bricks in order to build houses for shelter; the speakers in Gen. 11:4, the first place where the tower is mentioned, are the higher classes, who wish to create

exegetes, the Tower of Babel stands as a monument to overweening pride and, not surprisingly, becomes the locus of social unrest and internal warfare.

In the political understanding of the tower episode, the utilization of the unique human ability to speak and persuade for nefarious, instead of potentially elevating, purposes, foreshadows the story's denouement: the multiplication and confusion of human languages.[20] On the practical level, the proliferation of language makes it harder for people to unite politically and even socially.[21] This negative outcome has at least one positive ramification, however: the multiplicity of languages blocks, even if not completely, the practical realization of the despotic tendency to consolidate power on a worldwide scale.[22] Thus, from one vantage point, this trajectory exhibits symmetry and closure, as the absence of moral unity necessitates a corresponding decentralization in the social sphere. At the same time, the ambiguity exemplified in the Tower of Babel episode also highlights the indeterminate implications of the proliferation of languages: according to certain readings of this episode, absolute monarchy actually does develop at this juncture, but not universally. Its manifestation only in discrete locations occurs precisely in order to control the social unrest that results from miscommunication.[23]

The ambiguity characterizing the Tower of Babel episode makes the sense of moral closure in this text hard to define: the positive implications of the story are reflected in the presence of unified and cooperative people, who display the ever-burgeoning human spirit to seek out new frontiers, grow, and develop. At the same time, the political implications of the Tower

---

the physical trappings for political domination. In a more general sense, Kli Yakar uses the same hermeneutical principle to note that there is more than one group speaking, which indicates that several classes entered into this dialogue of wishes and desire for domination.

20. Cf. Abarbanel on Gen. 3:5: "And you shall be like God."

21. At the same time, it should be noted that social communication is depicted in the Bible as resulting from difference: Isaiah's vision of peace is styled as the coming together of opposites—or at least of formally discordant entities (e.g., the lion and the lamb; cf. Isa. 11:6).

22. Importantly, the Midrashic reading (Bereshit Rabbah 37:2 on Gen. 10:8) conflates the deliberate misappropriation of language with the establishment of absolute monarchy, locating them in the person of Nimrod.

23. For example, Ibn Ezra and Sforno. Ibn Ezra highlights the political exemplification of localized absolutism (Nimrod) and, by implication, the other political possibilities that potentially might manifest themselves in the absence of universal absolutism. Sforno points to the moral implications of absolutism that would admit of only one ethical understanding for all human beings (which for Sforno translates into idol worship); by implication, the lack of universal absolutism in that realm allows for the possibility of mankind's return to monotheism, according to Sforno.

of Babel itself may be presented as largely negative, with the tower sym-bolizing state or class oppression rather than humanitarian guideposts.[24] By contrast, in the Book of Judges, the image of the tower takes on a surprising liberatory twist. The conclusion to the Jotham narrative re-verses the dictatorial implications of the Tower of Babel, as the Tower of Tebetz is where the Israelites in Shekhem are freed from tyranny: it is from this tower that a millstone is thrown, killing Avimelekh.[25] Tellingly, the site of Avimelekh's death is a tower that symbolizes his own overweening pride, which, like the millstone, is finally brought low. Thus, images do not remain frozen in the Bible: the freedom inherent in the text enables these tropes perennially to metamorphose, such that their essential ambi-guity presents the possibility of both indeterminacy and freedom for their interlocutors.

The Politics of Trees

In Jotham's parable, figuration is similarly complex. The trees in his para-ble are depicted not just as unidimensional groups, typified only by the presence or lack of fruitfulness. The trees are also portrayed as engaging in extended conversations on the issue of political rule, with each type exhib-iting a different attitude toward political power and the acceptable ration-ale(s) for its possession. Likely as a result of this textual construction, one scholarly approach to the figuration of trees in the Jotham parable identi-fies each category of tree with a different kind of ruler, with the corre-sponding strengths and weaknesses of each type.[26]

In this view, the text highlights three categories of political leaders: those who are spiritual in nature, those emphasizing physical pleasure, and those who are elegant social and political operators. This approach argues that the best type of political leader is one who emphasizes spirituality; this type finds its exemplification in the olive tree, one use of whose products

24. In his commentary on Gen. 11:2, Ibn Ezra locates the humanitarian impetus of the desire to build a tower with the ordinary people of Babel. They wanted to build a structure that would orient them homeward when they would round up their cattle at night from the pastures outside the city.

25. An interesting parallel to this scene is found in Jth. 14:1 (Deuterocanonical Apoc-rypha), where Judith urges the display of the head of Holofernes, the Assyrian general whom she had just slain, on the gates of the city of Bethulia.

26. Cf. Malbim on Judg. 9:8–15.

is for illumination.[27] The second type of political leader (less ideal) is one who exhibits a tendency toward the luxurious and easy life. Although this type of leader manifests some animallike characteristics, its general bent is to realize what is aesthetically pleasing—therefore, this approach to leadership remains within the realm of what is morally acceptable, even if it is not preferred. This leader is typified by the fig tree, whose fruit is sweet (though perhaps less necessary to the conduct of life than the light and nutrition provided by the fruit of the olive tree). Proceedingin this vein, the third type of leader is presented as a cross between the first two categories. This is the advantageous/useful leader, the ideal (Weberian) political type—"the genuine official"[28]—because this kind of person can make things work. Not as obsessed with comfort as the second type of leader, this sort of ruler is also not as completely dominated by idealistic imperatives as the first type. This leader is identified in the text with the grapevine, whose product synthesizes spiritual joy (the reference is to wine used for sacramental purposes) and social conviviality, if not ecstatic abandon.[29]

Importantly, however, none of these types, as exemplified by the various species of trees, agrees to take on the position of political leadership in Jotham's parable. Consonant with the approach identifying each species of tree with a specific category of leader, each tree presents a particular reason of its own for refusing political power, related to its individual conception of the political role proper to it. The olive tree declines the crown because it does not want to stop its perpetual quest for spiritual perfection; the fig tree does not want to divert its attention from its own pursuit of luxury; and the grapevine does not want potential political involvement to lessen its happiness-enhancing product. As readers of the text, it is possible to regard any one or even all of these rationales as being completely self-regarding, refusing all responsibilities other than those that contribute to one's personal welfare. Alternatively, we may view each expressed motivation as extremely altruistic, declining to participate in anything that would

27. According to this reading, the specific reference is to the menorah in the Tabernacle/Temple. Olive trees are also a source of food, thus adding a complicating notion to the sustenance afforded by that tree, which turns out to be physically, as well as spiritually, nutritive.

28. Max Weber, "Politics as a Vocation," in *From Max Weber*, trans., ed., and with an introduction by Hans H. Gerth and C. Wright Mills (New York: Oxford University Press, 1975). But see also 125–28, on the heroism of the "principled politician."

29. Malbim is decidedly not talking about the solitary drunk.

promote individual self-aggrandizement at the expense of the fulfillment/ realization of their expected tasks.[30]

At this juncture, the interpretational approach equating disparate kinds of trees with different types of political leaders broadens to refer to the diverse groups within the citizenry. The logic is that the existence of different categories of rulers implies their origins in various groups of citizens, each of whom supports the ruler whose style reflects its own dominant characteristics. Thus, the most spiritually distinguished people gravitate naturally to the elevated leadership symbolized by the olive tree, while the rich people, focused on luxury, will seek a leader sympathetic to their economic and social interests (the fig tree). Similarly, those citizens interested in a practical combination of spiritual and economic pursuits will search for a leader who combines these two goals (the grapevine). The specificity of this approach, grounding leadership in the citizenry, underlines an important point, because it understands politics to be concerned not just with the exercise of political power, but also with its legitimation. By contending that rulers can function effectively only if they maintain their links to the people whence they sprang, this approach reveals a complex understanding of the role of the people, both in theoretically legitimating their rulers and in practically enabling them to govern.

The fundamental link connecting leaders to their people assumes that leadership is neither inevitably unitary nor absolute: in effect (successful) leadership reflects the makeup of the people that it governs.[31] But this point

---

30. Malbim actually takes both of these viewpoints but attributes them individually to the different prototypes of rulers that these trees represent. Thus, the olive tree, by virtue of representing the spiritual elite, refuses the leadership position because it understands that true happiness is antithetical to power. Instead, the olive tree recognizes that true happiness is realized by the pursuit of wisdom (*hokhmah*). This interpretation reflects the classical definition of happiness attributed to the Guardians in Plato's *Republic*, who themselves are impervious to political corruption because they truly do not want power (the exercise of which they view as detracting from their pursuit of wisdom). Plato, *The Republic of Plato*, trans. Francis MacDonald Cornford (New York: Oxford University Press, 1962), 231–32. On the other hand, the refusal of the fig tree to rule is understood just as a function of its own selfish desire to maintain personal luxury. As for the grapevine, its unwillingness to engage in politics stems from its reluctance to lose its connection to increasing both spiritual and social happiness.

31. Cf. Rousseau's *Social Contract*, which closely links the best form of government and, implicitly, the best leadership for any particular state, to the type of people that are to be governed: "*Comme avant d'élever un grand edifice l'architecte observe et sonde le sol . . . le sage instituteur ne commence pas par rédiger de bonnes loix en elles-mêmes, mais il examine auparavant si le peuple auquel il les destine est propre à les supporter*/As before putting up a large building the architect observes and sounds the site. . . . The wise Institutor does not begin by laying down law good in themselves, but examines first whether the people to whom he ordains the laws is fit to support them." *Social Contract*, bk. 2, chap. 8, in *Oeuvres complètes*, 3:384–85.

also carries with it specific moral consequences, for by extension, the type of leadership tolerated by the populace serves as its moral marker, indicating the people's level of ethical attainment. Consequently, the implied call to arms at the end of Jotham's parable is not just a political challenge, but a moral one as well. What is tolerable politically actually reveals the quality of the people's moral stature.

In addition, the interpretational approach identifying diverse social groups with their chosen leaders contains an implicit critique of this process of political selection—that, as a whole, society lacks consensus and is riven by social factions. This interpretation is mirrored in the events later described by the text: despite Jotham's invitation to the people (through the medium of the parable) to create a plurivocal discourse, reflected in the implied union of the interpretational activity that the parable *should* (but does not always) engender—subsequent events in the historical part of the Biblical narrative of Jotham reveal the (short-term) failure of his project. Like the parabolic community of trees, the Shekhemites are divided on the question of power: some of them champion Ga'al ben Eved,[32] who does not support Avimelekh, and others are loyal to Avimelekh's own appointee, Zevul.[33]

With the presentation of these various interpretations of the different levels and types of political power, one might expect the text to resolve the complexities raised by the possibilities of politics. One way to effect this would be to introduce a fourth type of tree, which would present the "correct" elucidation of the complexities within the political sphere. Interestingly enough, the Biblical text presents no such resolution. Instead, all the trees in unison approach the lowliest plant growth, the thornbush, and ask it to rule over them. After a short exchange, the thornbush agrees to be their king. Fittingly, the totality of trees—identified traditionally with the common (lowest) people—finds a leader in its own image: the unproductive thornbush.

---

32. Ironically, this name translates as "disgusting, the son of a slave," thereby lending a disreputable air to the arguments he advances against supporting Avimelekh. In brief, Ga'al argues against the inevitability of dynastic rule to provide moral justification for political power (Judg. 9:31–45).

33. Interestingly, Zevul's name here may be read as another permutation of a word denoting "garbage" (*zevel*), although this word may also be associated with the term connoting "a place of settled habitation." In the context of the Book of Judges, it would seem probable that Avimelekh may have bestowed the latter meaning on the name of his appointee, with its connotations of the royal palace, and hence the legitimation of his own power. His opponents, however, would as likely have delighted in the earthier implications of the former interpretation.

Of all the trees mentioned, the thornbush is the only one not concerned with the duties of kingship or how it may distract him from his erstwhile productivity. The reason for this is obvious in the text: The thornbush produces no fruit. In addition, unlike the other trees, the thornbush is the only one to threaten the other trees with destruction if they do not acquiesce to *his* vision of power. Thus, the thornbush is portrayed as possessing only the dubious distinction of exhibiting an arrogant sense of pride (recalling the extreme ego manifested by the people of Babel).

The dissonance between the theoretical possibilities evoked by the parable and the conclusion of actual historical events as presented in the Biblical text is underlined by the final image of the parable, when the thornbush exhorts its fellow trees to "come, take refuge in my shade." The meaning of these words in the parable and in its application to the actual events described by the text (the *nimshal*, or practical interpretation/application) remains characteristically indeterminate: we do not know for certain whether the tone of the bush's remarks is serious or sarcastic. Is Jotham hinting that just as it is impossible for tall trees to find refuge in the (nonexistent) shade of a low bush, so monarchy (recalling the situation of the parable, where the trees are seeking a king) as a method of rule will *never* work? In this view, monarchy is understood as an inherently flawed system of government, because the monarch is concerned only with his own well-being and will therefore inevitably harm (with his thorns) all those who come into contact with him.[34]

On the other hand, perhaps Jotham's words can be interpreted more circumspectly, suggesting that it is Avimelekh's tenure as king—that is, *this* particular thornbush—that will not succeed. In that reading, the image of the bush's thorns is taken as a harshly corrective method—"tough love"—employed by an abrasive but just king in order to ensure social decorum. In Jotham's opinion, however, Avimelekh is not equipped to be a good monarch, because he is likely to misuse the monarch's great powers for his own purposes (as evidenced, for example, by Avimelekh's slaughter of nearly all of his siblings in order to ensure his own political domination). In this view, it is not monarchy as a form of government that is disavowed; it is merely Avimelekh's (proven) unsuitability for the position that is emphasized.

Alternatively, is Jotham pointing out that monarchy is morally and politically a poor form of government? According to this logic, monarchy ought

34. In his later incarnations, Saul may be viewed in this light.

to be avoided not because it can never work—and not necessarily because of Avimelekh's poor leadership qualities—but rather because it inevitably cripples the people over whom it extends its power. In this reading, Jotham is arguing that monarchy may function at the *minimal* level of providing security for its subjects, but that it can never afford them all the possibility of reaching their full potential. In the parable itself, this is symbolically evoked by the implication that the tall trees will have to cut themselves down to size (in order to be able to shelter in the shade of the thornbush). The image utilized implies that the political system of monarchy inevitably eradicates all creativity and individuality from its citizens, because they are dominated by a disabling fear of punishment (the bush's thorns). As a result, all citizens are forced to subsist at the level of the lowest common denominator. The ambiguity of the parable's interpretation extends itself to its *nimshal*, the practical application of the parable to possible future actions recommended to the people of Shekhem. Is the point of Jotham's parable to inform the people of Shekhem that they are stuck with the monarchy and with Avimelekh—that having made their bed, now they must lie in it? Or is he painting such a bleak picture for them that he may be understood as surreptitiously encouraging a rebellion against Avimelekh?

Radicalizing the Parable

A radical reading of Jotham's parable goes beyond the interrogation of monarchy as the preferred system of government. Unlike the traditional defense of monarchy, which points to it as the best guard against the social chaos that is sure to ensue without the monarch's powerful presence, Jotham's parable emphasizes the multivalent resonances of the Biblical tree imagery. By implication, Jotham argues that political solutions can take many different forms and lead to various sorts of positive results.[35] The fruitful abundance of the Promised Land, which the Bible imputes to its

35. This anticipates a similar argument made by Rousseau in the *Social Contract*: "*Quand on demade absolument quel est le meilleur Gouvernement, on fait une question insoluble comme indéterminée; ou si l'on veut, elle a autant de bonnes solutions qu'il y a de combinaisons possibles dans les positions absolues et relatives des peuples*/If you ask absolutely which is the best government, one asks a question that is both unsolvable and indeterminate; or, if you want, it has as many good solutions as there are possible combinations in the relative and absolute positions of peoples" (bk. 3, chap. 9, 3:419).

fecund—and politically nuanced—trees indicates that for the Bible, politics and governance have important positive potential. Unlike Augustinian thought, which equates politics with unavoidable spiritual degradation, the Hebrew Bible suggests that politics may even be redemptive.

The key element in the Biblical text distinguishing between politics' contradictory oppressive and redemptive implications is the nature of the chosen leader. Although it is possible to interpret Jotham's parable traditionally, and to impute ideal leadership (only) to systems that limit voting power to the elites,[36] one may also draw a more radical conclusion. This aspect of leadership is hidden in plain sight within the text of the parable. Careful reading of the text reveals that all the types of trees that refuse power are gendered in the feminine. At one level, this point is merely grammatical and hence may appear to be substantively irrelevant—all nouns in Hebrew are gendered, some in the feminine and others in the masculine. However, the text could have chosen to highlight trees gendered only in the masculine, or to focus on trees that include both types of gendering. The fact that the text names trees that are gendered *exclusively* in the feminine implies a link between women and the exercise of political power.

This connection may be variously interpreted. The text may be hinting that women as a group are most likely to recognize the folly of power, and thus are best inoculated against its abuse. Taking this point one step further, one could argue that women as a group may therefore be the most inclined to the principled exercise of power.[37] The text might even be hinting that men should become more like women, at least in the implementation of political power.[38] On the other hand, one could explain the refusal

36. Malbim on Judg. 9:8–15.

37. In this reading, the women mirror the moral echelon of the Guardians in Plato's *Republic:* they are best fit to rule because they are impervious to corruption (see above). I return to this point later in this chapter.

38. This suggestion is made by Diotima in Plato's *Symposium,* when she argues that love is the pursuit of wisdom, not its incarnation, and that it is the process of man's quest for it, and not its absolute (and also dubious) achievement, that holds hope for humanity. Diotima holds that because love is the product of plenty (a male figure embodying realization) and penury (a female figure exemplifying deficiency), it must consequently be characterized in his pursuit (but not necessarily in his achievement) of the ideal. For Diotima, it is through love that "God mingles . . . with man." *The Symposium,* ed. Benjamin Jowett (New York: Anchor, 1973), 354. In other words, it is through what man *lacks* that he approaches most closely the Divine. This counterintuitive pairing of the consciousness of what is lacking and the apprehension of the Divine (which itself is traditionally identified with overflowing presence or perfect completion) is echoed in the dialogic dynamic between Diotima and Socrates. It is the woman and stranger Diotima who initiates the man and citizen Socrates into the (philosophical) mysteries of love. The radicalism inherent in this juxtaposition—traditional

of power by these particular trees as establishing a general political principle, indicating that it is *never* possible to ensure the moral implementation of power. Alternatively, one could view this general rule more narrowly, understanding the argument of the text to be that true fruitfulness (all the trees cited in the parable are fruit trees) is not coupled with political power; therefore, truly productive people tend to shy away from politics. Finally, the text may have a particular historical referent, alluding to the identity of a previous leader, Deborah, who had tried mightily, but in vain, to unite the Israelites in common action. In this connection, it is worthwhile noting that Deborah's judicial function is textually associated with the fig tree, under which she sat in judgment of the Israelites.[39] Interestingly, none of these possible interpretations are mutually exclusive: they may be cumulatively adduced as expressing different aspects of the same truth. By way of complete contrast, the Biblical text presents the desire for raw power utilized just for self-aggrandizement as associated with the grammatically gendered male *'atad* /thornbush, which is portrayed as barren, possessing only negative and hurtful qualities (thorns), contributing nothing to society.

It would be simplistic to read the Biblical text as recommending the exclusion of all men from political rule on the basis of the (moral) weaknesses attributed to their gender. An important aspect of the parabolic form, and the reason that Jotham uses it here, is that no text, and no reality, can

---

Greek thought defined women largely by the extent to which they did not fit the masculine "ideal"—finds its parallel in the Biblical linkage between outsider and community. Just as Diotima, the *"stranger* of Mantineia," is able to transmit to Socrates the spirit of love—which is the founding essence of community—so the Bible presents the outsider as the individual best able to apprehend and reveal the essence of the internal cohesion of community. For further development of this concept, see Chapter 6, on Esther; its more negative incarnation is presented in the discussion of the concubine at Gibeah in Chapters 2 and 6.

39. This tree has become known as *Tomor Devora*. Traditionally, it is held that this tree is named after the Biblical Rebecca's nurse, also called Deborah (Gen. 35:8). The implications of the later Deborah's judging under just this tree indicate that, contrary to accepted patriarchal notions, it is not necessary for political leadership to be imbued with military values in order to be successful. On the contrary, Deborah's parental/motherly concern for her flock does not prevent her from planning the successful Israelite military defense: it is the general Barak who follows her lead, not the other way around (Judg. 4:6–7). Similarly, Sisera himself is felled at the hands of a woman, Yael, in her tent, traditionally a feminine location. Cf. Laura Shaw-Frank, "From Under the Palm Tree: The Model of Devorah," *Jewish Orthodox Feminist Alliance Journal* (Winter 2004): 3–4. While the literary identification of the judge Deborah with a particular tree in Jotham's parable may seem far-fetched from a logical and textual point of view, it should be noted that Rashi's textual commentary, citing a Midrashic reading, does identify the fig tree with Deborah. Similarly, the olive tree is identified with Othniel ben Knaz and the grapevine with Gideon (Rashi on Judg. 9:8–12).

be reduced to such one-dimensional neatness. The parable makes us aware that the process of interpretation always uncovers successive layers of meaning requiring subtle elucidation. Ideally, the parable forces us to re-think the standard way that we interpret the world around us.[40] In the con-text of Jotham's parable, one is invited to ponder the nature of political power: Is power irremediably bad? Can it become redemptive—that is, can politics point the way to the higher expression and development of humanity? Can it do so through the inclusion of women, a group not tra-ditionally associated with power?

The Book of Judges does not end on a positive note regarding the tran-scendent possibilities of power. Neither does it reflect positively on the traditional male exercise of power: to the extent that women are excluded from and even oppressed by the process of decision making on the part of males, who (nearly) exclusively exercise this prerogative, that power is portrayed as inherently negative and even corrupt. The very next story in the Book of Judges centers on Jephtah, a man caught in the coils of his vow, resulting in the sacrifice of his daughter in repayment for his military victory against the enemies of the Israelites. Surprisingly, the Biblical text records no effort on Jephtah's part to try to nullify his vow, as Biblical law provides.[41] The Midrashic reading of the text further emphasizes the neg-ative behavior of Israelite leaders at that time, reporting that Pinhas, the high priest, similarly does not exercise his option to nullify Jephtah's vow.[42] Understanding what women as a group potentially symbolize, it is not just the individual daughter of Jephtah who is lost, but also the possibility for re-forming the Israelites into a whole and integrated community. A similar point is highlighted in the final narrative of the Book of Judges, the concubine in Gibeah, whose cut-up body metaphorizes the dismembered state of the Israelite community.[43]

40. "My suggestion is that parabolic narrative has as one of its functions subversion of the conceptual scheme in terms of which its hearers construe the world and their lives in it. . . . The parable thus compels its hearers to transcend the limits of their ordinary con-ceptual vocabulary; to grasp a new concept." Bernard Harrison, "Parable and Transcen-dence," in *Ways of Reading the Bible*, ed. Michael Wadsworth (Totowa, N.J.: Harvester, 1981), 196, 200.

41. Cf., for example, Lev. 27:1–34 (which cites several instances of the substitutions that may be used for redeeming vows); also Deut. 23:23 and Num. 30:2–17.

42. The comment of the Midrash on the behavior of both leaders is searing: "*bein din l'din ne'evda haNa'ara*/between the two, the girl was lost." This Midrash appears in different ver-sions in Bereshit Rabbah 9:39; Tanhuma Behuykotai 5; and Yalkut Shimoni 68.

43. This point is further analyzed in Chapters 2 and 6, on Esther.

The Politics of Hope

In the connection that Jotham implicitly makes between women and the morally coherent exercise of power, Jotham's parable may be read as a counterweight to the hopelessness and social anomie that seems to overtake the Israelite community at the end of the Book of Judges.[44] Both Jotham's words and the literary form that he employs insist that difficult circumstances need not result in morally or politically illegitimate outcomes. Ideally, the dissonance between the parable and reality as perceived by its audience (should) evoke responses of purposive questioning, as they strive to resolve the perceived incongruence between theory and reality. This response can subsequently engender a potentially radical subversion of the accepted moral and political truths, as well as the desire to integrate the new order of meaning and significations created by the world of the parable.[45] For example, Jotham's interlocutors might have reflected, "If the trees do not want a king to rule over them, perhaps human beings shouldn't acquiesce to monarchical government either." Alternatively, the interlocutors might have surmised that human beings, like trees, may not need any ruler at all in order to flourish. Each of these seemingly antithetical reactions is the result of the yearning of the audience to understand their world and then order their circumstances according to this comprehension. Crucially, the literary structure of the parable activates this longing. Viewed in this manner, the literary techniques of the parable—rhetoric, gaps, and ambiguities (among others)[46]—function as acts of persuasion aimed at its audience.[47]

The passion that enables the parable's audience to utilize the parables as a new way of seeing the world may also inspire them to conceptualize, through that same parable, a way of arriving at the ultimate level of meaning. One scholar of the parable has described this process as the "reconstitut[ion of] the gap left by the use of figurative language."[48] To be sure,

44. This applies specifically to the social and moral disorder portrayed at the end of the Book of Judges, particularly as reflected in the rape-and-mayhem consequences of the concubine in Gibeah narrative, ending in these words: "Each man would do what was right in *his* eyes" (21:21; my emphasis).

45. Harrison, "Parable and Transcendence," 196.

46. Gila Safran Naveh, *Biblical Parables and Their Modern Re-creation* (Albany: SUNY Press, 2000), 14; David Stern, *Parables in Midrash* (1991; Cambridge, Mass.: Harvard University Press, 1994), 63–101.

47. Naveh, *Biblical Parables*, 15.

48. It is important to note that Naveh ends the citation with these words: "[Which] . . . is [however] . . . perennially subverted" (ibid., 28).

the weight of signification thus imposed on the parable may cause it to disappoint its audience, because the *multiple* interpretations of the parable belie the existence of just *one* definitive import. Still, the very existence of this multiplicity points to a certain measure of hope inherent in the parabolic form: the never-ending search for meaning that is characteristic of parabolic discourse means that the parable avoids an ultimately deconstructive theory of language which contains no outside referentiality at all except to its own powers of deception.[49] In other words, the fact that the ultimate meaning of the parable remains unattainable does not imply that the existence of meaning itself has come into question. To a large extent, this is because the parabolic form, by maintaining its ties to the reality of the surrounding world (in the guise of the *nimshal*/application of the parable) continues to insist that language, even if mysterious and ultimately incomprehensible, can serve as the key to derive meaning from that world. In that sense, parables are a Midrashic exegesis of existence itself.[50]

Etymologically, the simultaneous presence of this literary form—multiple layers of meaning together with the human search for "the" ultimate level of signification—is represented in Biblical Hebrew by its word for parable: *mashal.* Importantly, this term connotes both the literary device itself and the root word for "dominion." Their juxtaposition in Hebrew suggests that the parable, by encouraging interpretation, allows people to dominate (*m'sh'l*) their surrounding environment. In its specifically political implications, the form of the parable as utilized in this narrative, as well as the parable's etymological tonalities, invites the people to exercise their own sovereignty.[51] Thus, contrary to postmodern indeterminism, this understanding of the parable presents language as a means for human beings creatively to control and organize their world.[52]

49. This is a major theme of Paul de Man's *Allegories of Reading* (New Haven: Yale University Press, 1979); see his chapter on "Metaphor (Second Discourse)," especially 152–58.

50. It is therefore possible to characterize parables, like Midrash, by their exhibition of polysemy—multiple layers of significance—while at the same time insisting on the capability of language to produce ultimate meaning: "Midrash is predicated upon the existence of a point of view . . . upon . . . an omniscient, merciful, and eternally present God. Because of this feature, *Midrash* is one method that can destabilize all actuality but itself, one language to govern understanding" (Naveh, *Biblical Parables*, 22).

51. This is not to exclude the potential political implications and complications of the parable. It could very well encompass not only control of one's own environment (domestic political control), but international political control as well. In the context of this narrative, however, the implications seem more domestically related than internationally referenced.

52. In this connection, it is important to note that the Midrashic commentary on the Song of Songs, *Shir haShirim Rabbah*, identifies King Solomon as having recounted one parable

In this context, Jotham's choice to utilize the parabolic form in speaking to his fellow Israelites is crucial. The very name of this literary category focuses the Israelites' attention on the immediacy of the subject at hand: the issue of political domination. Moreover, in presenting his speech as a parable, Jotham demands the participation of the audience in an interpretive act that can also serve as a paradigm for their future communal political activity. In utilizing the parabolic form of speech, Jotham performatively demonstrates that his interlocutors should likewise not be passive in the face of Avimelekh's demand for absolute sovereignty. Thus, by soliciting an interpretive response on the part of the people, the parable becomes not just a mode of narration, but a method of discourse. Through his aesthetic choices, Jotham sends a message to the Israelites to insist on an active role in the determination of their political future.

Jotham's allusion to the complexity of trees indicates that even if the political realm is mistakenly considered a venue of only power concerns, the need for power to be rendered legitimate means that politics may not be conducted with only concerns of power in mind. The Jotham narrative emphasizes the negative moral cycle repeated in (Israelite) history: in this context, the Israelites' lack of kindness to Gideon's sons (Judg. 8:35) is repaid through the violence that they, in a sense, self-inflict through their voluntary acceptance of Avimelekh as their ruler. The more general consequences of this act also contribute to the future communal chaos among the Israelites. Thus, much of the ensuing violence involving Avimelekh centers around the city and area of Shekhem, because the Shekhemites are depicted as (wrongly) acquiescing to the murder of Gideon's sons (Judg. 9:18). At the same time, the Bible structures its description of events to hint at a possible solution for this moral and political displacement. By placing misogynistic words in the mouth of the tyrant Avimelekh, as he comments on his own death at the hands of a nameless woman (Judg. 9:54), the Biblical text emphasizes the importance of recognizing the redemptive role that women in general—not just exceptional heroines—have to play on the political scene.[53]

---

after another in the quest to understand the entire Torah. Thus, the figure of King Solomon combines three forms of mastery: political (Solomon's monarchy was domestically extensive and also encompassed wide-ranging international alliances), exegetical (Solomon's engagement with the Biblical text), and verbal (Solomon's control of his environment through the use of the parable). We may add to this list Solomon's social/sexual mastery, as implied by his many marriages.

53. Cf. also Judg. 4:9 and, in the apocryphal writings, Jth. 13:15.

In that connection, the Biblically allusive metaphor of trees indicates that moral distinctions have an *irreplaceable* function that may not be ignored, even in such extreme political situations as open warfare (Deut. 20:19). In the context of Jotham's own parable, utilizing the trope of trees informs his interlocutors that selecting a political leader does not absolve them from making difficult moral choices. On the contrary, the political arena remains, even if not a Hobbesian war of each against all, potentially a minefield of complex moral choices with unforeseen and unforeseeable implications.

Contextualizing the Parable

The positive use to which the parable may potentially be put requires a thorough understanding of the historical context within which parables are recounted. The circumstances of Jotham's speech reveal important aspects of the nature of Israelite communal life at that time. Jotham's focus on the inhabitants of Shekhem hints that much degeneration has taken place in the communal life of the Israelites. This is best seen when the anomic nature of collective existence under Avimelekh's rule is contrasted with the cooperation that had existed under his father's leadership. When the story of Gideon opens, the text presents a solitary man secretly threshing wheat, which, at the time, was an activity forbidden by the Midianite overlords and, hence, fraught with peril.[54] As the story unfolds, however, Gideon is able to raise troops from the tribes on whom he calls in order to defeat the triple alliance of Midian, Amalek, and Bnai Kedem.[55] This is in pointed contrast to the previous narrative, recounting the experience of Deborah, whose lack of success in this area is marked by her cursing of those tribes who chose not to respond to her appeal.[56] In Gideon's situation,

54. The Biblical text (Judg. 6:3–6, 11) explains that this situation is the result of the economic strictures that Midian had placed on the Israelites to ensure their continued economic, and hence political, subjection.

55. Menasseh, Zebulon, Asher, and Naftali are the tribes on whom Gideon calls and who respond.

56. Although the conquest of the Promised Land had been accomplished by all the tribes working in unison much of the time (cf. Josh. 1:13–16), communal solidarity quickly begins to fade. By the time of Deborah's tenure as the leader of the Israelites (Judg. 4, 5), the military and political threat presented by the Canaanite general Sisera evokes no concerted effort or even sympathy on the part of those Israelite tribes not in his direct path. Issakhar, Reuben, and Dan are the tribes who refuse to help and are therefore cursed by Deborah (Judg. 5:15–23).

it is precisely the tribes not called at the beginning of the battle—specifically, the tribe of Ephraim—who feel rejected and left out (Judg. 8:1).

More telling are the individual reactions to situations of potential discord, which reveal an increasing importance placed on promoting national unity. In Gideon's time, the Ephraimites feel personally affronted by being overlooked, even disrespected, and consequently having to forfeit the glory that might have accrued to them in defeating a major enemy of the Israelites.[57] Potentially, this might have caused a major rift among Gideon and some of the Israelite tribes, which could have led to a mutual parting of the ways or even a civil war. This actually happens in the post-Solomonic era, resulting in two Israelite kingdoms split along the ancient Joseph/Judah divide, with the Ephraimites in the north and the Judahites in the south.[58] Importantly, Gideon averts this division by choosing instead to pacify the insulted Ephraimites by minimizing the contribution of his own tribe (Menasseh) to the battle and exalting the Ephraimites' endgame strategy of capturing two of the enemy kings (Judg. 8:2–3).

This compromise alludes to—and repairs—a historic imbalance between the two tribes. This asymmetry traces its origins to the Bible's presentation of Jacob's deathbed benediction of his children, at which time Ephraim and Menasseh, grandchildren of Jacob, are included in the official tribal count.[59] This historically tardy addition may well have engendered a feeling of tenuousness on the part of these grandchildren of Jacob regarding the stability of their place within the Israelite constellation, especially when contrasted with the "full" tribal status held by the recognized sons of Jacob. In the scene recorded in the Bible, this feeling of insecurity takes on an extra dimension as Jacob blesses Joseph's younger son, Ephraim, as if he were the older son (Gen. 48:17–19). By giving Ephraim precedence over Joseph's older son, Menasseh, Jacob sets up a potentially explosive situation in the future relationship between the tribes of Menasseh and Ephraim, which comes close to the boiling point in the aftermath of Gideon's battle against Midian. Importantly, by his fulsome praise of the Ephraimites, Gideon diffuses the latent tensions of this encounter by reassuring them

57. Cf. Malbim, on Judg. 8:1.

58. In fact, civil war does divide the Israelites at different times in their history. Some examples include the civil battles that occur during the judgeship of Jephtah (Judg. 12:4–6); the civil war that breaks out after the incident of the concubine in Gibeah (Judg. 20:1–25); and, most famously, the rift after the death of Solomon (1 Kings 12:4–17).

59. "They are mine, Ephraim and Menasseh; they will be to me as Reuven and Shimon" (Gen. 48:5).

that even though the leadership position is held by a member of a tribe that is their closest potential rival, the Ephraimites' primacy as a tribe continues to be assured by the critical nature of their contributions.

Gideon's judicious application of praise is more than a gesture of political prudence. It also alludes to a Biblical model of leadership that valorizes national well-being above personal stature. The modesty that allows the leader of a beleaguered nation to make light of his personal and tribal status in favor of his familial tribe's closest rival recalls Moses's refusal of leadership in the Exodus narrative when he is called on to lead the Israelites out of Egypt.[60] To be sure, individual abnegations of leadership in the Biblical text may be seen as instances of the folkloric motif of leaders who refuse political power when first approached (but who subsequently do fully exercise this power). Gideon and Moses are not the only leaders to accept authority in the Biblical text, however, and the more closely drawn textual parallels between them indicate that something else is going on.

The parallel between their approaches to leadership is textually indicated by God's first response to Gideon's protest of unworthiness to lead. In His reply to Gideon, God insists, "For I will be with you/*ki ehye 'imakh*" (Judg. 6:16), which precisely echoes the response to Moses at the beginning of Moses's own call to leadership (Exod. 3:12). As with Moses, this answer to Gideon is followed by a series of signs attesting that God has indeed chosen him as the vehicle to deliver the Israelites from their oppressors. What unites Gideon and Moses is their unswerving devotion to the nationhood of the people whom they lead. In the case of Gideon, the last half of the verse addressed to him is even more pointed than the words directed at Moses: "And you will smite Midian as one man/*vehikita et Midian k'ish ehad*" (Judg. 6:16). This verse may be read as guaranteeing an easy military victory over Midian (they will be as easy to conquer as if they were just one man); at another level, however, this verse may be said to promise a strong unity among the Israelites, which itself will improve their chances for military success. In this reading, the verse may be understood

60. The reference here is to Moses's refusal to assume the mantle of leadership as the Israelites leave Egypt (Exod. 3:11). In that passage, Moses argues that he will be ineffective as a leader and thus hamper the fulfillment of the Israelites' national destiny. Importantly, this dialogue is later cited as a rebuke to all those who might assess Moses's motivations for leadership as self-interested (Num. 12:3, 7–8). The rebuke to Miriam and Aaron serves also as a generalized warning to the rebellion engineered by Korah, whose major complaint against Moses and Aaron was that they "raised themselves above the congregation of the Lord" (Num. 16:3).

to say that the Israelites will be united as one man in their conquest of the Midianites.

The creation of a national consciousness does not occur of its own volition. Gideon's nurturing of a national, trans-tribal identity finds its first deep roots in the aftermath of his first encounter with the angel, when Gideon, in obedience to God's request, smashes the altar of Ba'al. Upon discovering that Gideon had destroyed the altar and the Asherah tree (contemporary forms of idolatrous worship), Gideon's irate fellow citizens demand that he be put to death. But Gideon's family does not give him up to the people's anger. This reveals an emotional unity on the individual/familial level that bodes well for the incipient feelings of national solidarity that develop later under Gideon's leadership. To be sure, family solidarity does not necessarily lead to national identification: literary texts and narratives of political theory abound with counterexamples of families who uphold values that question automatic obedience to the state.[61] On the other hand, the ability to expand on a family connection may serve, as it does here, to generalize a dynamic connection in the context of the political state.[62] Thus, in response to his angry neighbors, Gideon's father in effect taunts them with their own logic: let the Divinity in whom you believe fight his own battles (Judg. 6:31).

This response may be said to replay the Midrashic narrative, in which the young Abraham smashes the idols of his father; Yo'ash (Gideon's father), however, unlike Terah (Abraham's father), does not deliver his son into the hands of the irate townspeople.[63] In keeping with the political context of the narrative, it is more relevant that the text inversely anticipates the incident in which Saul prepares to put his son, Jonathan, to death for inadvertently failing to adhere to the terms of the vow that Saul had enjoined on the Israelites in the course of a particularly difficult battle (1 Sam. 14:28–30; 38–45).[64] A man who cannot practice love and understanding for his

61. An obvious example is Sophocles' *Antigone*. More modern examples include the sustained questioning by modern political theorists (e.g., Rousseau) of whether primary identification adheres to the family or to the state.

62. Thus, Rousseau: "The good son, the good husband, the good father . . . make the good citizen" (*Émile*, bk. 5, 4:700).

63. Bereshit Rabbah 38:13. This Midrash portrays Abraham as systematically discouraging people from buying/worshipping idols from the workshop of his father, Terah. In the Midrashic narrative, Terah hands over Abraham to the "tender mercies" of Nimrod's justice, from whose fiery furnace Abraham is miraculously saved.

64. While on that occasion, Jonathan is saved by the voice of the people and does not die, the immediate juxtaposition of that narrative in 1 Samuel to the subsequent account of

own son in difficult circumstances will also misappropriate feelings of kindness towards an avowed enemy of his people.[65] By contrast, in the Gideon narrative, Gideon's father, Yo'ash, exhibits feelings of empathy for his son (even though he personally does not share in Gideon's belief system) and, consequently, does not betray him to the indignant townspeople. Such interaction between people, who value each other individually more than they honor their own particular ideological loyalties, indicates strong roots of interpersonal solidarity. This sympathy can be nurtured to form a group whose members operate successfully as a unit, because what unites its constituent parts is greater than what divides them, even in matters of ideology and belief. In such a situation, a nation can be forged.

Forging a Nation

Traditional political theory tends to conflate the creation of a nation with the determination of its mode of governance: thus, in *The Republic*, the Guardians are charged with bringing together the requisite workers and professionals needed to constitute a (more-or-less) autarkic city-state, while at the same time they are given the power to rule the polis in line with their highest philosophical ideals.[66] Similarly, in more modern times, liberal political theory unites the formation of a people (its constitution, describing the conditions that constitute the citizenry of the state) with the document that sets down its method of governance (its Constitution).[67]

Because of the close juxtaposition depicted in the Bible between the Divine choice of the Israelites and the bestowing of the Torah on Mount

---

Saul's failure to fulfill the Divine command regarding the Amalekites gives rise to the suspicion that it is perhaps the lack of judgment already displayed toward his own son that lies equally at the root of the mistake that would eventually cost Saul his kingdom.

65. The verse records, "But Saul . . . had pity on Agag/*va'yahmol Shaul . . . 'al Agag*" (1 Sam. 15:9).

66. It seems possible to argue that the myth of birth—that the rulers all emerge directly from the soil of Greece—spoils the concept of the simultaneity of the formation of a people and their government. It should be remembered, however, that the propagation of this false myth is urged on the Guardians once they have indeed established a polis and are concerned about its future transmission and existence. Plato, *The Republic of Plato*, 106.

67. In this context, I utilize the term "liberal political theory" to refer to a political theory predicated on a limited and not absolute government. An obvious example of unity of word and purpose is the Constitution of the United States. The same document formed (constituted) a nation—the preamble speaks of the Constitution that will "form a more perfect Union" (i.e., a nation that will be better than the one that existed before, under the Articles of Confederation)—and that will at the same time determine its system of governance.

Sinai, it is easy to assume that this same conflation obtains in the Biblical view of the formation of the Israelites as a nation. A closer look, however, reveals that this is not the case. Although the proclamation of the Israelites as a nation is accompanied by a plethora of laws regarding the conduct of daily life and even the details of social bienséance, this is not yet the stuff of political governance.[68] The Bible remains peculiarly quiet on this subject until the Deuteronomic verses elaborating on the establishment of kingship (17:14–20). Even here, however, the language is not absolute. To be sure, the traditional interpretation has always understood these verses to command monarchy as the preferred form of government —albeit one limited in privilege and mindful of ultimate Divine sovereignty.[69] More modern scholars, however, have pointed to the word that introduces this section—"ki"—as indicating the tangential nature of this enterprise: in the context of the verse, "ki" can mean "when" or, alternatively, "if."[70] According to the latter understanding, monarchy is only one of a range of power arrangements—and not necessarily even the best one—available to

68. On the formation of the Israelite nation, see Exod. 19:6: "You will be *for Me* a king-dom of priests and a holy nation" (emphasis mine). On rules of propriety, see, for example, many of the warnings on the just and kind treatment demanded for the defenseless in society, particularly widows and orphans: Exod. 22:21; Deut. 10:18, 24:17; Jer. 7:6; Isa. 1:17.

69. Sifrei 28–29, on Deut. 17:14–20, and Rashi ad loc.; cf. TB Sanhedrin 20a. The tradi-tional interpretation of this verse tends to follow Maimonides, who, in *Hilkhot Melakhim* (in the *Mishneh Torah*), promotes a view of the king as all-powerful. In fact, however, there are traditional sources that insist that his acceptance by the population is part of the king's legit-imacy. This approach is seen even in the Malbim's comment on Jacob's sons' sneering ques-tion to Joseph when he first reveals his dreams to them: "Will you reign over us and lord it over us?/*Hamalokh timlokh 'aleinu; 'im mashol timshol banu?*" (Gen. 37:8). Malbim comments that there is a difference between *malokh* and *m'shol:* the root *m'l'kh* refers to accepted rule and *m'sh'l* to enforced rule. Even later in history, Saul had to be accepted again by the entire nation before he could legitimately rule them: this is what leads to his second coronation (*hidush hamelukha*) in the Gilgal. The comment of Gersonides (Ralbag) on this incident in 1 Sam. 11:15 is very telling: "As if to show that until now, Saul did not fully reign/*k'iluy her'ah she'ad 'ata lo haya melekh b'shelmut.*" This comment is not just a matter of positivist tautology. Rather, it points to the people's consent as indispensable to the creation of political legitimacy. In a similar vein, the Pirkei d'Rabbi Eliezer states: "The nation appoints the king; the king does not crown himself if the people do not crown [i.e., consent to] him/*l'fi sh'ha'am mam-lichin et hamelekh, v'ein hamelekh mamlikh et atzmo 'im ein ha'am mamlikhin oto.*" Abarbanel, commenting on Deut. 17, insists that, due to the tendency of human nature to oppress any-one over whom they have absolute power, the best arrangement for monarchy is for there to be term limits for rulers. In this connection, Abarbanel praises what he thought he saw in the cities of Venice and Florence (although he also voices his discomfort with enunciating too many general rules for the conduct of kingship; as he puts it, so much depends on the specific circumstances and on the individual abilities of the king).

70. Cf. Malbim, on Deut. 17:14–20; and also Sifrei 28. Abarbanel ad loc. views this commandment as conditional, meant to "counter man's evil tendency." Abarbanel bases his

the Israelites once they settle their land.[71] Read in this light, the Deuteronomic verses on kingship emphasize the extent to which the people must
have a role in choosing their leader and participating in their own governance. If you choose to establish a monarchy, these verses seem to warn,
take care that you choose a monarch from one who is your equal ("from
among your *brothers*," which is to say, not from a person who is socially your
superior).[72] Thus, the text in Deuteronomy foregrounds the challenge that
Jotham presents to his fellow Israelites to take an active role in the creation
of their own political future.

At the historical juncture when Jotham is speaking, the form and content
of the Israelite political community remains in doubt. Through the parable
of the trees and the nature of its setting, Jotham attempts to solidify Israelite political identity in two ways. Most obviously, Jotham endeavors to
unite the community by offering them a common text for their joint interpretation. In terms of material practice, this communal text aims to galva-
nize the people into working through the text together and, in so doing, to
recreate the dynamic of their own community formation. Second, through
this independent act of interpretation, Jotham also wants to orient the
Israelites toward their own political future by inviting them, implicitly, to
seize responsibility for the nature of their own political governance.

In this way, Jotham activates the forces of history in two directions.
First, in attempting to center the Israelites around a text, he performatively
recalls the first instance of permanent national consolidation on the part of
the Israelites when they received the text of the Torah at Mount Sinai.[73] At

---

contention on the fact that the Israelites are depicted as desiring a king just to be "like all
other nations." According to him, this is not a sufficient moral basis for a Divine commandment. In his terms, this commandment at best serves as a means (*Kli*), although not necessarily the preferred one, to further the Israelites' achievement of moral excellence.

71. This point is emphasized by Thomas Paine in *Common Sense* (1776), when he argues
that kingship is not Divinely ordained; on the contrary, it is Divinely despised as a form of
governance for a free people.

72. Professor Joshua Berman (SBL conference, Washington, D.C., November 2006) has
highlighted the egalitarian implications of the preposition "from among/ *mibein*." I thank
Professor Berman (Bar-Ilan University) for this insight.

73. It is important to note that the location where Jotham speaks his parable also contributes to the foundational and national nature of his enterprise. The Biblical text (Judg.
9:7) describes Jotham's declamation from atop Mount Grizim, a location laden with historical significance for the Israelites. At the time of the Israelite conquest of the Promised Land,
this mountain had been the venue of the proclamation of blessings and curses, serving both
to guarantee and to warn the Israelites of what would befall them if they ignored the word
of God. It is not happenstance that this ceremony is considered so important that it is
twice mentioned in the Biblical text. It is first commanded at the time of Moses, before the

the same time, Jotham anticipates those future Israelite leaders who likewise leave their imprint on the character of Israelite national identity and self-consciousness through the establishment of a text. Notably, this refers to Esther, whose purpose in writing her eponymous book centers on the reconstitution of Israelite national identity to withstand even the rigors of political exile.

In line with the indeterminate nature of the parable, Jotham's evocation of history yields its own ambiguous implications. Although Jotham anticipates the liberating activity of Esther, his appeal to common Israelite historical experience also foreshadows Samson, whose activities call into question precisely the valorization of exclusive national identity on the basis of historically established, unique national practices.

Parabolic Implications

Unlike most of the narratives in the Book of Judges, which finish with the (at least temporary) cessation of travail and disorder, the end of the story in which Jotham's parable figures highlights ever-widening ripples of social unrest and open warfare. To be sure, a ray of hope may be glimpsed at the last event of the Jotham narrative: a woman literally seizes opportunity in her hands and throws down a millstone from the besieged Tower of Tebetz, killing Avimelekh (Judg. 9:53). The jarring nature of the episode's conclusion—a far cry from the conventional endings of the crisis-and-salvation cycles in this Biblical book—emphasizes the necessity of taking up the parable's political and moral challenges.

Jotham's parable highlights important themes in the construction of Israelite political discourse and the establishment of a legitimate mode of governance. First, politics is revealed as the art of the possible. In dealing with the realities of human self-aggrandizement and the search for power,

---

Israelites' official entry into the Promised Land (Deut. 11:29). It is actually realized once the Israelites and Joshua commence their conquest (Josh. 3:30–35). This point is both concretely symbolized and spiritually referentialized by the raising of a monument in Shekhem, which commemorates the Israelites' covenant to follow God's word. It also reenacts, as it were, the previous occasion during which they first operate as a nation: when they receive the Torah at Mount Sinai. Significantly, Mount Grizim is located just opposite the city of Shekhem, the focus of Jotham's words. By choosing this same Mount Grizim, overlooking Shekhem, as the location of his own speech, Jotham evokes the trace of the original act, thus signaling that his words are of major historical and moral significance for the entire Israelite community.

the constraints of politics often require choosing a solution that is morally less than ideal in order to prevent an even greater calamity: thus, the tower, originally (in the Biblical text) a symbol of human reification and self-aggrandizement, becomes the means for preventing even further consolidation of power on the part of the despot Avimelekh. Second, the reality and meaning of words and symbols remain fluid, with the ambiguous implications inherent in this formulation. Language serves as the means of both establishing a society based on justice (the aim of Jotham's parable) and legalizing social and economic exploitation (e.g., the society of the Tower of Babel; similarly, Avimelekh's attempt to force the people of Shekhem to transfer all of their freedom to him in perpetuity).

Finally, salvation may come from where it is least expected: the young, the weak, the dispossessed, and the disrespected. In this episode, it is Jotham, the youngest and weakest of Gideon's sons, who declaims a parable underlining the importance of accepting political responsibility. The centrality of what is commonly held to be marginal is a crucial part of the historical reality of Israelite leadership: Gideon, himself a younger son, and Jephtah, the son of a prostitute, rise to become judges of the Israelite tribes. Likewise, the position of king is often awarded to a person whose background gives no hint of the aptitude to lead: Saul comes from the least consequential family of the youngest and smallest of the tribes, and David is a lowly shepherd when he is anointed as the king of the Israelites. Support for a counterintuitive source of leadership is also reflected in the substance of Jotham's parable, where women, a group often disregarded, are symbolically depicted as untainted by the desire for political power; hence, they represent arguably the best hope to form a morally acceptable polity. In this connection, the staunch refusal of the parable's fruit trees to accept power unless it conforms to what they regard as their moral raison d'être leaves the reader with a lingering and revolutionary thought regarding the future construction of Israelite power. Is it possible to understand the *nimshal* of this parable as advising that a morally just and hence politically stable Israelite leadership will be fully established only with the conventional admission of women into the circles of political power as a normal measure (in the manner of Deborah, who was an accepted judge of her time), and not merely as a stopgap measure in times of emergency (as exemplified by Yael)?[74]

---

74. Note the simple past tense used to introduce Deborah as judge—"and she judged Israel at that time" (Judg. 4:4)—as a simple fact, rather than as an unusual event requiring a complicated explanation.

Closely connected to the establishment of power in unexpected places is the role of God in the Bible's presentation of the formation of Israelite political discourse. Jotham's personal situation hints at the Israelite national imbalance of perception in both the political and the religious realms. Jotham's relegation to the margins of politics alludes to the underlying rationale of Israelite political persecution as explicated by the narrative voice of the Book of Judges, which attributes Israelite political troubles to their ensnarement in the surrounding polytheistic culture. The sidelining of Jotham models the placement of God at the (neglected) periphery of Israelite consciousness; thus, it literally embodies the paradox of marginality in the contexts of both the material (political) and the ephemeral (spiritual). In both cases, what is conventionally considered tangential may really be centrally determinative.

The Biblical portrayal of what appears to be the marginalization of God on the Israelite political scene (as opposed to God's portrayed central role in Israelite nation formation at Sinai, for example) is evident in the relative lack of consideration that the Israelites show God in their daily trafficking with political power. At the same time, the Biblical text portrays God as playing a significant, even if obscure, role behind the scenes in the development of Israelite self-awareness and political identity. For example, in the course of the Jotham narrative, in the midst of what often appears to be nothing more than an ill-tempered, small-time squabble about who gets to rule over a relatively small amount of land, God is described as directly "sending an evil wind" to discombobulate Avimelekh and his desire to wield ever-increasing amounts of power (Judg. 9:23). In the Jotham story, it is this evil wind that accounts for the otherwise unexplained change of heart that the Shekhemites evince toward Avimelekh.

But the results of this "evil" wind are not so easily categorized. The wind that hastens Avimelekh's demise is not purely benign: this negative spirit also ignites a series of civil disputes among the Israelites, which do not really end until the establishment of the Israelite monarchy. In like manner, the subsequent narratives of the Book of Judges depict the Israelites as deeply divided both on how to deal with their enemies and whether, in fact, the occupation of the Land of Israel by other nations (notably, the Philistines during the era of Samson) is something worth fighting about. To be sure, the activity of this spirit does not cease even during the period of the monarchy: the evil wind noted here foreshadows the evil spirit (the word for both of these is the same in Hebrew: *ruah*) that destabilizes Saul and eventually destroys his hold on power from within (1 Sam. 8:10).

The presentation of the direct, albeit hidden, nature of Divine intervention in political affairs allows this text to go further than other Biblical narratives that acknowledged the potential of politics to ameliorate human welfare beyond simply justifying the already existing arrangements of political power (such as the Joseph narrative, discussed in Chapter 1). This text also expands on narratives that had foregrounded the "strangeness" of the political realm as safeguarding equal rights even, and especially, for all Others (as in the alienated leadership narratives presented in Chapter 2). With the Jotham narrative, the figuration of Divine influence as a wind/spirit directly affecting human actions also reveals the ambiguity of the results, which are left squarely within the range of human choice to develop further. Thus, the effect of Divine action, even if pivotal, is still subject to human direction. Similarly, in the Jotham story, while God's "evil wind" precipitates the events that conspire to throw Avimelekh from power, the full-scale acknowledgement of Jotham's message by his fellow Shekhemites/Israelites—the imperative for them to take responsibility for their own political future—is not fully manifest. In this regard, the Jotham episode ends with a resounding silence.

The implications of the Jotham story may also highlight the potential subversion of the positive moral connotations of Otherness: thus, the radical Otherness of the Divine may be manipulated to facilitate the maximization of power in the hands of those individuals claiming to know the exact nature of Divine demands. In that event, God becomes the excuse for human exploitation. Kant writes of a not-dissimilar situation in *Perpetual Peace*.[75] Recalling the imagery utilized by Jotham, Kant expands on the comparison of each nation to a tree and writes that the human ability to manipulate even nature to its desires—to graft the limb of one tree onto the trunk of another, thus producing a diversity of hybrid vegetation that

---

75. In *Perpetual Peace*, Kant writes: "Since, like a tree, each nation has its own roots, to incorporate it into another nation as a graft, denies its existence as a moral person, turns it into a thing, and thus contradicts the concept of the individual contract." *Perpetual Peace and Other Essays* (Indianapolis: Hackett, 1983), 108. Kant continues: "The sole established constitution that follows from the idea of an original contract, the one on which all of a nation's just legislation must be based, is republican. For first, it accords with the principles of the *freedom* of the members of a society (as men), second, it accords with the principles of the *dependence* of everyone on a single, common [source of] legislation (as subjects), and third, it accords with the law of the equality of them all (as citizens)" (112).

can be exploited for commercial purposes—actually indicates not the ulti-mate attainment of human prowess but the actualization of the inhuman inversion of moral means and ends. While the Biblical text does not utilize Kant's particular imagery, its referencing of God and the accompanying demonstration of the propensity of moral ideals to be misused makes a related point. The Bible goes on to add that that even when the concept of God is misused, the struggle to maintain the idea of the Divine still allows for a greater play of free will. This, in its turn, facilitates the further exer-cise of moral choice, which for the Bible is the quintessential and defining human activity, because it allows for the development and expression of the human soul.[76]

From the Biblical perspective, viewing politics as an arena for human and Divine interaction has the potential to yield both a positive notion of community and a dynamically interactive political system. Jotham's procla-mation of the parable, and the bloody events that bracket it, focus Israelite attention both on the moral claims of political life and on the inability of power to elide the principled demands of moral choice, which are an inex-tricable part of national identity. How the question of national identity can be further solidified is the riddle that continues to torment even Samson, the last major judge of the pre-monarchic period.

76. Václav Havel makes similar arguments, particularly in his essays arguing for a tran-scendent, perhaps Divine, element in human politics. See especially *The Art of the Impossible: Politics as Morality in Practice* (New York: Knopf, 1997).

5

SAMSON: THE POLITICS OF RIDDLING

As we have seen, Jotham's parable presents a challenge to the Israelites, whose sense of (political) identity is largely overshadowed by Avimelekh's tyranny. While the Biblical text informs us of the death of Avimelekh, the broader question of whether the Israelites take the words of Jotham's parable to heart is not (openly) treated by the text. Subsequent chapters of the Book of Judges largely reinforce the impression that these issues remain unaddressed.

In this context, one way of reading the Samson narrative is to view this story as a meditation on the necessity of possessing a unique communal identity, particularly in times when this difference arguably seems to provoke more trouble than it is worth. Strangely enough, the Bible locates these questions within a narrative whose protagonist appears to personify a very superficial type of difference—that is to say, difference limited to flagrant physical markers. Thus, conventional wisdom understands Samson's physical prowess to be the center of the story. Some critics delight in Samson as mighty hero, while others denigrate him as a leader with a tendency to reduce interpersonal relationships to brute force. While these approaches differ fundamentally, even contradictorily, in their respective assessments of Samson's character, what unites these divergent evaluations is even more noteworthy: in all of these appraisals, Samson is reduced to a remarkably simple—not to say simplistic—figure.

In this chapter I offer a fresh look at Samson as political leader. His self-understanding as a political actor is complex: he consciously grapples with the Israelites' as-yet-incomplete idea of their own national identity, while coming to grips with his own sense of estrangement. Samson's strangeness makes him difficult to comprehend. As such he remains a problematic figure for both his contemporaries and for later readers of his saga. At the same time, Samson deliberately utilizes his strangeness to deepen his own and, hopefully, his people's understanding of the paradoxes of nationhood. Samson does this in order to enable the Israelites to create a dynamic sense of national identity that can respond to the ever-changing challenges of the different eras in which Israelite national identity plays out. Samson's ability to define the interactions and extent of these issues marks his accomplishment as a leader in the development of Israelite nationhood.

Conventional Readings

At first glance, the Biblical text seems to present Samson as an embodiment of the Peter Principle: the individual who is promoted beyond his level of competence. With his acts of seeming buffoonery and apparently senseless violence, Samson appears to lack sufficient dignity to hold the position of Israelite judge. Samson has been categorized by scholars as manipulative and deceitful;[1] his tenure as judge seems to yield no permanent improvement in the political and economic well-being of the Israelites.[2] That four chapters of a relatively laconic narrative of Israelite judges is dedicated to an apparent political disappointment explains perhaps why some scholars have chosen to see the Samson story as a compilation of various earlier histories, serving as a recapitulation of the pre-monarchic experience in ancient Israel.[3]

A brief summary of the surprisingly complex Samson narrative follows:

Against the background of the Philistine domination of ancient Israel, the Biblical text focuses on Manoah, a Danite whose wife is visited by an angel foretelling the birth of a son who will "begin to save the Israelites

---

1. A typical assessment is found in Samuel Sandmel, *The Enjoyment of Scripture* (New York: Oxford University Press 1972), 23. Also see Edward Greenstein, "The Riddle of Samson," *Prooftexts* 1, no. 3 (1981): 239–41.

2. Cf., for example, James L. Crenshaw, *Samson: A Secret Betrayed, a Vow Ignored* (Atlanta: Scholars Press, 1978), 20. Ulrich Simon describes Samson as "unstable." "Samson and the Heroic," in *Ways of Reading the Bible*, ed. Michael Wadsworth (Sussex: Harvester, 1981), 157. Similarly, Yairah Amit classifies Samson as an "unbalanced hero" and questions his efficacy as a judge. *The Book of Judges: The Art of Editing* (Leiden: Brill, 1999), 288.

3. Cf. Greenstein, "The Riddle of Samson," 248.

from the Philistines."[4] This child, Samson, must adhere to the restrictions of a Nazirite and neither drink wine nor cut his hair. Subsequently, the text highlights certain events in Samson's life featuring his unusual strength and cunning. Several of these stories center on Samson's marriage plans, which, to his parents' consternation, involve a Timnite (Philistine) woman. During the journey to arrange the details of the marriage, Samson tears apart a lion surging forth in his path. Upon returning on the same path several days later, Samson discovers a nest of bees in the dead lion's chest cavity. He eats the honey as he walks home.

It is at the wedding festivities that the text shows Samson displaying his craftiness vis-à-vis the Philistines. He challenges them with a riddle that they "solve" only by threatening Samson's new bride with death if she does not provide them with the solution. This exchange sets off a cycle of violent revenge. Samson's wife is eventually given to another (Philistine) man, whereupon Samson destroys a large portion of the Philistine harvest. Later, the Philistines send an army to Ramath-Lehi, demanding that Samson be delivered to them. The Israelites comply with this request, but by the text's account, Samson's bonds melt off him and he slays one thousand Philistines (this time with the jawbone of an ass). The Philistines finally manage to capture Samson when he reveals to Delilah, a woman in the pay of the Philistines, the secret of his strength: his hair that had never been cut. After Delilah cuts his hair, the Philistines successfully capture Samson, blind him, and make sport of him during a thanksgiving festival to their deity, Dagon. Samson's final act is to bring down the temple of Dagon on himself and his Philistine captors.

Thematic links in the Biblical text give Samson's picaresque adventures some unity. One of these is Samson's physical prowess; another is Samson's recitation of riddles. To be sure, these themes are narratively interrelated: most often, the riddles are a pretext for the display of Samson's strength. But the riddle does more than serve as a device to move the narrative forward.[5] First, the riddle allows conventional ideas to be reexamined and questioned:

4. Judg. 13:5.
5. In emphasizing the centrality of the riddle in the structure and content of the Samson story, I am utilizing Mieke Bal's notion of *mise en abyme*, particularly as it is understood by Claudia Camp. While Camp focuses on the microstructure of the riddle as highlighting the values/themes of strangeness, however, I expand on the notion of the riddle as a pivotal microstructure to emphasize the political issues of power, knowledge, and difference. Mieke Bal, *Lethal Love* (Bloomington: Indiana University Press, 1987), 756–76, 788; Claudia Camp, "Riddlers, Tricksters, and Strange Women in the Samson Story," in *Wise, Strange, and Holy* (Sheffield: Sheffield Academic Press, 2000), 94–143, especially 95–96.

Samson uses the act of riddling to question the notion of national exclusivity and the proper relationship of the personal and the political realms as these are advanced by the Biblical text. In addition, the form of the riddle serves as the means to explore issues of personal identity and the extent and limitations of knowledge. As we will see, the consequences brought about by Samson's riddles can themselves be understood as attempts on his part to generate a discourse about the quality both of nationhood and communal life. Finally, the riddle (and it will become evident that there is more than one riddle in the story) exemplifies the strangeness emblematic of Samson's life and political destiny.

Relating the Riddle: The Personal Is Political

The lion's share of critical attention regarding riddling in the Samson narrative has been devoted to the nature of the riddle with which Samson challenges his Philistine companions at his wedding celebration: "Out of the devourer came forth food, and out of the strong came forth sweetness" (Judg. 14:14).

Much has been written about whether the content of this riddle makes it fair—that is, if it can be solved without the specialized knowledge of the particular adventure that had befallen Samson before the wedding festivities—and whether it even can be considered a riddle at all.[6] But the utilization of the riddling structure can also be seen as a method of interrogating power relationships and presenting the various techniques that can be employed as a means of dealing with power inequities.

Analysis of the riddle as a genre[7] of literature and social interaction reveals that the issue at the heart of the riddle is not merely the answer to a

6. The argument here is whether a "neck riddle," properly speaking, is a true riddle. For general commentary on this issue, see Roger D. Abrahams and Alan Dundes, "Riddles," in *Folklore and Folklife*, ed. Richard M. Dorson (Chicago: University of Chicago Press, 1972), 129–43. For a negative reply on this question, see W. J. Pepicello and Thomas A. Green, *The Language of Riddles: New Perspectives* (Columbus: Ohio State University Press, 1984), especially 87–88. Regarding the issue about whether it is a fair riddle, see also Crenshaw, *Samson*, especially 111–20. For a negative answer to this question, see Mieke Bal, *Death and Dissymmetry* (Chicago: University of Chicago Press, 1988), 136.

7. This discussion of riddles will not include the differences among the various genres of riddles; rather, it will concentrate on their social and political implications as reflected in the Samson story. For more on the various genres of riddles and the cultural accounting of riddles, see Annikki Kaivola-Bregenøj, "Riddles and Their Use," and Richard Bauman, "'I'll Give You Three Guesses': The Dynamics of Genre in the Riddle-Tale," both in *Untying the*

specific question. Indeed, the way of posing the question itself attempts to prevent, rather than facilitate, the discovery of an answer. To this end, the riddler transforms the usual categories in which the items forming the riddle are normally placed, rendering them strange, or uncanny, such that information nominally presented in a straightforward manner is actually transformed in a veil of misinformation. The riddle therefore always contains (at least) two objects that seem unlike, incompatible, or contradictory. The juxtaposition of these categories within the context of the riddle demands that these seemingly dissociated entities be connected in a novel manner, which is accomplished by reconceptualizing the essence and boundaries of the items in question.[8]

The new way of thinking suggested by the riddle can have important positive consequences; its questioning of the status quo can open up a more benign way of looking at the world. In other words, the strange juxtaposition of normally unconnected objects[9] (in Samson's case, the eater and the eaten; the strong and the sweet) can allow for an ambiguity in approaching the world that can prove liberating.[10] In this vein, the riddle can be used to mediate between diverse and even opposed categories of a cultural system.[11] That Samson is able to pose the question to the conquerors of his homeland points to the fact that boundaries in daily life between victor and vanquished are not strictly drawn. This becomes apparent when the riddle is viewed in context: the occasion of the riddle is Samson's marriage to a Philistine woman, which is officially celebrated in a Philistine city, and to which Samson brings his own Philistine companions.[12]

But the destabilization achieved by questioning accepted categories, while liberating, also has a darker, more ominous side.[13] Just as the riddle reveals that verbal classifications are not unassailable, the riddle also implies

---

Knot: On Riddles and Other Enigmatic Modes, edited by Galit Hasan-Rokem and David Shulman (New York: Oxford University Press, 1996).

8. Don Handelman, "Traps of Trans-formation: Theoretical Convergences," in *Untying the Knot,* ed. Hasan-Rokem and Shulman, 44. In the context of the Samson riddle, the connection between the strong and the sweet is unanticipated; likewise, the derivation of food from what is normally associated with the eater or consumer par excellence is so farfetched as to be labeled oxymoronic, or even impossible.

9. Ibid.

10. Ibid., 48; Dina Stein, "A King, a Queen, and the Riddle Between: Riddles and Interpretation in a Late Midrashic Text," in *Untying the Knot,* ed. Hasan-Rokem and Shulman, 129.

11. Stein, "A King, a Queen," 128.

12. Cf. Camp, "Riddlers, Tricksters," especially 94–105.

13. Handelman, "Traps of Trans-formation," 41.

that the institutionalized order is not immutable.[14] In other words, the estrangement that obtains between the description vouchsafed by the riddle and the actual referent itself implies a parallel disjoining of the commonly accepted connection between power and its possessors. Consequently, a riddle is potentially revolutionary; as such, it poses a distinct danger to the party in possession of political power.

Thus, the presentation of the riddle is a calculated challenge on Samson's part. The riddle's origin with a member of the subordinated Israelite tribes poses an implicit challenge to the Philistine interlocutors: Is their superiority an accepted benefit of their elevated political and economic status, or can they defend their position in the context of current and dynamic interchange? In other words, who is really the "dull giant": Samson, who appears motivated by nothing apart from what his eyes see; or the bloated Philistines?

More complicatedly, it becomes evident that riddling actually highlights an *ambiguity* in the location of power. Although the riddle nominally privileges the position of the questioner, who turns out to possess (at least one of) the solutions to the problem posed by this challenge,[15] it turns out that there is a danger for the riddler as well. In posing the riddle, Samson risks the possibility that the Philistines may indeed solve it, thus depriving him of any tactical political advantage. In the context of the narrative in Judges, then, the question is double-edged: Why would the Philistines agree to take part in a dialogue in which they have everything to lose? And why would Samson subsequently run the risk that they may discover the riddle's solution?

In effect, the riddle reflects the internal contradictions of Samson's position in the context of his larger historical role. For Samson, the strangeness and the tragedy of his situation is that the ambiguity of the riddle permeates his political position, not allowing him to be identified clearly with either side of the Israelite-Philistine encounters. Samson is strange to both sides and therefore defended by neither. The complexities of the narrative reveal that Samson's ambiguity cannot be interpreted as a "bridge"

14. Stein, "A King, a Queen," 128–29, 136; also Handelman, "Traps of Trans-formation," 48.

15. Dan Pagis, "Toward a Theory of the Literary Riddle," in *Untying the Knot*, ed. Hasan-Rokem and Shulman, 83; and Handelman, "Traps of Trans-formation," 53. In the context of the riddle, it is the questioner who holds and strives to maintain his position of power; the respondent at best either avoids ridicule (in Finnish riddling contests, this is expressed as avoidance of banishment to Hymylä; see Handelman, "Traps of Trans-formation," 45) or is validated in the estimation of his intelligence.

between exclusive antinomies: the various binary oppositions in the narrative do not resolve themselves so easily.[16] While Samson's marriage to the Timnite woman appears to have the potential to mediate the deep cultural differences between the Israelite and Philistine peoples, Samson's persistent riddling challenges the oppressive Philistine authority, which devalues the character and identity of Israelite nationhood.[17] Thus, Samson is the

16. Susan Niditch, "Samson as Culture Hero, Trickster, and Bandit: The Empowerment of the Weak," *The Catholic Biblical Quarterly* 52 (1990): 613. The riddle reflects a situation even more complex than the acknowledgement that Samson lives in a mediated state between the Israelites and the Philistines, or, as Niditch expresses it in anthropological terms, between the raw and the cooked (616). To be properly appreciated, Niditch's understanding of Samson performing a mediating function should be compared to assessments of Samson that emphasize his actions as taking one side of a binary struggle. Thus, J. Cheryl Exum in *Fragmented Women: Feminist (Sub)versions of Biblical Narratives* (Valley Forge, Pa.: Trinity Press International, 1993) writes about the string of exclusive oppositions that make up the Samson tale: Israelites versus Philistines, female versus male, circumcised versus uncircumcised, and nature versus culture (72–77). While Exum mentions (once) that Samson "crosses boundaries . . . mediating between them" (77), her actual analyses of Samson and his actions range him along one side of a struggle between opposites. Thus, for Exum, the Samson saga "functions . . . to control women and justify their subjection" (62). While it is certainly true that the Samson narrative exhibits an androcentric view of reality, that is not the same thing as insisting that "the story of Samson is a story about women," and, by implication, about little else (61). To be sure, there are feminist analyses of the Samson story that take account of the ambiguity within the narrative while retaining their critical stance regarding the story's treatment of women. Thus, for example, Mieke Bal in *Lethal Love* views the cutting of Samson's hair as a symbol of castration (following Freud), which means that Samson, the figure of the virile male par excellence, in fact becomes a woman (55, 57–61). See also Edmund Leach, "Magical Hair," in *Myth and Cosmos*, ed. John Middleton (Garden City, N.Y.: American Museum of Natural History, 1967), 77–108. Bal explains this apparent contradiction by reading Samson's life as focused on the "fantasy of rebirth," which, in the manner of Freudian longings, is both feared and desired (59–63). For her part, Claudia Camp reads the Samson story as including a series of gaps ("Riddlers, Tricksters, and Strange Women," 117) into which she interjects the figure of the Wise/Strange Woman to help elucidate the resultant ambiguity. This approach builds on Bal's suggestion that "woman represents the Other who gives access to the symbolic order" (60), which is itself a reworking of Lacan's pronouncement in "Le non du père" that it is the Father (*"le nom/?non? du père"*) that is the desired source of such access. Neither Bal nor Camp loses sight of the androcentric view of the universe present in the Biblical text while continuing to emphasize the often ambiguous view that the text presents of power and human relationships within the shifting landscape of politics and personal identity. We may add that one such example that has received rather little attention is Samson's remark, "Had you not plowed with my heifer, you would not have discovered my riddle" (Judg. 14:18). Most critics read this as a (typical) misogynistic response on Samson's part. On the other hand, the image of plowing—of exploiting another creature for one's own material enrichment—may have been Samson's way of acknowledging Philistine abuse of one of their own, just for reasons of gender. For another nuanced view of feminist analysis and the ambiguity of the Biblical text, see Carol Smith, "Samson and Delilah: A Parable of Power?" *Journal for the Study of the Old Testament* 76 (1997): 45–57; and "Delilah: A Suitable Case for (Feminist) Treatment?" in *Judges*, ed. Brenner.

17. This is expressed in the Biblical text by use of the word "m'sh'l," which connotes oppressive rule against the wishes of the subjected group (cf. Malbim on Gen. 37:8).

focal point of anxiety as the contradictions of nation, religion, family, and belief play themselves out in the text. While theoretically the riddle might serve as the locus of negotiation between two disparate groups, the riddles in the Samson story do not actually serve this peaceful function at all. Instead, they reflect and even exacerbate the pressures rumbling just beneath the surface. These tensions present themselves in diverse ways and are not restricted just to the obvious dissonances between the Philistines and the Israelites. Rather, the riddles expose the ongoing interrogation that Samson conducts regarding the accepted truths of his own culture; they also present his own—albeit idiosyncratic—notion of what constitutes salvation.

Interrogating the Personal and the Political

Samson's first reported excursion as an adult is one that bursts boundaries: he seeks marriage with a Philistine woman. To his parents' protests that there surely is no dearth of Israelite girls for him to marry, Samson responds only that he has chosen the girl that he wants, for "she is right in my eyes" (Judg. 14:3). While at a certain level this episode may be seen as an instance of youthful rebellion, it can also be viewed as an attempt on Samson's part to determine the measure and limits of national exclusivity. To what extent is national uniqueness determined by exogamous restrictions? At what point does physical propinquity make social isolation impossible?[18] Can moral and religious independence be maintained in a situation of complete social integration?[19] To what degree does personal feeling (love) mitigate the demand for national exclusivity? To be sure, the text does not overtly frame the issues along these lines: the narrative itself hastens to point out that these seemingly bizarre requests on Samson's

18. The text of Judges reveals that various Canaanite nations still remain, even after the (partial) Israelite conquest of Canaan (1:27–36).

19. Cf. particularly Josh. 24:14–21, where Joshua warns that the Israelites must be exclusive in their worship of God. In his speech to the leaders and elders of the tribes, he warns against accepting any of these neighboring nations' social or religious mores (23:7). The Biblical text in Deuteronomy (a particularly potent example is 7:1–11) insists that the only way to ensure national solidarity and unity of purpose with God is to adhere to the received endogamic strictures. In this connection, the apparent counterexample of Ruth, a Moabite who marries into the Israelite nation and is credited with being the ancestress of King David (Ruth 4:17–22), actually serves to reinforce this point; the text in Ruth openly records her acceptance of the Israelite strictures and way of life (1:16) before her marriage to Boaz (4:13).

part actually are part of God's plan. Careful parsing of the relevant verse, however, leaves extremely unclear the identity of the plan's originator, as well as the extent and nature of the plan itself. That Samson appears ready to forgo these long-held sanctions of marital endogamy and look among strangers for a bride indicates that this narrative also explores issues that continue to elude modern theorists and practitioners of nationalism, who might attempt to give positive expression to inclusive and multiple forms of nationalities under conditions where land is scarce. At the same time, the denouement of the Samson narrative reveals that crossing borders, regardless of whether these are clearly demarcated, carries with it consequences of its own. Arbitrary violence easily overtakes relatively innocent people, who remain unaware of the larger issues at stake against which their lives figure merely as pawns. In the end, the Samson narrative warns against easily traversing received lines of demarcation to integrate with other groups, no matter what the motivation.

The consequences of crossing boundaries manifest themselves in a seemingly benign conversation whose resolution foreshadows a later interchange (with Delilah) that results in Samson's capture by the Philistines. This first discussion takes place between Samson and his Timnite bride, when Samson refuses to divulge the secret of the riddle with which he had challenged the Philistines. Closer analysis of the conversation reveals a level of discourse remarkably disconnected, not just on the personal level (she pesters him), but also on the logical one: "And Samson's wife wept before him, and said, 'You do but hate me, and do not love me; you have propounded a riddle to my compatriots, but have not told it to me.' And he said to her, 'Behold I have not told it to my mother and father, and shall I tell it to you?'" (Judg. 14:14).

The interchange between Samson and his wife seems to focus on a disconnected series of issues: she weeps because she thinks Samson hates her, since he hasn't revealed to her the riddle's solution. For his part, Samson is amazed that she considers herself a sufficiently intimate connection of his to be privy to this information, especially since he hasn't relayed this information to his parents either. The disjunction here is between competing concepts of intimacy and privacy, as well as the proper boundaries (if any) between them. In other words, at what point does a socially recognized form of intimacy (marriage, for example) mandate the erasure of the lines that delineate the intimate sphere vouchsafed only to the self (privacy)? The argument of Samson's wife is that the relationship of marriage precludes any separate sphere of privacy for its participants. Samson's view, revealed in his response, is that different relationships require different measures of closeness, and that there is no privileged sphere of intimacy with immutable demands. Thus, the intimacy of marriage does not mean that there will be no secrets or, in this case, riddles between its partners; furthermore, it does not necessarily preclude the (perhaps greater) loyalty or intimacy that is obligatory toward one's own parents.

The divergent views between Samson and his wife regarding the implications of the marital bond are further explicated in the words chosen by Samson's wife in her first statement on this issue. She starts with a fact: Samson had engaged her fellow Philistines in a riddle but didn't reveal its solution to her. She concludes from this not only that Samson does not love her, but also that he hates her. Interestingly, she states the conclusion before the facts that motivate this conclusion, giving the impression that she is dominated by her emotions. In addition, when parsed logically, the statements that she makes do not follow: why does Samson's withholding the riddle's solution from her betoken his hatred? After all, Samson had not told the other Philistines the solution either. The conclusion that follows from the context of her statement is that the (other) Philistines at least were invited to participate in his riddle dialogue: in other words, they are part of the conversation. His wife, on the other hand, is excluded, and it is this that she equates with lack of love (and even hatred).[20] This unstated assumption is the basis for Samson's explicit response to his wife: I did not reveal the riddle's solution to my parents either; that is, they too are excluded and (this is the part that is unstated: since I love them) it does not therefore follow that love must be equated with constant inclusion.

At this level, the conversation seems to reach an impasse. What makes this dialogue of more than theoretical interest is that there is more at stake than a philosophical evaluation of a relationship or even the identity of the winner of Samson's challenge, with its prize of thirty sheets and thirty changes of clothes. Indeed, Samson's wife has received a threat from her fellow Philistines, who inform her that she and her father's house will be burnt if she does not inform them of the riddle's solution (Judg. 14:15). The

20. The equivalence that she draws is well understood by minority groups in the Western world, where exclusion is often the weapon of disempowerment. Samson's response, on the other hand (and it must be remembered that culturally, Samson is not of the Western world), attempts to elide this issue by arguing that exclusion does not always carry with it connotations of disempowerment: in the same way that a cigar is sometimes just a cigar, Samson's argument is that, at times, not being included means just that and nothing more.

logic in this seemingly inapposite consequence for what is not a specific action, but rather the absence of a desired outcome, is terrifyingly simple and belies the apparent ease with which Philistine and Israelite society are supposedly integrated. The Philistines make this connection clear when they accuse Samson's wife of having brought them to the marriage festivities in order to chase them out (i.e., of their landholdings and dominant economic position). In the Philistines' reading of events, the supposedly benign celebration of a wedding marking the union of two people, and even two distinct social and religious groupings, is really an excuse for economic colonization of one (the stronger Philistines) by the other (the weaker Israelites).[21] According to this understanding of the passage, the Philistines may be seen as blaming Samson's wife for having engendered the chain of events that places them in danger of failing to answer the riddle, and thus losing items of monetary value (the sheets and the changes of clothing). Following this logic, they can feel justified in threatening the Timnite woman and her family with a fiery death if she does not reveal the riddle's solution to them. In this scheme, Samson's wife seems to serve the function of a Trojan horse.

Samson's wife refuses this appellation. She insists on her overriding fidelity to her nation of origin; as she remains physically ensconced in her father's house even after her marriage to Samson, this patrilocal conception of marriage works to ensure this ordering of her loyalties.[22] She openly alludes to this by referring to the Philistines as "my people," ironically demanding that Samson privilege the marriage bond with her over all other and prior connections in his own life (Judg. 14:16). For Samson's wife, marriage to her entails the loss of Samson's social and political individuality: henceforth, all loyalties must be to her clan and people. As far as she is concerned, Samson possesses no reciprocal right regarding the primacy of his own social background and identity. Still, it is possible to excuse the Timnite woman's one-sided view of the primacy of her social origins

21. Cf. Kimhi (Radak) on Judg. 14:15. The text (*Judges* 14:15) uses the verb "h'r'sh," which connotes chasing another out of his/her economic possession.

22. In *Death and Dissymmetry*, Bal argues that the narrative of the Book of Judges presupposes and masks the social system of marriage changing from patrilocal to virilocal residence (80–93). Certainly taking note of these two models of marital residence elucidates the tensions evident in different sets of married couples. In terms of the historical development that she posits in her reading of the Book of Judges, however, Bal fails to take into account the stylistic analysis that I undertake further on, which calls into question the strictly chronological composition of the text (see note 64).

by pointing out that she is put into a frightening position. When her life is threatened, it is indeed understandable that her own identity, and the method by which she thinks she can safeguard her life, become the over-riding concerns for her. In that context, the fact that the Timnite woman does not make the most reasoned moral choice, or indeed the one that the reader of the text might consider morally preferable, fades into the shadow of the stark terror that she faces.[23]

Samson, however, is subject to no such fright. Indeed, one of the motifs of the Samson narrative is that he evinces no fear. Even when at the total mercy of the Philistines in the Temple of Dagon, he manages to conquer what must have been a considerable amount of despair to effect a certain measure of victory over them. Thus, while it is possible to find an excuse for the Timnite woman's lack of moral acuity, no such rationale justifies Samson's inability to interpret the situation around him. He is deaf to his wife's verbal tone. He is not cognizant of her real motivation (even though it is plainly alluded to in her careful choice of words), perhaps because he is unaware of the implications of his own response to his wife regarding intimacy and privacy. The question of Samson's wife—What is the solution to your riddle?—itself becomes the riddle by which Samson is stumped, because he does not recognize the political ramifications of revealing his personally held secret.

To be sure, Samson had already exhibited a singular lack of sensitivity when it came to understanding the political effects of the choices in his personal life. When his parents remonstrate with him on the unsuitabil-ity of intermarriage with the Philistines, they identify them as "'arelim," meaning uncircumcised. Although the usage of this particular locution may seem to indicate nothing more than the notation of a physical marker, the parents' citation of this term is fraught with meaning. The term 'arel

23. In terms of strict logic, the Timnite woman has another (set of) option(s) beyond the two offered to her by her countrymen: she can refuse the duality of the choices offered to her by the Philistines and invoke the aid of a third party (Samson comes to mind, for example). The fact that the Timnite woman discovers the solution to Samson's riddle means that she also is aware of the previous set of circumstances that had given rise to the terms of the riddle, circumstances that themselves reveal the great extent of Samson's physical power. Thus, it can be argued that the natural reservations against involving Samson—the Philistines threaten her and her father with death if she fails to reveal Samson's riddle—do not apply, because Samson's knowledge of the real circumstances behind her wish to discover his secret would arouse his natural sympathies against the Philistines. In addition, Samson's great phys-ical strength (which fact is an integral part of the special set of circumstances giving rise to his riddle) would stand the Timnite woman in good stead against possible vengeance by her Philistine compatriots.

recalls with special force the Biblical episode in which Abraham is commanded to differentiate himself physically from his neighbors in preparation for the birth of Isaac, which would mark the establishment of the Abrahamitic clan as a nation of its own.[24] Their focused terminology reveals that Samson's parents are displeased with Samson's choice, but not on the grounds of idiosyncratic taste or preference. Rather, they instinctively react to the larger issues of national identity that lie at the core of this action that seems exclusively personal. Their incredulous questioning reveals their disappointment—like Samson, they are aware that it is not the lack of available Israelite women that motivates Samson in his choice of whom to marry—and also recalls the unusual circumstances surrounding Samson's birth.

For his parents, Samson's national duty is obvious even before he is born. The first chapter of the Samson narrative describes Manoah's wife as "barren, and bore not," which implicitly identifies her with Sarah, Abraham's wife (Gen. 11:29).[25] By contrasting their son's selection of a foreign spouse with the national exclusivity and endogamous patterns of marriage championed by the Abrahamitic clan, Samson's parents reveal their profound disappointment in their son's choice. With her own individual situation recalling that of the matriarchal ancestress of the Israelites, Samson's mother had been able to remain confident in the Divine messenger's prediction of her son's redeeming destiny until this moment of directed choice on the part of her now-adult child. At this point, however, Samson seems to repudiate the values that the founding members of the Israelite nation had embodied and, by implication, all that the circumstances of his birth had appeared to promise.

Samson's parents' implicit identification with the larger national destiny of the Abrahamitic clan thus serves to rebuke to Samson for failing to live up to both his national heritage, and his own prophetically directed destiny. For his parents, and for countless readers of the Biblical text, Samson's

24. Gen. 17:4–19. See also Judg. 14:3.
25. Source-critical commentaries often impute the apparent redundancy of this text (if she is barren, obviously she has not given birth) to two differing sources for the finished form of the redacted text. Cf., for example, Robert Alter, "Samson Without Folklore," in *Text and Tradition*, ed. Susan Niditch (Atlanta: Scholars Press, 1990), 48. On the other hand, the Midrashic reading is sensitive to the linguistic complexities of the text and thereby discovers new information in the apparent redundancy: it is not just that Manoah's wife had not *yet* given birth (*lo yalda*); rather, she was incapable of *ever* giving birth (*'akara*). Cf. Midrash Bahayai on Gen. 11:30 (Jerusalem: Blum, 1988), 71.

actions, and indeed his entire existence, represent a riddle. How can a savior flout the very laws enshrined by the legal code of his nation? How can a person who seems to disregard the methods (as enshrined in the largely endogamous marriage laws) by which this nation historically had maintained its own notion of national identity and exclusivity, be heralded as the savior of that same nation? More generally, how can salvation at all be achieved if the protagonists of the story seem remarkably unaware of the larger historical forces shaping their destiny? Or if they are aware, if they willfully disregard fundamental aspects of their national identity? This point regards not just Samson, but the entire Israelite nation: this is the one episode of foreign oppression recounted in the Book of Judges when the Israelites do *not* beseech God for salvation.[26] In that context, why is deliverance predicted for that particular era in which Samson is judge?

Answers to these questions can be found by reexamining Samson's riddles. Instead of emphasizing just the structural understanding of the riddle and the way in which it can destabilize heretofore fixed relationships, I will focus on the content of Samson's riddles and the discourse that it engenders among him, his Philistine companions, and the Israelites.

Riddling the Solution

We now return to the first riddle: "Out of the devourer came forth food, and out of the strong came forth sweetness" (Judg. 14:14).

Commentators and critics alike have been puzzled by these images. To be sure, the very wording of this statement itself reveals an assumption— that riddles do possess meaning beyond their structural functions, which, in this case, is as a device to move the plot ahead. Although there are critics who classify Samson's riddle as a "neck riddle" and therefore not "authentic," rigorous analysis demonstrates that Samson's riddle functions very much at the center of the narrative and indeed holds the clue to the meaning of the entire story.[27] Several major differences distinguish Samson's riddle from the typical neck riddle. First, unlike the typical neck riddle,

26. The quiescence of Manoah and his wife reflects this national passivity on the personal level. Unlike their erstwhile childless progenitors Abraham and Sarah, Manoah and his wife do *not* pray for children (Judg. 13:2).

27. In this context, Bal's insistence that the riddle functions as the mise en abyme of the Samson narrative, while she at the same time denigrates the riddle as being "inauthentic," seems a contradiction in terms.

whose solution serves to bring the events of the story to a final (and more or less satisfactory) close, Samson's riddle unleashes a complication of events that threaten to derail the entire enterprise toward which Samson's entire life had been geared. Also, the prevalence of mysteries, or riddles, that entangle all major episodes of Samson's career, which make his actions appear both arbitrary and self-destructive, indicates that riddles hold the clue to understanding Samson both as an individual and as a political leader. In addition, the argument that Samson's riddle can be solved only with reference to and prior knowledge of the bizarre discovery of honey in the lion's cavity makes little sense in a story where personal relationships are characterized by complicated posturing (and rarely by univocal shades of meaning). In separate articles, Camp and Crenshaw both contend that in the context of the wedding festivities, Samson's riddle is eminently solvable: the riddle's combination of strong and sweet naturally gives rise to thoughts of love or sex.[28] Crenshaw even claims that the ancient Philistines must have shared a common fund of cultural images with the neighboring Israelites and so would have been able in all likelihood to decipher the riddle.

Despite this proposed commonality of cultural symbols, careful analysis of the text reveals that in fact the Philistines do not solve the riddle that Samson poses to them. To be sure, the Philistines do offer a response and, in so doing, appear to have solved the riddle. But their answer corresponds neither to the actual occurrence recounted in the text just prior to the wedding festivities, nor to the actual content of the riddle. In their answer to Samson's implied request for the citation of a specific occurrence, in fact, the Philistines never describe any particular event. Instead, they simply set forth their own images of strength and sweetness, which Samson then

28. Cf. Claudia V. Camp and Carole R. Fontaine, "The Words of the Wise and Their Riddles," in *Text and Tradition*, ed. Niditch, 141–42; Crenshaw, *Samson*, 112–17; Exum, *Fragmented Women*, 82. In "Riddles, Tricksters, and Strange Women," Camp extends the list to include domesticity, desire, and women (132–33).

In "Samson and His Riddle," Professor Tur-Sinai suggests that one answer to this riddle is the Torah. He derives this from a set of linguistic parallels, noting that in Hebrew the word for "lion" and the word for "honey" (albeit a lesser-known locution of the latter term; ur-Sinai bases this similarity on a citation from Song of Sol. 5:1) derive from the same root, *ari*. As for the identification of these two with the Torah, Tur-Sinai points out that in Aramaic, a language spoken early on by far-flung kin of the Abrahamitic clan (Laban, living in Mesopotamia, is just one example of a relative speaking Aramaic), the word for Torah is *oraita*, which similarly derives from the root *ari*. In *Iyyunim b'Sefer Shoftim* [*Considerations on the Book of Judges*] (Jerusalem: Kiryat Sepher, 1966).

accepts as the riddle's solution. Rather than solve the riddle, the Philistines merely react to the images of "strong" and "sweet."

But Samson does not ask about strength or sweetness: instead, he demands that his interlocutors describe a situation where sweetness results from strength and where food is derived from a devourer/eater. The fact that the Philistines neglect the actual structure of Samson's riddle and ignore the element of dynamic action at its core reveals that they have missed entirely its true import. Samson's use of the verb "y'tz'a"—whose translations include the connotations of "result" or "become"—indicates that he is meditating on the nature of human existence. Is it possible, he wonders, for strength to be transformed into sweetness and for a devourer to become a food product that is itself eaten? In other words, can theoretically antagonistic antinomies successfully be resolved in real life?

Read in this way, Samson's riddle can be understood as examining the possibilities of change and of mediation in a world that, by actualizing all options in their most extreme incarnations, seems bent on self-destruction. In this context, Samson's search for a wife among the Philistine women can be seen as an attempt to mediate this radicalization, perhaps in an effort to establish a new combination that would work to diffuse the Philistine threat—or perhaps it is because he simply could not find a bride to his liking from his own people who would be able to aid him in his effort to begin the process of salvation. The riddle, then, presents what Samson was seeking: sweetness (a personal companion) from the strong (the Philistines). The text, however, reveals this effort to be doomed.

But the riddle may also be read as a meditation on styles of leadership.[29] Leadership may present itself as strong and unforgiving, much in the manner of the Philistines, who deprive the Israelites of any type of metal implement so that they cannot even cultivate their own soil.[30] In addition, leadership may look mighty and uncompromising. But its reality may be sweet: its primary concern may be to care for its people and their welfare. Indeed, Samson manifests this type of concern for his people even when they are ready to surrender him to the Philistines. He agrees to be ignominiously bound and handed over; he asks only that they not harm him physically (Judg. 15:12–13). In this reading, then, it turns out

29. For much of what follows, I am indebted to the suggestions of Sarah Rosen in reaction to the lecture in which some of these ideas were first presented.

30. The text in 1 Sam. 13:19 describes the political, military, and economic oppression perpetrated by the Philistines even as late as the period of Saul's monarchy.

that the riddler and the riddle are one: the answer to the riddle is Samson himself.

The situation becomes even more complex, however, because Samson does not recognize that he is the answer to his own riddle. In effect, then, Samson stumps himself. This explains why he remains unaware of the implications of his personal decisions for the larger political and social framework against which he operates. It also explains why he himself is unaware of his strength (Judg. 16:9) and the true source of his power. When his hair is shorn, Samson thinks that he can still escape the toils of the Philistines. The words he uses are significant: "*etzei k'fa'am b'fa'am*/I will escape/go out as before" (Judg. 16:20). The use of the root *y'tz'a* (to leave/go out/result) forcibly recalls the verbal construction of the riddle. Samson's inability to recognize himself as both the subject and solution to his own riddle prefigures his incapacity to wrest himself from the Philistine trap in which he is enmeshed.[31] One might even argue that the riddle foreshadows this turn of events. This aspect of the riddle's meaning is contained in the much-ignored first section (to which the Philistines never respond): "From the eater/devourer came forth food" (Judg. 14:14).[32] While it is possible to argue that the double imagery of the riddle has only one static (or iconic) referent,[33] my reading of the solution being Samson himself deepens the dynamic complexity of that image. It is Samson, appearing as the devourer (read: aggressor) throughout the Samson saga, who actually winds up captured by the Philistines, the subject of their mirth (i.e., "food" for their collective appetites) in the Temple of Dagon.[34] In that

31. A riddle, as Handelman has written, "is a process that must move from 'here' to 'there.' . . . Any riddle presents this movement as puzzling and problematic. . . . As long as no solution is found, the problem remains impenetrable, *the protagonist is trapped in the riddle*" (Handelman, "Traps of Trans-formation," 43; emphases mine).

32. Cf. also Yair Zakovich, *Hayyei Shimshon* (Jerusalem: Magnes, 1982), 116.

33. This is the position of Philip Nel in "The Riddle of Samson," *Biblica* 66 (1985): 534–45, especially 539.

34. In this connection, the understanding of Samson as a "loose cannon" who unleashes limitless violence on a group of unarmed civilians is a serious misreading of the text, as it disregards repeated textual evidence (Judg. 13:1; 14:4) of Philistine domination and oppression of the Israelites. Taking these statements into account, the willingness of the Israelites to deliver Samson into the hands of the Philistines does not therefore reflect their "relief" at ridding themselves of such a "loose cannon." Rather, as the text puts it, it is an expression of their perceived vulnerability to the Philistine reading of events, because the Philistines, by virtue of their oppressive rule over the Israelites, likewise posses the power of determining the acceptable and unacceptable versions of the "truth" of events (Judg. 15:11; the term used is again "m'sh'l," denoting aggressive force on the part of the Philistines). It is in that sense that the Israelites remonstrate with Samson: do you not know that the Philistines are oppressing

context, perhaps it is less painful in the end for Samson to be mystified by his own riddle.

Samson's mystification, however, can also be viewed in another context: as an integral part of his own awareness of the limits and imperfections of politics. Samson has certainly been roundly criticized for his lack of statesmanship, but it is possible to view the "messy" or un-statesmanlike quality of Samson's leadership as his own commentary on the true nature of political life.[35] In his capacity as leader, Samson unmasks the received pieties of leadership: that it is always possible to effect political solutions that are morally perfect. The moral and political ambiguities of Samson's solutions characterize the realities of politics as situations of imperfect closure. As such, they prefigure the flawed situations that would mark even the height of the Israelite political system under David and Solomon. Thus, the Samson narrative reveals politics to be characterized less by the constraints of absolute force[36] than by the actions of the highly imperfect human beings that populate its structures, a situation that demands sympathy, if not complete understanding.

---

us and that your actions in killing several of them have rebounded onto us, potentially resulting in an even greater loss of Israelite life? Finally, in terms of the Philistine presence in the House of Dagon, the text carefully notes, "And all the Philistine [military/political] leadership was there" (Judg. 16:27; the term "s'ranim" denotes leadership that is a combination of the two categories), as was to be expected on a holiday of religious and political import. Thus, Samson's action in "bringing down the house" can be seen as a calculated attempt to destroy the leadership of the nation that was oppressing his own. In that context, the accompanying deaths of the other civilians in the building underlines a theme present in the Samson narrative from the beginning: crossing borders, an idea that in and of itself can have creative implications of its own, can also engender arbitrary violence that easily overtakes the lives of people not fully cognizant of the larger issues at play.

35. In this sense, Samson's understanding of power may be not unlike that of Machiavelli, as expressed in *The Prince*. In that work, Machiavelli analyzes the minimal expectations for a leader to be able to retain his power. He expresses no illusions about a leader being a perfect being either morally or strategically: the important point, Machiavelli emphasizes, is to "avoid the public disgrace of those vices that would lose him his state" (45). Consequently, says Machiavelli, a ruler must learn "how not to be good," not in any hedonistic celebration of evil, but rather in pursuit of the necessary imperative to maintain his power. In the end, concludes Machiavelli, the art of politics is to learn to "accept the least bad as good" (65)—due not to any mistaken equivalence of the moral standards of good and evil, but rather as the reflection of a practical understanding of what is possible.

36. In Anthony Low's understanding, this is Milton's portrayal of the Philistine nation: "Philistia's rulers are destroyed because they have arrogated power to themselves . . . in particular the policy of tyrannizing over the Jewish nation, holding its people in captivity, and attempting to force or seduce them from their duties to the God of Israel." *The Blaze of Noon* (New York: Columbia University Press, 1979), 122.

Samson's general lack of awareness regarding the forces that propel his destiny reflects the general tenor of human existence. Indeed, Samson is not the only person in the narrative to be thus caught unawares. His father, Manoah, seems to be the prototype for the hopelessly clueless individual. At the beginning of the story, Manoah does not perceive the uniqueness of the individual who informs his wife of the impending birth of their son: he asks for a repetition of the special instructions that are given to his wife and insists on inviting the Divine messenger for a meal without realizing that the angel would not be able to eat with them.[37] Even Samson's mother, who at the beginning of the narrative is the only person to interpret correctly the substance as well as the implications of the angel's message,[38] falls prey to doubts about Samson's choice of a foreign bride and fails to recognize the historic hand of God, which she had correctly identified many years earlier. To be sure, it is not difficult to understand why she does not see Divine guidance in everyday affairs: the text informs us that the Divine spirit influenced Samson only intermittently.[39] In these circumstances, how is it possible to know when unusual efforts are called for? How can one differentiate between extraordinary circumstances and the overwhelming force of personal desires?

The story of Samson reveals that human beings often cannot tell the difference. The text's portrayal of the limited state of human knowledge[40]

37. According to Judges, "Manoah did not know that he was an angel of God" (13:16). While it is possible to classify this comment as merely informational, the remark of the Talmud leaves no doubt as to the quality of his intelligence: "Manoah was an ignoramus" (BT Brachot 61a).

38. On the other hand, Manoah's wife understands immediately the import of the Nazirite strictures that devolve on her and the unborn child (she needs no repetition of the instructions). Similarly, when her husband fears death from having seen a heavenly creature, she logically proves to him that this would not happen: "If God had meant to kill us," she tells him, "He would not have accepted our sacrifices nor shown us all of these things" (Judg. 13:23). In this connection, Robert Polzin's position (*Moses and the Deuteronomist*, 184), that Manoah knows while his wife does not, appears difficult to sustain on the basis of the textual evidence. Similarly, Bal's contention (*Death and Dissymmetry*, 74), that Manoah's wife (in terms of her function as wife and mother) is erased because she remains the nameless prize tugged between the (impotent) husband and all-powerful father, does not take account of the fact that the beginning and end of the Samson narrative are marked by the awareness of his Nazirite status "from the *mother's* belly" (Judg. 13:5, 17:17; emphasis mine). Crucially, those statements appear when Samson's savior status is prophesied and when he consciously identifies his uniqueness to Delilah.

39. Judg. 13:25. The root *p' 'm* occurs rarely as a verb in the Bible. Different commentators derive its meaning in context to mean "from time to time" (Rashi) or irregularly, imitating the movement of a bell, or *pa'amon* (Ralbag).

40. Arnold Stein's *Heroic Knowledge* (Minneapolis: University of Minnesota Press, 1957) presents a different understanding of the role of knowledge in the Samson narrative. According

demonstrates that human beings often work in circumstances whose appearances mask the truth; therefore, people are frequently misled regarding the nature of the reality that lies just beneath the surface.[41] But the Samson narrative takes these constraints one step further. Human beings are restricted not just by their limited ability to evaluate correctly the information made available to them. In addition, they themselves adversely affect the outcomes of their own projects by deliberately minimizing the knowledge that they make available to their own people, even their own families. Samson purposely does not tell his parents of his miraculous encounter with the lion or of the resultant provenance of the honey; certainly none of Samson's women openly reveal their own arrangements with the Philistines. Ironically then, the riddle that appears to be a perverse use of language, obfuscating instead of communicating clearly, in fact precisely mirrors the true state of human language and, thus, human perceptions as they actually occur. The uncanny and misleading language used in the riddle exactly imitates the nature of dialogue in the entire Samson story: the surface exchanges of words yield no true meetings of the minds.[42] Samson and his parents, no less than Samson and his wives/women, hold conversations with each other, but little of import gets transmitted between the two sides. In terms of the quality of discourse, the narrative reveals that the nature of its interpersonal relationships—on the personal level between parents and children, between the partners within a linked couple, or on the communal level between leader and people—is anomic instead of responsive. At the end of the Samson narrative, a national discourse among the Israelites has yet to be established.

The perceived dissonances in the Samson story stem from the disjunction that develops between the structural role that Samson plays in the narrative—he is the leader who is destined to begin to save the Israelites—and the content of that role, which, at the very least, must include the (partial) revelation of salvation to the people that he will (at least begin) to save.

---

to Stein, Samson's "heroic knowledge" allows him, through "the terrible knowledge of guilt and . . . suffering," to rise above individual despair and act in affirmation of his religious beliefs and national identity. In Stein's words, "Despair convert[s] itself into a necessary transition to humility" (210), which in turn brings with it "a heightened vitality and clarity of vision" (208; see, on this topic, 206–15).

41. In *The Particulars of Rapture*, Avivah Zornberg highlights the theme of "not knowing" as a motif of human limits (210–13).

42. The opaque nature of language, as manifest in the Samson episode, calls to mind the manipulative possibilities of language underlined in the Tower of Babel narrative (see Chapter 4).

Complicating the matter still further, as we have seen, Samson himself at times appears curiously unaware of the larger implications and goals of his own actions. At one level, as already noted, this is explained by the indeterminate quality of Divine influence on Samson. The text references this negatively, recording the moment when Samson is unaware that the spirit of God is no longer with him. For the reader of the text, it is logical to conclude that if Samson does not realize when God has left him, he also does not know when God is with him (Judg. 16:20). The text itself figures in an unusual way the intermittent manner in which God's spirit descends on Samson: in an elliptical verse that may be read as a meditation on the extent of Divine intervention in human history. Appearing unexceptional at first glance, the verse seems to explain why Samson's desire to marry a Philistine woman is misunderstood by his parents: "And his father and mother did not know that this was from God as he sought a pretext against the Philistines; and at this time the Philistines had dominion over Israel" (Judg. 14:4).

Samson's parents do not appreciate that Samson's desire to marry the Philistine woman derives from God, the verse argues; God had set up the situation so that Samson is seeking an excuse to aggravate the Philistines, who at that time "had dominion over Israel." Careful attention to the language in the verse, however, reveals that the antecedent to (and therefore the referent for) the word "he" is actually not "Samson," but "God." Read in that way, the verse delivers another, or additional, message: God is seeking a pretext against the Philistines. He is setting up a situation in which Samson would marry a foreigner in order to bring to a head a predicament in which He, God, might intervene.[43]

The image of God debating whether and in what measure to intervene in human affairs is both mystifying and energizing. The Biblical text portrays God as being held in thrall, as it were, to human imagination and actions: God is waiting for the Philistines to act in a certain fashion so that He may, in turn, respond in a way that would ease the situation of Philistine domination in Israel. The Biblical casting of God's projected actions in this relational manner—as opposed to the more conventional portrayal of Divine actions as absolutely autonomous—implies a trenchant questioning of the nature and extent of Divine action in human history.

43. In this connection, the correct translation of the term "m'vakesh" is important. The English word "seeking" conveys some of the tentative quality of the root, *b'k'sh*. Thus, God *might* intervene, but there is no guarantee that He would.

Interestingly, this text is not the first to question elliptically the nature of God's actions. The Midrash records that in the course of Moses's remonstrations with God about the ramifications of his mission to free the enslaved Israelites in Egypt, Moses says to God: "I know that You will save them [i.e., the Israelites], but what of those set under the building!"[44] In this Midrashic reading, Moses does not deny the efficacy of God's future salvation; he questions its ability to redress past moral wrongs. With these words, Moses queries—and perhaps even doubts—the ability of the Divine act (at least this one in particular) to pass beyond the restrictions of time.[45] In the Samson narrative, it is not just the extent of God's ability and intervention in human history that is at issue. The nature and exclusivity of Israelite nationhood are likewise questioned and put at stake, and by none other than the person who is supposed to be the instrument of national salvation.[46] In view of the earlier questions advanced by Moses, the paradigmatic figure of salvation, the Biblical text appears to suggest that salvation is figured by radical questioning coupled with unswerving devotion to the national good.[47] Crucially, salvation is not equated with success in any particular national or personal endeavor: neither Moses nor Samson actually complete their tasks. For the Bible, it seems emblematic of salvation that it never be fully attained and that it never be ascribed to the actions of any one particular individual.

In the more restricted context of the Samson narrative, the indeterminate quality of both the narrative and the discourse that it encompasses

44. Anthony Low develops the parallel between Moses and Samson in *The Blaze of Noon*. Low argues that Samson, like Moses, performs extraordinary feats as a warning to the Philistine nation to end their enslavement/exploitation of the Israelites (118–23). For the Midrashic quotation, see Shmot Rabbah 5:22. The translation is adapted from Zornberg, *The Particulars of Rapture*, 37. The reference is to the Israelite children who, in the Midrashic recounting of events, were deliberately asphyxiated by the Egyptian taskmasters in the walls of the storage cities that the enslaved Israelites were forced to build for the Egyptians (Yalkut Shimoni, Shmot 247; Pirkei d'Rabbi Eliezer 48; cited in Zornberg, *The Particulars of Rapture*, 39–40).

45. The succeeding verses of the text do not directly answer Moses's charge (which, as we have already noted, is not set forth explicitly in the text). But one may read those verses, which speak of the covenantal promise that God had established with the forefathers of the Israelite nation, as a hint that its fulfillment will result in a new discourse about, and therefore understanding of, past historical events. For more on how discourse can change the understanding and even the reality of past events, see Chapter 1.

46. The irony of these questions is highlighted by another Midrashic text (Bereshit Rabbah 98:14) which points to Samson as a (failed) Messianic figure.

47. The Biblical text relates these questions in the context of Moses's concern for the safety of his people. Similarly, the Samson narrative reveals a leader who never demands anything of his people relating to his own comfort; on the contrary, he is willing to be presented ignominiously to the Philistines as a captive in order to avoid retribution against his people.

also emphasizes the extent to which events are murky and give rise to ambiguous interpretations. This makes the elucidation of human deeds, as well as Divine actions, a complex activity. In view of the inability of the protagonists even to conceive of or appreciate the larger forces propelling their destinies, the attention of the reader in arriving at a judgment of these same characters naturally takes on a reflexive cast.[48] After all, to what extent can we as readers of the text ever be certain that we can evaluate properly the actions of leaders like Samson? Can we be sure that he accomplishes nothing during his twenty-year stewardship? Does he remain merely the conventionally perceived oversexed buffoon lacking any redemptive value?

The Nation and the Other

In answering these questions, it is well to consider another aspect of Samson's riddling. This refers not to the content of the riddles themselves, but rather to the riddles' outcomes and the way in which these are utilized. On a superficial level, the consequences of the riddling act seem always to involve a measure of violence, ranging from Samson's killing of thirty Philistines (Judg. 14:19) to his burning of a portion of the Philistine harvest (15:5). While it is easy to attribute this to an overwhelming predilection for violence on Samson's part, this interpretation fails to take seriously both Samson's position as judge, itself an office of public stature, and the characterization of Samson as savior (not strongman) by the Divine messenger at the beginning of the narrative.[49] The aftermath of the riddles, and especially Samson's reaction to the Philistine response, can be more fruitfully understood, and more directly integrated into the thematic topoi of the Samson narrative, if we view them as the demonstrations of the logical reactions to the exploits of each riddle's subject.

48. In *The Poetics of Biblical Narrative*, Meir Sternberg analyzes the ambiguity of the Biblical text, which requires the (moral) involvement of the reader (209–13; see also 179, 326).

49. Cf. also Low's evaluation in *The Blaze of Noon:* "Samson's inward suffering, depicted so vividly by Milton, is left by *Judges* largely to the reader's imagination" (186)—on which point it is well to cite Erich Auerbach's mention of the laconic quality of the Biblical text (*Mimesis*, 6–12). Further on, Low notes, "While he mentions only what appears to be a device for personal vengeance, a higher spiritual motivation cannot be ruled out" (186–87). Low cites Samson's position as judge and designation as savior as the basis for his conclusion: "As Judge of Israel, Samson has the right to execute vengeance on any who persecute or tyrannize over his nation, attack its religion, or seduce the people from their God. He is . . . commissioned by God . . . to bring back her people into the right way" (193–94).

In this context, Samson's responses to the Philistines may be considered not just personal expressions of his fury, but also practical examples of the ultimate outcome of the Philistine rule of terror over the Israelites. Samson's seemingly variable reactions to what he perceives as Philistine trickery illustrate the inherent consequences of arbitrary violence that the Philistines perpetrate upon the Israelites. By his actions, Samson performatively illustrates the inherent reactions of an oppressed people toward their tormentors; thereby he consciously invites the Philistines to consider the ways in which their own enforced supremacy over the Israelites may elicit further violence.[50]

Like Samson, however, the Philistines do not recognize that they too are the subject of the riddles. Thus, they do not respond to this invitation with intense scrutiny of their own activities.[51] Instead, they view Samson's frankness as tantamount to a declaration of war (to which end they demand that he be delivered up to them, Judg. 15:9–14). Eventually, through the machinations of Delilah, the Philistines meet Samson's challenge by outriddling the riddler. This enables them to neutralize the threat of violence that Samson presents on the personal level, and thus to subvert the greater logical and national challenge that he embodies.

The Philistines are not the only group to misread Samson's riddles and the consequences that they engender. The Israelites do not understand Samson's riddles either. To be sure, one may well ask: What riddle does Samson ever ask the Israelites? What is it that they have to misunderstand? And in truth, Samson does not ask them to solve any specific riddle, although in fact the Israelites do face a riddle posed by Samson. The mystery that the Israelites fail to grasp is the same one that eludes Samson: the riddle of Samson himself. The Israelites do not understand the nature of his leadership and the goals toward which he is striving. Interestingly, the Israelites are given the opportunity to compensate for this omission. This is evident when the Philistines demand that the Judahites hand Samson over at Ramath-Lehi.

> Then the Philistine army came up . . . and ranged themselves against
> Lehi. And the men of Judah said, "Why have you come up against

---

50. Cf. the terminology of the Judahites in 15:11 and the implications of the verb "m'sh'l" in the analysis of Malbim (Gen. 37:8).

51. Low puts it this way: "Because the Philistines continue to oppress Samson and the Jews, because they ignore events . . . [a] miracle becomes a means of condemnation only when the individual exercise of hardening his heart or closing his eyes and ears" (*The Blaze of Noon*, 122–23).

us?" And they answered, "To bind Samson." And three thousand men of Judah went to . . . Eitam and said to Samson, "Do you not know that the Philistines rule over us? What have you done to us? . . . We have come to bind you that we may give you over to the Philistines." And Samson said to them, "Swear to me that you will not harm me." And they bound him with two new cords . . . and they melted off his arms. . . . And he slew one thousand men. (Judg. 15:9–15)

This situation could have been the opportunity for the Judahites to reflect on Samson's actions and their own political situation. It could have afforded them the occasion both to think about the meaning of their national existence and to open a collective discourse on the quality of their national life. Instead, the Judahites automatically adopt the Philistine interpretation of events, consigning Samson to capture and, for all they know, death. Samson manages to escape the machinations of the Philistines in this instance, but his failure to establish among his people a robust discourse on topics of national import marks his lack of effectiveness as a leader. To be sure, one may note that Samson is not destined ultimately to redeem his people: he is charged only with beginning their salvation. Still, the question naturally arises: why can't Samson even begin to redeem them?

One answer to this question may well be that Samson does not redeem his people—that is, he is not successful in inviting them to join him in a national discourse—because, ultimately, as we have already noted, he is himself stumped by the riddle that he represents. This may be because Samson's personality appears to defy received categories. He is the embodiment of strangeness. The Biblical text reveals that the social structures of everyday life among the Israelites and among the Philistines, as well as the realities of political power that form their respective existences, are singularly ill equipped to deal with the challenges of difference. Samson continually breaches the boundaries of proper social etiquette and expected political performance. Consequently, Samson's enactment of performative strangeness continues to mystify all of his interlocutors, Israelites and Philistines alike. Even in the contemporary era, more cognizant of the (political) significance and (moral) justification of difference, modern critical evaluations of Samson have focused on the extent to which the flamboyance of his actions seems to polarize people along the lines of mutually exclusive dualities. In this reading, Samson's alienating actions, which highlight

the Otherness of the adversary, are themselves the problem.[52] This understanding attributes Samson's failure to a purely practical reality: a leader
who demonizes and radicalizes his opponents is not a likely candidate to
achieve salvation.[53]

Notwithstanding the morally deleterious effect of deliberately rendering
people Other, it is important to note that the text itself does not display the
category of Otherness in so simplistic a fashion. The actual structure of
the narrative reveals that the Other is not automatically demonized as the
Philistine enemy; often, the Other is the Israelites themselves. On the individual level, the first person to be declared Other is Samson, who receives
Nazirite status even before his birth. The ongoing characteristics of the
Nazirite status—the prohibition of cutting one's hair, for example—mean
that these differences continue to manifest themselves physically throughout Samson's life, thus increasing his sense of alienation.[54] By the same
token, the continuing bewilderment of Samson's parents reveals that even
for them, he remains Other. Finally, the political situation plays itself out
as a deliberate demonization of Others, as the Philistines render the Israelites alien in their own land.

Importantly, the Samson narrative does not automatically declare all
manifestations of Otherness to be inherently suspect and therefore to
defy salvation.[55] Events in the narrative make it clear that difference and

52. In *Lethal Love*, Mieke Bal expresses the polarization this way: "A tension develops
between *own* and *alien*" (43). In *Fragmented Women*, J. Cheryl Exum argues that the Samson
narrative represents a structuring of reality as "binary opposition" (72). Many critics impute
to this what they consider the narrative's misogynistic tone. Thus, for Bal, "The Philistines
now receive a clear meaning. They represent the feminine. On the other side, and at the end
of the episode, is the masculine occupying the arbiter position" (64). Similarly, Exum writes
of the "negative image of the foreign woman" (*Fragmented Women*, 68), although the account
given of the Timnite woman is substantially different from that of Delilah. More specifically,
Exum writes, "The Philistines are enemies, alien, the other. Women are also enemies, alien,
the other. Philistine women are doubly other. . . . The Philistines are permanently identified
with otherness . . . and they appear more negatively in the story because women are their rep-
resentatives in their most important dealings with Samson" (76, 85).

53. This is not to say that polarizing leaders make bad military leaders. On the contrary,
history is replete with leaders who excelled in leading their people into battle, encouraging
them by demonizing their opponents. Carrying over these attitudes to the postwar structuring of peace, however, often resulted in laying the foundations for the next war (the roots and
causes of World War II are the paradigmatic examples of this for the twentieth century).
Thus, polarizing leaders by definition cannot bring about salvation.

54. In his commentary on Judges, Abarbanel describes Samson's unshorn locks as serving
symbolically as his "cloak of mourning" for the oppression suffered by the Israelites at the
hands of the Philistines.

55. A similar distinction underlies the narrative in the Book of Ruth. A major source of
the tension in that text concerns the place of difference in Israelite national life: should it be

sameness are not correspondingly "bad" and "good" characteristics. To the extent that "difference" may exacerbate tensions, Samson does try to bridge boundaries and resolve differences, even if not always successfully (his marriage with the Timnite woman is one example of his efforts). Ultimately, the Biblical text's subtle analysis of the various characteristics of difference and sameness emphasizes that each permutation of these elements must be judged in its own context. Seen in that light, the Samson narrative presents both individual and communal existence as enterprises of ongoing moral and political discovery.

In this connection, the Samson narrative treats the concept of Otherness in a distinctly political manner—as central to Samson's understanding of the integral requirements of leadership. In his role as a leader, Samson operates as Other, in an inexplicable and nontraditional fashion, because by Samson's era, the problem that he faces—the brutal domination of the Philistines over the Israelites—has become the status quo. As such, the nature of the situation is by definition morally and politically ambiguous. It is not obvious to everyone—or perhaps even to anyone—who or what the problem is. The text reports that the Philistines dominate Israel at the time (Judg. 13:1), but this fact is not greeted with universal consternation: in fact, when there is a clash between Samson and the Philistines, the Judahites parrot the Philistine reading of events.[56] In such a situation, being the recognized savior of the Israelites is not a secure position to occupy.[57] Thus, Samson must profile himself as Other—as different—because he is forced to operate at a time when the meaning of salvation, and even its necessity, is not universally acknowledged. At that level,

---

automatically incorporated or rejected? In the end, difference retains an important place in the construction of Israelite national life, although it never does receive an absolute moral value, either positive or negative. As in the Samson narrative, the question remains one of context. In this connection, Exum's remark that "exceptions [to the negative image of foreign women] like Ruth only prove the rule" (*Fragmented Women*, 68) overlooks much of the nuances of the Biblical text. For more on this issue, see my "Ruth and the Sense of Self: Midrash and Difference," *Judaism* (Spring 1999): 131–45, and chapter 3 in this book.

56. One could argue that the Judahites, like the Timnite woman, are constrained by Philistine domination and so are obliged to agree with the Philistine version of what happened. Still, if another reading of events (that of Samson, for example) were accepted, they might have engineered an alternate approach to the Philistines instead of agreeing to hand him over exactly as demanded.

57. In his commentary on the Samson story, Abarbanel adduces that as the reason for Manoah's wife not revealing to her husband that the unborn child would (begin to) deliver the Israelites from Philistine oppression (Abarbanel on Judg. 13:5).

the very maintenance of the struggle against the Philistines in the face of Israelite quiescence is a great achievement.

Samson's failure to establish a national discourse that includes and thus unites all the Israelites leads to an intensification of his Otherness. As a result, Samson must devise an alternate method of fighting for Israelite freedom, without letting the Philistines discover his true aim. This requires a leader who does not look like a leader, who behaves erratically, in self-directed ways that seem to belie his primary concern for his national task.[58] Samson therefore chooses to fight an "undercover" revolution for Israelite freedom. This "stealth" insurrection has the advantage of fooling both Israelites and Philistines regarding the very real political and military changes taking place in their midst; at the same time, it protects the Israelites against reprisals had the Philistines perceived any challenge to their domination.[59] Samson operates as a disguised deliverer, a masked bearer of salvation. By accepting the brunt of Philistine ire on himself, Samson protects the Israelites, whose (contemporary) sense of national identity and military knowledge is still quite untested.[60] In figuring himself as strange (the indeterminacy of the Biblical text leaves ambiguous the degree to which Samson specifically intends this result), Samson implicitly runs the risk of alienation from his own people, in order to safeguard their existence on all levels: individual and physical, communal and national.

In this context, the episode of Samson and the Judahites at Eitam/Ramath-Lehi is important not only as it reflects the Judahite state of mind, but also for its commentary on the alienation of a leader from his people. The situation is complicated by the fact that in this case, the people do not even recognize Samson as their chief. Instead, they are politically and

58. Abarbanel remarks that at times, God chooses to act through people who are not perfect (Abarbanel on Judg. 14:1). In this regard, Abarbanel is sensitive to the amorphous quality of the Samson narrative, an aspect that has received attention from modern commentators as well. Thus, for example, Crenshaw (*Samson*, 73) points out that the designation of a name in the Samson story does not necessarily connote positive importance (e.g., Delilah), while the absence of such designation does not necessarily signify a lack of importance (cf., for example, Samson's mother). Likewise, Sternberg draws attention to the indeterminacy of the Biblical text (*The Poetics of Biblical Narrative*, 176–79, 228, 326).

59. The measure of Philistine vindictiveness is revealed by their treatment of the one prisoner that does fall into their power. Philistine treatment of Samson reveals not a decision to dispose of a feared enemy (in that case, the Philistines simply would have killed him), but rather a conscious effort to humiliate and torture a person who represented an idea that they deemed culturally inferior. That is why the grand celebration takes place in the House of Dagon, to whom the Philistines attribute their victory; that, too, underlies their call for the blinded and enslaved Samson to "play/make merry before them" (Judg. 16:24, 25).

60. Cf. in this connection Malbim on Judg. 14:4.

morally passive before the realities presented to them by the Philistines. Thus, the Judahites make no attempt to evaluate morally the actions of either side. Instead, they accept unquestioningly the version presented to them by the Philistines—blaming it all on Samson (Judg. 15:11)—even though it is clear from the text that the Philistines exert their domination on the Israelites by force, not by consent.[61] Similarly, the Judahites never question the justice of an entire population being made to suffer for the actions of what appears to be an individual renegade. Despite this, Samson does not remonstrate with his fellow Israelites. His innate sympathy for their plight and his understanding of how the situation must have appeared from their distinct vantage point allows him to accept the humiliation of being bound and handed over to the Philistines (although in the end, the bonds dissolve so easily as to render laughable the entire notion of anyone trying to subdue Samson).

This episode, contained as it is in a few laconic verses, reveals a concept of force and political power that flies very much in the face both of contemporary exhibitions of Philistine military might and of the future manifestations of monarchical power in the Israelite kingdoms. The example of Samson, who closes the period of the Judges in Israel, stands as a warning to all those who view political power as a source of personal prerogative. For all of his individual strength, Samson utilizes his power to serve his people, not as a source of personal aggrandizement. Contemporary (Philistine) and future (Israelite monarchical) exercises of might would be accompanied by far greater arbitrary demands for even more power based not on political or military necessity, but rather as expressions of personal will. Thus, when the Israelites in the future demand a king of Samuel, he meets their request with precisely these warnings of capricious royalist exploitation at the expense of the Israelite people (1 Sam. 8:11–17). In direct contradistinction, Samson's approach to power, historically placed to serve as a warning to future Israelite kings, is symbolized in Samson's name, whose root derives from the verb denoting "service."[62]

61. The root *m'sh'l* indicates rule that is forcibly exerted, in contradistinction to *m'l'kh*, which indicates the rule accepted by the people (which thereby invests it with legitimacy). For further elucidation of this point, cf. Malbim on Gen. 37:8.

62. Abarbanel derives this reading from the root analysis of Samson's name (cf. Abarbanel on Judg. 13:24). This is in contradistinction to the approaches that claim that Samson's name is rooted in an antique solar myth (Crenshaw, *Samson*, 16). For an opposite approach, cf. Zakovich, *Hayyei Shimshon*, 70–71. Greenstein, understanding Samson to be "everyman," similarly reads his name as a play on the Hebrew word for "name." Cf. Greenstein, "The Riddle of Samson," 241, 248.

Despite Samson's appreciation of power in its best Socratic sense—in terms of the interests of its object—the fact that the narrative ends with a description of his place of interment, instead of an account of his political/ historical legacy, indicates that he brings about little concrete change. To a large extent, Samson is caught in a double trap of alienation: he is alienated from his own people, who do not perceive him as their leader; and he is consequently estranged from the realization of power in the fulfillment of his national objectives.[63] Ironically, this double alienation comes about as a result of the *lack* of emotional distance between Samson and the Israelites (as manifested by his overpowering sympathy for them in the Ramath-Lehi episode). Because Samson cannot communicate politically with the Israelites, he becomes politically estranged from them and is not accepted as their leader. Consequently, he is not perceived as invulnerable (as indeed he is not); thus, he is prevented from completing the process of political liberation.

The estrangement exhibited both by Samson (exemplified in his marriage to the Timnite woman) and the Israelites (who give him up to the Philistines) find its expression in the Talmudic assessment of his character (TB Sotah 9b), which links his rationale for his actions—"For she is right *in my eyes*" (Judg. 14:3; emphasis added)—to his eventual downfall (being blinded by the Philistines). In this context, Samson's moral exceptionalism may serve as a warning both for designated leaders and ordinary citizens. As presented in the Book of Judges, this has salience for the common run of Israelite life, which is dominated by a morally atomistic attitude.[64] This point is articulated in the text by the formulaic expression "each man would do what was right in his own eyes." In addition, the moral tone of Samson's

63. This parallels and is a manifestation of the phenomenon of the double estrangement of the leader described in Chapter 2.

64. Judg. 17:6; 21:25. Although the two incidents cited in these verses are found in the last chapters of the Book of Judges, there is a textually based linguistic reason to locate the actual occurrence of these incidents already at the beginning of this period. The Tribe of Dan had not yet been assigned its land portion at the time that the incident of the graven image of Micah takes place, which would seem to locate this episode toward the end of Joshua's life or the very beginning of the period of the judges. Similarly, the fact that Phineas, the son of Elazar (the son of Aaron) is the high priest at the time of the story of the concubine in Gibeah indicates that this episode must have occurred fairly early within the era of the judges (cf. Abarbanel on Judg. 17:1). In sum, the tendency toward atomistic moral judgment seems to characterize the attitude of both lay Israelites and their judges/leaders. In this connection, it is important to note that the text does not condemn using one's own judgment. Rather, what corrupts human motivations and actions is using one's own judgment to the exclusion of what the Biblical text deems the Divinely mandated priorities.

personal life, reflecting the community-wide moral atomism of the time, functions as a warning to future Israelite monarchs, who would justify with impunity their disregard of the legal strictures placed on them by arguing that those laws were rendered moot by the individually unique and extraordinary circumstances in which they found themselves.[65] In this reading, Samson's failure on precisely those grounds—his substitution of personal desire for revealed law, replacing known moral directives with ephemeral sentiment—reveals the Biblical view of the moral and logical weakness of that rationale.

It may seem obvious to interpret Samson's tenure as a judge exclusively as one of failure and missed opportunity. Not only has salvation not been achieved, but it does not seem even to have been begun. Rethinking the essence of that promise of deliverance, however, suggests a different evaluation of Samson's life. The human condition of imperfection and lack of closure, reflected in the charge and promise that heralds the beginning of Samson's life, is also encompassed in the Talmudic remark, "All beginnings are difficult" (BT Ta'anit 10b). The story of Samson clues us into the fact that new beginnings are hard because they are not recognized as beginnings. At the time of its unfolding, the new beginning appears an assemblage of senseless phenomena. Because it is not clear that something new is being experienced, it is easy to misunderstand the ensuing circumstances. Thus, Samson's lack of definitive attainment may be interpreted as emblematic of the existential human struggle to attain a larger context for meaning and comprehension. In that context, the beginning of salvation is all that can be promised, because once salvation has been achieved, there is no further need for human action. At that juncture, the only response can be death.[66]

The Samson narrative does end with death. But it is the death of an individual only, not a nation or the idea embodied by that nation. Fittingly, the person who during his life holds himself to be exceptional, and who exempts himself from many of the requirements of Israelite law and practice, dies admitting his own fealty to that tradition. In saying, "Let my soul die/*tamot nafshi*," Samson harks back to an ancient distinction (mentioned

65. Thus, for example, Solomon is charged with having too many wives, in contradiction to the Deuteronomic strictures (Deut. 17:16–17). According to the text in 1 Kings, these wives in fact do turn Solomon's heart away from God, which in turn is adduced by God as the reason that Solomon's son finally would inherit only a reduced kingdom (11:1–13).

66. Indeed, Samson is buried in the grave of his father, whose name, fittingly, means "resting place."

already in Genesis) between the "life/soul/*nefesh*" and the "life/spirit/ *neshama*."[67] At his moment of death, Samson acknowledges that while his physical life is over, the idea for which he had been fighting his whole life— the unique nature of Israelite nationhood—will survive him. The story of Samson is a valedictory to this early stage of Israelite nationhood in preparation for its future complicated expression on the national scene.[68]

67. Compare Gen. 1:24 (the creation of animals: "nefesh haya") and Gen. 2:7 (the creation of human beings: "nishmat hayyim").
68. Cf. Greenstein, "The Riddle of Samson," 238–41.

6

ESTHER: THE POLITICS OF METAPHOR

In a study focusing on the development of political discourse in the Hebrew Bible, it seems counterintuitive to analyze a text like the Book of Esther, whose overriding theme explicitly seems to elide the notion of establishing political discourse for a self-identified nation. In the world in which the Book of Esther finds itself, the Israelites have lost any semblance of independence and no longer inhabit an autonomous homeland. Instead, they are styled "Jews" and are (at times, unwelcome) guests in the multiethnic and very powerful Persian Empire.

In this context, the Biblical Book of Esther seems to have little to contribute to the analysis of the actual workings of power.[1] The plot of this latter-day Biblical tale does not appear to contest the conventional structures of political power at all: at the end of this narrative, the current regnant power is not deposed; in fact, it appears to be further solidified in its dominion (Esther 10:3).[2] The Book of Esther seems to be nothing more than a fairy tale overlaid with a masquerade: the narrative gives stylistic

---

1. At the same time, it should be noted that the political implications of literary texts have long been recognized as powerful. Even works of a putatively religious nature—ostensibly beyond the sordid reaches of the claims of power—can contain explosive political implications: in contemporary times, for example, certain Biblical narratives have been interpreted in "liberationist" ways that challenge established power hierarchies in both the religious and political realms. Cf. Michael Walzer, *Exodus and Revolution* (New York: Basic, 1985), especially "Introduction," 3–17, and "Exodus Politics," 133–50.

2. Arguably, this may be imputed to Mordecai's advice to King Ahaseurus (Esther 10:2–3); this trajectory calls to mind Joseph's role in the increasing centralization of Egyptian royal power (Gen. 47:13–26), which paves the way for the centralized royal enslavement of the Israelites in Exodus (1:9–14).

evidence of being concerned primarily, if not exclusively, with the externalities of luxury and power. Indeed, the text's ostentatious descriptions look closely linked with its cultural assumptions about social order. In this scheme, opulence functions to delineate a subject and an object of power, ranged along the lines of the gender divide: the connection drawn between luxury and place seems to support the conventional understanding of the role of extravagance. Emphasizing this traditional configuration of power, the main interest of the story popularly continues to be the sexual tension evoked by its account of lavish court life, piqued by the personal intrigue of an imperial beauty contest. In that context, the "magical" quality of its resolution seems fitting: the orphan girl becomes a queen, and the persecuted Jews are saved from annihilation. Intensifying the wizardly aura of the denouement is that one half of the improbable plot—the unknown girl chosen as queen—resolves the other: Esther conceives and executes the strategy that leads to the salvation of her people.

But the conventional reading of this Biblical narrative as just a magical fairy tale neglects the story bubbling just beneath its surface. The sexual tension and nuanced artistry of the text overlay an additional source of pressure that motivates both the structure of the text and the actions of the characters. The book is preoccupied with the use of metaphor to fashion an understanding of both political power and the power of the text, which permits political plurivocity and an inclusive sense of empire.

In this chapter, metaphor—the application of a word or phrase in a nonliteral, allusive manner—is understood primarily in the light of Aristotle's definition in the *Poetics:* "the application to a thing of a name that belongs to something else."[3] This understanding foregrounds both the strange quality of metaphor and the sense of displacement that it brings to life in the individual and political arenas. As we will see, many characters in the Book of Esther feel alienated, obviously or not, and this displacement informs their self-understandings as well as their interactions with other personages in the narrative. In addition, the presence within metaphor of elements that are both like and unlike informs Esther's recalibration of text from a monosemic dead letter that eradicates community to a polysemic entity that constitutes community.[4]

3. This particular understanding of Aristotle's definition of metaphor in *Poetics* (chap. 21) is offered by Paul Ricoeur in "Metaphor and Symbol," in *Interpretation Theory* (Fort Worth: Texas Christian University Press, 1976), 47.

4. The contradictory elements of metaphor as presented here find literary parallels in Dmitri M. Slivniak's notion of "reversal and subversion" in the (carnivalesque) Book of Esther.

The Metaphor of Power

How does the literary trope of metaphor, whose nature appears indirect and evanescent, relate to the tangible exercise of power? In *The Genealogy of Morals*, Nietzsche writes about the ability of the [historical] Jews to "invert all [their enemies'] values . . . the aristocratic value equates good/noble/powerful . . . and maintain [that] 'only the poor, the powerless are good.'"[5] Nietzsche goes on to trace this inverted dialectic to the development of Christianity as the full realization of this paradox. The Book of Esther does not (only) utilize metaphor in the way here outlined by Nietzsche, as a tool of indirection that subverts power. More complicatedly, Esther understands that the power of metaphor lies in its ability to reconstitute meaning.

Thus, as we will see, the Book of Esther implicitly rejects the notion, assumed in Nietzsche's text, that texts and values have only one meaning. (This postulation allows Nietzsche to attach just one obvious meaning to the "rejection" and "inversion" of what he considers the elevated ethic of power.) Instead, the Esther story proposes that texts are themselves multivalent in meaning, and thus that their theoretical interpretations, as much as the practical reactions to the realities that they describe, alter over time. Consequently, metaphor in the Book of Esther is not just a stratagem utilized by the weak in order to make their way in the world. In addition, the Book of Esther argues that metaphor organizes the very essence of human existence. In the course of its narrative, the Book of Esther moves between both senses of metaphor, seamlessly and often confusingly (for the modern reader) alternating between them. Thus, we will see that Esther, who incarnates metaphor in her name, will also utilize metaphor as a tangible strategy in negotiating the complicated politics of the Persian royal court.

Metaphor and the Constitution of Meaning

The ability of metaphor to reconstitute meaning is perhaps best expressed by Aristotle in his *Poetics*, where he defines metaphor as a fusion of sameness

---

In "The Book of Esther: The Making and Unmaking of Jewish Identity," in *Derrida's Bible*, ed. Yvonne Sherwood (New York: Palgrave Macmillan, 2004), 143.

5. Friedrich Nietzsche, *The Genealogy of Morals*, in *The Birth of Tragedy and the Genealogy of Morals*, trans. Francis Golffing (New York: Doubleday, 1956), 167.

and difference, each of which, by their presence, implicates the other.[6] Inevitably, much critical debate has focused on whether the essence of metaphor lies in sameness or difference.[7] Regardless of the particular interpretational emphasis, however, it is apparent that Aristotle's definition—centering on the introduction of strangeness into a preexisting framework of sameness (and arrived at in a historical time frame contiguous to the events depicted in the Book of Esther)—has a political analogue that directly links to the events described in the text: the introduction of the stranger (that which "belongs to something else") into the polity (the "thing"). The Esther narrative centers on the introduction of strangers into a milieu organized before their entry into it. Oddly enough, the historical background to the Esther story is specified only once the first set of events have gotten underway—the account of the king's series of parties throughout the empire and in his capital city, together with the royal domestic contretemps, which is the narrative device for introducing a newcomer into the king's palace. It is precisely after the presentation of what seems like irrelevant, gossipy detail that the element of history is introduced, in the guise of an autobiographical detail: Mordecai is identified as being one of the Benjaminite exiles from the kingdom of Judah (Esther 2:5). This marks the first open interpolation of a stranger into the text. Rather than echoing the dissonance of Vashti's (perhaps surprising?) disobedience at the royal court, it prefigures the introduction of yet another stranger into that hermetically sealed environment, where even a conversation with one's royal spouse requires an official invitation (4:11).

The embeddedness of both the theme of the stranger and the function of the metaphor grows out of these seemingly disjointed introductory paragraphs of the Book of Esther. The identification of Mordecai as a product

6. In *The Slayers of Moses*, Susan Handelman distinguishes metaphor from metonymy, identifying them with Christian and Rabbinic interpretations, respectively. Handelman's distinction, even on her own terms, however, is not absolute: she too acknowledges that metaphor implies *both* similarity *and* difference. See, for example, her understanding of Derrida: "This wandering life of the letter expresses itself above all in metaphor, metaphor as the origin of language" (176). Handelman's desire to distinguish absolutely between Christian and Rabbinic approaches often leads her to characterize only plurality as metonymic, simplifying the polysemic qualities of metaphor to the manner of the Church Fathers with regard to the Christian Bible (and as such, ceding to them the interpretational framework; cf. 144 in her discussion of Freud). The Book of Esther emphasizes that metaphor conveys a multiplicity of meaning; thus, the ambiguity of the text carries over to the variable nuances and functions of language.

7. Cf. Paul Gordon, *The Critical Double* (Tuscaloosa: University of Alabama Press, 1995), 19–37.

of deportation, a description that immediately follows the report of the extent of Ahaseurus's empire and his unimaginable wealth (his parties, all told, last over six months), gives rise to the suspicion that the grandeur described at the beginning of the narrative has been acquired through the (unmentioned) suffering of other people.[8] Also, the juxtaposition of Mordecai's introduction with the seemingly needless recitation of luxury that begins the Book of Esther plants the idea that perhaps all these details are not as inconsequential as they might appear; consequently, the key to the interpretation of the Book of Esther might lie with a deeper understanding of the function of metaphor within the text.

The allusion at the beginning of the text pointedly frames the Book of Esther as political. Right from the start, the reader is made aware that the Jewish national existence has been irrevocably altered by events occurring already before the narrative episodes of the book. No longer ensconced in their own land, the Jews are now forced to survive within an empire of diverse nationalities. Making matters more complicated, the requirements of political survival in this new reality arbitrarily begin to change. In the course of the narrative, the political nature of the empire is problematized by the new prime minister, Haman, who threatens the Jews by reconfiguring the notion of acceptable difference. Significantly, when Haman recommends their annihilation,[9] he does not present their difference as a characteristic that they share with the other nationalities populating the Persian Empire, although in fact, many of these groups persistently adhere to their own languages and alphabets (Esther 3:12; 8:9). Haman carefully avoids that connection because, in that case, the uniqueness of the Jews would be an indication of their essential sameness: like all other peoples of the Persian Empire, the Jews, too, possess distinctive marks of difference. Paradoxically, that would allow the Jews to fit seamlessly into the multiethnic composition of the Persian Empire. Instead, Haman adduces the difference of the Jews as proof of their danger to the political survival of Ahaseurus: their laws are different, they ignore the king's commands, and they are scattered throughout the empire. He posits that they can easily

8. Indeed, due to the contiguity of these two parts of the narrative, the Midrash, fixing on the wording of the verse describing the "diverse vessels" (Esther 1:7), opines that during these celebrations, the holy vessels and garments of the sacked Temple of Jerusalem were put on display. Cf. Esther Rabbah 1:12; 2:1, 11.

9. The text records the pretext for Haman's decree of annihilation for all Jews in the Persian Empire to be rooted in Mordecai's refusal to prostrate himself before Haman (as before a deity; the relevant verbs translate as "kneel and prostrate," Esther 3:2, 5).

spread their dangerous ideas and thereby destabilize the entire polity (3:8–9). In effect, Haman is arguing for a vision of empire that would parallel the new bureaucratic order he set up in Ahaseurus's court after being named prime minister: in both arenas, a tyrannically established uniformity is valorized over a pluralistic coexistence.[10] This is an idea of dominion that views difference as a threat and consequently feels compelled to abolish it.

In the Book of Esther, the definition of Mordecai by both his national/religious origins and his exilic experience reveals that Jews as a group function in the text as a metaphor for difference.[11] Similarly, Esther as an individual actualizes the metaphor of difference in her personal life. She is an orphan, and Mordecai takes her in "like a daughter" (2:7). But while Esther is *called* a "daughter" (recall Aristotle's definition of metaphor: "the application to a thing . . . "), Esther actually is *not* Mordecai's daughter (" . . . of a name that belongs to something else"). Esther is Mordecai's cousin, although she (at least in the beginning of the story) obeys him with filial piety. In short order, the doubly displaced Esther—from her land and from her family of origin—becomes triply estranged: she is removed to the Persian court, where she is forced to take part in the extended contest for the selection of Ahaseurus's new queen.[12] As presented in the text, Esther's life embodies the displacement of metaphor.[13]

Similarly, her name reflects the alienated structure of her life. The text tells us that, in fact, Esther is not her original name. Esther's Hebrew appellation is Hadassah, meaning a myrtle plant. By contrast, Esther's Persian name (which is Esther) has been traced to "ishtahar," the Persian word for "star." The combination of two members of the natural world in the name of one person—a plant, anchored close to the ground; and a celestial body,

10. Haman's projected revenge is noted in Esther 3:6. For an exposition on Haman's singular approach to governing, changing the cabinet-style government utilizing a group of advisors to one dominated by a primary advisor to the king, see Yoram Hazony, *The Dawn* (Jerusalem: Shalem, 1995), 50–58.

11. Anthony Appiah similarly points out the essence of race as a marker of difference: "Race, we all assume, is, like all other concepts, constructed by metaphor and metonymy; it stands in, metonymically, for the Other; it bears the weight, metaphorically, of other kinds of difference." "The Uncompleted Argument: Du Bois and the Illusion of Race," in *The Idea of Race*, ed. Robert Bernasconi and Tommy L. Lott (Indianapolis: Hackett, 2000), 134.

12. The text reads "and Esther *was taken*" (2:8); the Midrash adds that the passive tense indicates that Esther's participation was involuntary. See also Timothy K. Beal, *The Book of Hiding* (New York: Routledge, 1997), 35.

13. It is worth noting that Mordecai's genealogy is also consciously displaced: as a Benjaminite (the descendant of the Kish family), Mordecai is identified with the (first) displaced Israelite royal family, now (doubly) subsumed, in the regard of outsiders at least, with the appellation of the rival tribe for monarchical power, the Judahites (whence the term *yehudim*, Jews).

whose very distance renders it mysterious—recalls the definition of metaphor, which is also described as the placement of two things in (implicit) comparison with each other. In *The Critical Double*, Paul Gordon points out that the (metaphorical) juxtaposition of two items that are both like and unlike leads to "doubling," which implies that "the double is . . . neither one nor two . . . [and] . . . both one and two."[14] Esther embodies some characteristics of both myrtle plant and star but belongs wholly to neither category. People may think that they grasp the essence of what is apparently a simple girl ("a humble plant"), but, like the star, Esther's deceptively harmonizing appearance belies her distance—that is, the impossibility of grasping her essence. Complicating the metaphor, the name Esther actually connotes various things in different languages. Its Persian meaning derives from the word for star, but its Hebrew roots (in addition to the plant connection) allude to the quality of hiddenness (*s't'r*). Esther's name betokens both dazzling appearance and self-effacing modesty; the name is both/neither Persian and/nor Hebrew. Significantly, neither linguistic code succeeds in entirely encompassing Esther's essence.

This is not to say that Esther's essence, in being so readily metaphorized, is bereft of tangible content. On the contrary, the doubled metaphor of Esther's name highlights the nonconformity of her spirit. In practical terms, Esther's life seems to follow a ready-made plotline—whether in terms of the "obscure girl made 'good,'" or the "obedient daughter"—but in actuality, Esther defies all expectations.[15] Her complex political activity removes her from the category of "trophy queen," and the success of *her* plan (as opposed to Mordecai's) in saving the Jewish people emphasizes that the text does not unqualifiedly valorize obedience.[16] The extent to which Esther refuses to be limited by the accepted categories ready to encapsulate her indicates that metaphors do not function merely as interpretational tools. More profoundly, both characters and events in the book provide the opportunity for further reflection on the nature of metaphors and their implications for attaining philosophical coherence in both the minutiae of daily life as well the broader political arena.[17]

14. Gordon, *The Critical Double*, 19.
15. In Beal's words, Esther is "signed in" to play a specific role in a world to which she has not assented and over whose structures she has no control (*The Book of Hiding*, 60, 72).
16. Mieke Bal, "Lots of Writing," in *Ruth and Esther: A Feminist Companion to the Bible (Second Series)*, ed. Athalya Brenner (Sheffield: Sheffield Academic Press, 1999), 238.
17. Paul Gordon puts it this way: "Any definition of metaphor will . . . by offering a partial truth or resemblance . . . yield metaphors of metaphorization" (*The Critical Double*, 20).

Metaphor and Ambiguity

By going beyond the limits of conventional categorization, the dialectical nature of metaphor helps explicate the dual, or doubled, nature of Esther's essence. In addition, the "doubleness," or multivalence, of metaphor also hints at its uncanny nature.[18] This points to the "strangeness/uncanniness"—or, in Freud's terms, the "unheimlichkeit"—of metaphor.[19] But the meaning of this reference may also encompass Freud's referent of the uncanny, which is the body of the mother.[20] With this approach, and in this text, the "uncanny" metaphor reveals itself particularly as the province of women. More pointedly, the metaphor constructs the arena of the powerless.[21] Powerful people do not need the ambiguity or the allusiveness of metaphor to express opinion or desire: they can say directly what they want, without fear. It is the powerless who need the shadows of ambiguity to protect themselves as they speak truth to power or, alternatively, as they recognize that they themselves are manipulated by external powers. Haman, for example, speaks his mind directly throughout much of the Book of Esther; interestingly, it is only when he is aware of his fall from political grace that his parading of Mordecai through the streets of Shushan takes on the quality of a metaphor of foreboding.[22]

In the Esther narrative, the "doubling" aspect of metaphor is realized not just in the internal complexity of particular personages, but also through its array of characters and the complication of relationships among them. Each actor has one double, if not more. Befitting the intricacy of his character, Mordecai has more than one double: while his obvious counterpart

18. Ibid., 25.

19. In his essay on "The Uncanny" (1919), Freud explains that what we recognize (defensively) as "strange" or "uncanny" (*unheimlich*) within ourselves is actually the part of ourselves (*heimlich*) that we classify as "bad" and hence want to expel. Julia Kristeva expands on the political implications of this discovery in *Strangers to Ourselves*.

20. See Diane Jonte-Pace, *Speaking the Unspeakable*, 4–5.

21. Mieke Bal argues that the "opportunistic concept of metaphor" recapitulates the power structure that actually exists within the sociopolitical sphere. To the extent that the male voice reifies its own power, this results in women's voices being constricted, marginalized, and finally silenced. "Metaphors He Lives By," *Semeia* 61 (1993): 199, 202–5; for a similar point of view, see Claudia Camp, "Metaphors in Feminist Biblical Interpretation," *Semeia* 61 (1993): 17. Significantly, while Derrida defines the essence of metaphor as Hegelian "Aufhebung" or "sublation" (49), Bal insists that the most adequate metaphor is "sublimation" (205)—that is, the re-couching of language in the "acceptable" image in order to stabilize the current power structure. For Derrida, see "White Mythology," *New Literary History* 6 (1974): 5–74.

22. "If Mordecai is of Jewish seed . . . you will not prevail against him, but will surely fall before him" (Esther 6:13).

is Haman (both serve as prime ministers to Ahaseurus),[23] his double may be also construed as the eunuchs (like Mordecai, the eunuchs occupy a liminal position "on the threshold" and, like him, help to transfer women from outside the king's palace to the interior royal court).[24] In the Book of Esther, the eunuchs also provide the pretext for the reversal of fortune that marks the "salvation" aspect of the narrative: Mordecai's discovery of a plot to assassinate King Ahaseurus on the part of the two eunuchs, Bigthan and Theresh, is the pretext for his delayed royal reward (the procession through Shushan) that presages Mordecai's elevation in the imperial court and Haman's concomitant fall from power. Complicating things still further, the character of Mordecai may be seen as alluding to, and hence doubling, the deposed Queen Vashti; she is Other to Mordecai both in gender and national origin, and yet similar to him in flouting royal decrees of obeisance and obedience.[25]

By the same token, Vashti, the previous queen and royal consort, is also Esther's obvious parallel. Esther is described as attractive (Esther Rabbah 6:9), and the same may be inferred for Vashti: given the mechanism that Ahaseurus utilizes to find a new wife for himself, focusing almost entirely on sensual appeal, it is not unreasonable to suppose that it is on the basis of sexual attraction that he had made his previous choice of wife as well (Esther Rabbah 3:13; 14). In the course of the narrative, Esther consciously utilizes her attractiveness to Ahaseurus to gain access to him: she dresses up in her finest royal robes (Esther 5:1) and she cleverly manipulates her special invitation to the king to pique his curiosity (5:4, 8). To be sure, even in the deliberate utilization of her own powers of seduction, Esther is not Vashti. But neither is Esther the complete anti-Vashti: in the context of the Persian court, Esther utilizes their similarities to the advantage of her and her people (the Jews), while simultaneously alluding to the vast differences between them (Esther Rabbah 6:11). Indeed, Esther distinguishes herself from Vashti even as she alludes to her. It is precisely the highlighting of the differences in their similarities, and the similarities in their differences, that forms the basis of Esther's attractiveness for Ahaseurus. Thus, for example,

23. Little noticed is the fact that while Haman condemns Mordecai's people as "different," his own status, as an Agagite, is no less non-Persian (Beal, *The Book of Hiding*, 58, 116). In Freudian terms, Haman projects hatred onto an object that epitomizes his own fears and insecurities.

24. Ibid., 52.

25. Timothy Beal notes this affinity by tracing the textual similarities in the description of their respective refusals and (threatened) punishments (ibid., 55).

Esther, like Vashti, can be a negative presence: she refuses to reveal anything about her provenance, her people, even her mysterious party invitation. But, unlike Vashti, at no time does Esther flatly disobey the king, her husband.

Adhering to the multilayered concept of doubleness, however, it is also possible to argue that Esther has another counterpart: Haman's wife, Zeresh. The ambiguity derives from the fact that Zeresh is the one woman, apart from Esther, who offers an analysis of the current situation that counters the conventional wisdom as expressed by the central man in her life; moreover, her dissenting opinion is proven right by the ensuing chain of events. Thus, the phenomenon of doubling represents a paradox, because characters can be doubled in more than one way. There are many ways to metaphorize a person, none of which exclusively defines that character's truth or essence. This emphasizes the porousness of boundaries and, concomitantly, the tangential quality of identity. The surfeit of doublings, born of metaphor, yields an ambiguity of identities and an implicit questioning of clearly demarcated boundaries, culminating in disguise.

Metaphor takes advantage of this ambiguity by valorizing the masquerade. Indeed, intrigue—pretending to be what one is not—is the hallmark of the Persian court as described in the Book of Esther. Ahasuerus masquerades as a genial host but gets rid of his wife for not showing up on command; he is king of all his subjects but manifests no qualms about annihilating a particular group among them. For his part, Haman disguises his plan of genocide as a function of his concern for Ahaseurus's political stability, while the narrative points out that his real motivation is hatred of the Jews.[26] Importantly, however, the Esther narrative does not portray the wearing of masks as wholly negative. Probing more deeply, we see that the wearing of masks serves as a metaphor for political involvement in the Persian Empire: any political activity, particularly in the etiquette-driven halls of any imperial court, requires the wearing of masks. Thus, once Esther is taken to the royal palace, Mordecai advises her to keep secret her origins and identity, and indeed she does so for several years of her tenure as queen.[27]

26. As already noted, there are many disparate peoples in the Persian Empire who maintain their own linguistic and alphabetic distinctions; thus, Haman's singling out of the Jewish people as different is motivated not by real perplexity vis-à-vis a strange social phenomenon. Importantly, the introduction of Haman in the text reveals this rationale: he is presented as one of the Agagites (Esther 3:1), longtime enemies of the Israelites (cf. 1 Sam. 15:2).

27. The Book of Esther begins during the third year of Ahaseurus's reign (1:3); the contest occurs in the seventh year (2:15); Haman writes the decree in the twelfth year (3:7); the victory of the Jews over their enemies occurs during the following calendar year.

Moreover, the wearing of a disguise, in and of itself, is not portrayed as morally inferior. In urging Esther to action, Mordecai points out that all her years of subterfuge may well find their justification now, if she chooses to use her position to avoid the genocide of her people (Esther 4:12). Esther, as we know, does not disagree with Mordecai's reasoning, but it is clear that she values subterfuge more than he does. The structure of Esther's plan of approach to the king indicates her belief that indirection (rather than the open approach advocated by Mordecai) is the only method that will succeed.

In tracing the doubling of the narrative's array of characters, there is one protagonist who does not appear to have a double: King Ahasuerus. One may suppose that Ahasuerus represents absolute power and thus does not need a counterpart. At the same time, it is possible to contend that Haman represents the political/literary counterpart to Ahasuerus. This reading extrapolates from Haman's self-interested wish to destroy the Jews that he ultimately desires to wear the king's crown himself. According to this approach, Haman's advice to the sleepless Ahasuerus is a projected wish fulfillment, which is ultimately thwarted.[28] The Midrashic reading posits a different counterpoint to Ahasuerus: God Himself. But this seems textually as well as philosophically counterintuitive: because God is not mentioned at all in the Book of Esther, it would seem that God does not provide a counterpoint to any character in the text. According to the Midrash, however, God is in fact present in the Esther narrative, even if not obviously so: textually, the Midrash interprets every mention of the term "the king," without any specific appellation, as referring to both Ahasuerus and God.[29] It is important to note in this connection the specificity of the linguistic structure of the Midrashic interpretation. The Midrash does not attribute only one specific referent to the ambiguous term "the king." Rather, by imputing two different, but similar, meanings to the open-ended term "king" (the individual human Ahasuerus and the celestial Divinity God), the Midrashic understanding of this locution recalls the quality of

28. This is the underlying assumption of Malbim in his comment on Esther 6:6, where he interprets Haman's specification of the *royal* horse and the *royal* crown as betraying Haman's desire for royal power. For a similar approach highlighting Esther's awareness of Ahasuerus's psychological vulnerabilities, see Rabbi Dr. Joseph B. Soloveitchik, "In the Days of Mordecai and Esther," RCA Hashkafa Unit, 2nd series, no. 4, lecture transcribed by Rabbi Abraham Besdin (5734/1973–74).

29. Esther Rabbah 3:10. Also see Beal, *The Book of Hiding*, 116–20, where he questions whether the presence of God is hidden in the Book of Esther (and therefore implicitly there) or simply unavailable (i.e., in "another place," Esther 4:14).

metaphor, encapsulating both similarity and difference, highlighting the permeability of borders and, thus, the evanescent nature of meaning.

The doubled referent of "the king" also reveals the Biblical view of earthly politics. Unlike many other religiously inflected texts, the Book of Esther does not consider politics just as an onerous requirement to be fulfilled in a minimalist fashion. Instead, the Book of Esther suggests that politics may contain, at least potentially, elements of the transcendent and the spiritual. In the Esther narrative, this is signaled by the political activism of Esther and Mordecai, neither of whom disdains political activity for their people's survival, and neither of whom fades from public life once the emergency detailed in the Esther narrative is resolved.[30] The fact that the results of political action are neither uniform nor problem-free (careful readers note that Mordecai was not accepted by all of his community) does not excuse anyone from withdrawing from this demanding enterprise (Esther 10:3). Even with less-than-favorable odds given for the success of any particular political plan, the narrative in the Book of Esther contends that it is even more reprehensible to refuse to do anything at all. Mordecai makes this argument succinctly when he urges Esther to take action: even though the dispersal of the Jews in exile makes it unlikely that the destruction of Persian Jewry will result in the total annihilation of the Jewish people, Mordecai insists that Esther's first reaction—her refusal to act (i.e., her rejection of politics)—would result in her own (spiritual) destruction.[31]

Esther, as we know, does act in response to Mordecai's words, although the plan that she puts forward differs markedly from his. Consonant with the indirection of metaphor that typifies both her name and existence, Esther approaches Ahaseurus in a roundabout manner: she couches her politically motivated request as a social invitation to a cocktail party, and she piques the king's interest most when he thinks that Haman is after the queen's favors (Esther 7:8). But Esther does more than utilize the multi-valent and masquerading aspects of metaphor to engineer the salvation of her people. More importantly, she also changes the nature and substance of the metaphor used. In this, she reveals the extent of her power.

30. Mordecai remains prime minister even after the events chronicled by the Book of Esther are resolved (10:3).

31. The Hebrew verb *a'b'd* is taken to mean utter destruction in Esther 4:14. One proof-text for this interpretation is the utilization of the verb *a'b'd* in the Bible's description of Korah's oblivion as described in Num. 16:33.

The Book of Esther is most obviously concerned with questions of power: who has it, who wants it, who appears to have it, and who schemes to get it. But while power is most often exercised in brute (if not totalitarian) form, the Midrash's metaphorization of the term "king" informs us that power does not always reside where it is most obvious. In fact, there are hidden venues for the exercise of power that prove more central to power's actualization than its more public symbols. For her part, Esther describes the exercise of power by utilizing the metaphor of strength, which is figured most often in the text as "hand"; in the Book of Esther, the "hand" is contextualized by connotations of physical violence and utter destruction.[32] But she inverts this metaphor's traditional implications to emphasize another function of the hand: writing. Thus, Esther's response to the successful self-defense of the Jews in the Persian Empire is to write letters commemorating not the fighting, but the communal unity that allows them to act in concert against a common enemy. In addition, more letters go out to establish a national holiday marked by giving portions of food to one's friends and donating alms to the poor (Esther 9:22).

Text as Metaphor: Esther Writing, Writing Esther

The centrality of texts in the Esther narrative emphasizes writing as a metaphor for power, as this may be both positively and negatively understood. This complex understanding of texts is not universally shared: Ahaseurus, by virtue of his rigidification of texts, wants to deny their historicity, even while events demonstrate that texts are in fact never written on a tabula rasa: instead, texts and stories continually erase and rewrite earlier events.[33] In addition, writing texts is not presented as a common activity: in the Esther story, only Esther, Mordecai (to some extent), and Ahaseurus/Haman are described as authoring/authorizing texts. The Book of Esther demonstrates, however, that it is not just the act of writing that encompasses the text's metaphorization of political power. In addition, the manner of texts written reflect on their own nature as dynamic actors within the political sphere. In that understanding, reading can also become an important way of

---

32. See, for example, Esther 2:21 (describing Bigthan and Teresh's plot to assassinate Ahaseurus) and 3:6 (Haman's plan to murder Mordecai and his co-religionists).

33. In Beal's words, "The book of Esther [functions as] a kind of palimpsest" (*The Book of Hiding*, 29).

participating in the political act of forming community. In this way, reading opens up politics to the average (i.e., politically unconnected) individual.

The multiplication of texts within the Book of Esther generates two sets of reflections. First, the various texts that Esther, Haman, and Ahaseurus write all function differently. Second, no text is ever frozen in its final form. Mieke Bal has argued that a dissonance exists within the act of writing, stemming from the different interpretations of a text as it is first written and as it is subsequently read (often, these actions also involve different audiences).[34] Because (at least at the period of the events delineated in the Book of Esther) a considerable amount of time elapses between the reading and the writing of a text, writing loses its fixed quality even if the text is never officially altered. Thus, the central principle of the political functioning of the Persian Empire—the immutability of the written royal decree (Esther 8:8)—proves incoherent on its face, as decrees are never read as written, and never written as read.[35]

The fiction of the unchangeability of the text incites much of the narrative's tension. It first appears in the text, however, as a travesty of itself: a comic prefiguration that points to the logical incoherence of Ahaseurus's system of rule. This logical dissonance is figured in the law passed (after Vashti has been relieved of her crown) mandating the rules of linguistic engagement in the domestic sphere. Ahaseurus's profound misunderstanding of the uses of language and the tenor of private life casts doubt on his ability at all to write a workable law. He does not realize that for a law to be effective, its requirements must be based on actions that are subject to control. Ahaseurus does not understand that people in a private setting exercise their own desires in choosing which language to speak: their motivating factor in linguistic choice is not reinforcement of political power structures, but rather the maximization of personal communication between individuals. As a result, the hallmark of this first decree of Ahaseurus in the text is its nonenforceability.

The nonenforceability of Ahaseurus's royal edict sabotages its stated aim, which is to solidify the respect shown to the king. Ironically, Ahaseurus's

34. Mieke Bal, "Lots of Writing," especially 225–38.

35. Importantly, while the implications of decrees change as a function of the time and distance that they encompass, the letters detailed in the Book of Esther evince no such change: they are understood as they are written. (Thus, the two letters written by Esther and approved by Mordecai on the institution and perpetuation of the celebratory feasts marking the Jews' salvation are accepted without demurral or change.)

severe misreading[36] of the Vashti altercation, based on the mistaken notion
that the king's honor is at stake in *every* gendered encounter, leads to a law
that makes the king look ridiculous. Moreover, this law actually weakens
Ahaseurus's ability to administer his own empire. By insisting that domestic communication be governed by an inflexible rule, the king subverts his
own previous method of communication with the far-flung parts of his
empire, whose diversity he accepts, by writing to each group in its own
distinctive language and alphabet (Esther 3:12; 8:9). In imposing what the
king believes is uniformity of method (all households speaking the language of the husband), the decree inevitably gives rise to a cacophony of
voices, guaranteeing that linguistic misunderstandings and chaos will ensue.
The result is not pluralism, but rather the rule of the strongest (voice).

Esther subverts the legally proclaimed unchangeability of texts by mul-
tiplying them: that is to say, she writes even more. By increasing the instances of text, Esther demonstrates the ability of writing and the text to
evolve. Instead of remaining a dead letter or an implacable, murderous
device, the text becomes a living actor, reflecting and also affecting events.
Thus Esther's texts change reality for the slated victims of Haman's decree,
allowing the Persian Jews to defend themselves against their enemies.
Significantly, the new decree written at Esther's behest does not annul
Ahaseurus's previous one; rather, it loosens the bonds of permitted activity,
allowing for the reinterpretation of text. Instead of being imprisoned by
the words in which it is written, this new type of text utilizes the openness
and multivalency of its words as a promise of renewal.

Esther's insistence on writing serves to recreate political reality: the final
answer to violence in the Esther narrative is to reframe it as a quest for
national identity, which is constituted by text. At the same time, her response cannot eschew violence altogether, as armed self-defense in the
Persian Empire, as then constituted, is critical in order to physically survive. Survival in its turn, however, is not reified as a solitary goal in and of
itself. Importantly, it is valorized in the production of a (new) text.

In that spirit, Esther's letter on the annual commemoration of the historical events of the book differs in both form and effect from the conventional monosemic texts of the Persian Empire. In its form, Esther's letter rejects commemorative celebration in its (traditional) guise of mimetic

---

36. The term derives from Harold Bloom's "severe misprision" in *The Anxiety of Influence*,
19–45.

recitation. Instead, her new text expresses its sense of commemoration as the performative re-creation of community each year. This is accomplished through sending portions of food and giving charitable alms. These activities both recall and represent—in effect, they recall *through* re-presenting—the unity that allowed the Persian Jews to defeat their enemies.[37] As if to emphasize the living nature and permeability of text with the environment that it produces/reflects, this letter of commemoration is itself rewritten: the holiday of Purim is institutionalized permanently only after Esther sends the *second* letter (9:29).[38]

The newly energized textual form that Esther employs in her commemorative letter is echoed in the dynamic effect produced by the text. The required practice established by this communication is not one of formalized rote. Rather, this performativity emphasizes activities in which a constant measure of judgment is exercised, whether in "sending portions to one's friends" or by giving "gifts to the poor" (9:22). In addition, the members of one community are not viewed with flattening uniformity: it is frankly acknowledged that some people are friends with each other and, therefore, by implication, that some are not. Also, the text does not maintain the fiction of universal wealth. Importantly, in highlighting the requirement to give, the emphasis is placed on giving to each person what he needs to *receive*, instead of focusing on the desire of the donor, who may

37. On the notion of re-presenting community as a key to its dynamic renewal and perpetuation, see my *Rousseau and the Politics of Ambiguity* (University Park: Pennsylvania State University Press, 1996), especially 44–47.

38. The argument that Esther is not the true author of these letters/decrees, because Mordecai is also mentioned in the description of their origins, is specious: it adduces distinctions without any real difference. From the changed directives at the end of Esther 4, it is clear that Esther is at the forefront of the tactical and strategic planning regarding the approach to Ahaseurus; she remains at the helm even once Mordecai's identity is made fully known to Ahaseurus. It is Esther who approaches the king again, who frames her additional request (regarding the fighting in Shushan, 9:12–13). Even when Esther's authorship is cited together with that of Mordecai, her primacy remains unquestioned: her name precedes his (and that import is conveyed by the Hebrew grammatical construction of the verb, which remains styled in the feminine). The one time that Mordecai's name precedes Esther's (9:31) refers not to the authorship of any particular text, but to the observance of the commemorative celebratory days. (The solitary mention of Mordecai's writing in 9:21 has been adduced by traditional commentary to reflect his position as a member of the Jewish judicial body called Sanhedrin. But even without that detail, writing as practiced by Mordecai is presented in the text as commemorative; writing as practiced/inspired by Esther materially alters lives and political reality. Thus, their writings differ in structure, even if united in their aim.) Finally, as described in the Book of Esther, it is the decree (*ma'amar*) of *Esther* that is observed and *written* in the book (whether this refers to the historical chronicles of Persia or the canonical books of the Hebrew scriptures is secondary in this context to the primacy of Esther with regard to authoring texts).

be primarily concerned with his/her self-image. Thus, the act of giving requires a concerted effort on the part of the donor, who must individually and perennially adjust her/his effort at all times to correspond to the actual situation at hand.

This nuanced way of seeing other people dynamically counteracts the deadening "look/*regard*" by which Haman had endeavored to annihilate all those whom he regarded as Other. Esther, by contrast, understands that all people are Other to oneself, but she does not view that as a moral or political problem. Instead, Esther realizes that her new understanding of community can also metaphorically function to create a new concept of empire. More specifically, the notion that not all members of one community are transparently the same, yet they can still act in unison with one another to achieve greater communal coherence, can help in the figuration of difference within empire. Instead of utilizing (scarce) resources to destroy difference because of its (potential) challenge to the power base of its leader(s), difference can be nurtured, because these diverse populations provide a wider base for the flourishing and expansion of empire. Implicitly, Esther views empire not as a reification of its leader(s), but rather as an expression of its constituent members. By going beyond the stultifying uniformity enforced by Haman's totalitarian rule by decree, Esther prepares the way for a more inclusive concept of empire, where the exercise of individual or ethnic differences is harnessed to create a dynamic realization of community flexible enough to adapt to, and thereby survive, changing circumstances.

Esther demonstrates that, contrary to Haman's pronouncements, diversity does not represent a danger to the cohesion of empire. Rather, by presenting alternative methods for solving problems, diversity allows for empire's most constructive actualization of its creative potential. Esther's multifaceted categorization of community demonstrates that she views being different and dealing with difference as alternating aspects of the opportunity to expand one's own humanity. Just as the Other serves as an opportunity for the expansion of the "self," so the stranger represents an invitation to empire to achieve its ultimate greatness. For Esther, the fact of Otherness emphasizes the ongoing moral imperative and political opportunity that, by definition, applies to all participants in the social conversation.

It is easy to dismiss Esther's conception of empire as unrealistic and romanticized. But her understanding of the true sources of political stability is in fact validated by the Biblical text (Esther 10:3). Importantly, Esther's conception of empire as a function of its inhabitants, not (just) its chief(s), even functions to cast (some) doubt on the efficacy of monarchy as a method of rule. To be sure, the Esther text does not function as a call to democracy: political action is limited to elites, and "the people" are not portrayed as actively originating or justifying political action on their own. Still, Ahaseurus's misbegotten method of rule by decree, and his disregard of the limits of political control, merely emphasizes these political reservations regarding monarchy. In addition, these misgivings highlight Esther's consciously offered rethinking of her own national and familial origins: her examination of monarchy implicitly interrogates its political and moral effectiveness within Israelite history in general, particularly as exemplified by Esther's own Benjaminite ancestor Saul, the first king of the Israelites.

As we have seen, Esther's utilization of metaphor has both textual and political implications. These, in turn, operate in two different contexts: the power setting of the Persian Empire and the ancient framework of Biblical texts. In the contemporaneous construct of the Persian Empire, Esther expands the meaning of text, utilizing it as a positive metaphor for power and political rule. At the same time, Esther understands that, despite the pacific proclivity of words, texts themselves can be used to kill. Unlike the writings of Haman and Ahaseurus, Esther's texts (her letters) promote the harmony of many voices ("plurivocity") instead of the monotonic repetition of despotic pronouncements. In addition, Esther's self-conscious actions to rescue her own people places her (re)writing of text (in this case, the Esther-inspired decrees that allow for Jewish self-defense against their enemies) squarely in the context of the ancient roots of her national origins. In addition to their effect on the imperial power structures of the Persian Empire, Esther's writings function in the context of her tribal and national roots: Esther's reconstitution of the text stands in opposition to and fundamentally reorders (*tikkun*) some previous writings of her own national heritage and tribal culture (in the Book of Judges) that seem to valorize an exploitative understanding of writing text. In so doing, Esther is able (potentially) to restructure her community's understanding of the possibilities of politics.

Men and Misreading

The intertextual citation of the Book of Judges in the context of explicating the Esther narrative is apposite: the political disorder that typifies

Jewish communal life in exile as set forth in the Book of Esther is not dissimilar to the hesitant groping of the Israelite community toward political self-definition in the earlier days of the judges.[39] I will focus on one story in particular, the concubine in Gibeah incident, which highlights the propensity of gendered exploitation. In the Bible, the abuse suffered by women in the Book of Judges is figured literally as bodily inscription— more specifically, as the writing of Israelite political history on the bodies of women. Thus, the connotations of text are expanded to include the bodies of the Other (Israelite women), which are systematically utilized as palimpsests to reorder society and reify the locus of power. Significantly, this denatured writing is portrayed as the consequence of a severe misreading of the elements and implications of contemporary social/political issues. In this context, society in these Biblical writings is understood as a text that structures and reflects meaning; similarly, the understanding of the relationships among its people and its structures may be expressed as "reading," in the larger sense of that term.[40]

In the concubine in Gibeah narrative (discussed in detail in Chapter 2 as well), a Levite, with his concubine, is forced to seek shelter in the strange/unfriendly town of Gibeah (in the Benjaminite holding). Although the Levite and his concubine find housing for the night (an old man takes them in), men of the town soon come crowding around the old man's door, demanding to "get to know" the Levite (the intertextual resemblances to the Genesis narrative of Sodom leave little doubt that their intention here is to rape the Levite).[41] This encounter ends with the Levite thrusting his concubine outside, where she is gang-raped throughout the night by the "wicked men" of the town. As dawn breaks, the concubine crawls towards the threshold of the (old man's) house. The Levite, upon leaving the house, abruptly tells her to "get up and go." She no longer answers him, and the indication of the text is that she may already be dead. The Levite throws her body on his mule; upon returning to his home, he cuts up her dead body into twelve pieces and sends one piece to each of the other tribes as a clarion call to war against the inhospitality of the Gibeahites. What results is a civil war with many negative repercussions and implications, the

---

39. On intertextuality, see Daniel Boyarin, *Intertextuality and the Reading of Midrash* (1990; Bloomington: Indiana University Press, 1994).

40. Richard Harvey Brown, *Society as Text* (1987; Chicago: University of Chicago Press, 1992),

41. See above, note 39.

most immediate being the forced marriages of the kidnapped Shilohite maidens to the remaining members of the decimated Benjaminite tribe.

Many feminist critics of the Bible[42] have pointed to these tragedies as evidence of the misogynistic message of these Biblical texts, arguing that the narrator supports this dehumanizing treatment of the women.[43] But one can also interpret the texts as a devastating critique of that very socially accepted (dis)order.[44] These stories demonstrate that the negative treatment of women is a metaphor for the disintegrating Israelite body politic. As one reflects on these stories and the ensuing course of Israelite history, it becomes obvious that the extent to which men perpetrate violence on women also renders the men incapable of talking to each other. The lack of this fundamental act of political civility explains why no polity can be established at this juncture, because without the establishment of discourse, no community can cohere. Similarly, the cuts that the Levite inflicts on the body of his concubine prefigure the slashes to which the Israelites subject their own corporate body, depriving it of the power of speech and thereby transforming it into a headless monster capable only of violence.

The emphasis on discourse as central to the establishment of political community does not belittle the importance of a written legal code: the stability of a written legal code contributes an essential aspect of collective coherence that can override the vagaries of time and space. The point of these Biblical texts, however, is that rigid texts alone cannot produce a community vibrant enough to survive the various challenges to its existence. In various episodic narratives, and particularly in the Esther story, the Bible argues that it is the dialectical relationship between text and discourse—the dynamic generated among people and their various readings of the texts—that is the best guarantee of the vigorous existence of community.

By implication, the physical and moral disintegration of the Israelite body politic portrayed in the Book of Judges may be seen as an open condemnation of misogyny. Thus, the cut-up body of the concubine mirrors

42. Particularly noteworthy examples are Mieke Bal, *Death and Dissymmetry;* Athalya Brenner, *Judges;* J. Cheryl Exum, *Fragmented Women;* and Phyllis Trible, *Texts of Terror* (Philadelphia: Fortress, 1984).

43. Exum, *Fragmented Women,* 121–202.

44. See in this regard Carole Pateman's *The Disorder of Women* (Palo Alto: Stanford University Press, 1989), which analyzes the deeply rooted belief that women, largely because of their implication in romantic love and the family, are the source of the deep disorder with which they fundamentally imperil the rational arrangement of society as founded by men.

the disintegrating coherence of the Israelite body politic. In this narrative (the last one in the book), the exploitative inscription of narcissistic male violence directly on the bodies of women is not a solitary incident, reflecting a momentary lapse of decency or judgment (on the part of the Levite). Significantly, this action is proposed as a solution to what was viewed at the time as a problem of national proportions. Kidnapping the Shilohite maidens and forcing them into marriage with the remaining Benjaminite males is undertaken to prevent the tribe of Benjamin from dying out (which would have resulted in the fundamental alteration of the makeup of the Israelite community). Thus, the males in this narrative reduce the women to mute objects of male desire by writing on their bodies—by either physically dismembering them or forcing them to serve as vehicles for tribal propagation. In either case, writing functions as a destructive expression of what is otherwise a medium for human creativity.[45]

The Biblical text reflects this elliptically in its final comment on the concubine narrative: "In those days there was no king in Israel: each man would do what was right in his eyes" (Judg. 21:25). The multiple layers of irony that suffuse this verse—the fact that each man doing what is right in his own eyes really leads to moral anarchy, not dynamic or peaceful pluralism; the ostensibly sincere reference to a justice-imposing king inevitably recalls the actual history of Israelite kings, who rarely manage consistently to guarantee a fair system of justice for everyone—cast severe doubts on the contemporary moral integrity of, and even on the possibility of, a dynamic national existence for the Israelite nation. The subtle emphasis of each *man* acting according to what he *personally* finds acceptable hints at the source of the problem: by implication, the text accuses the Israelites of ignoring a Divinely mandated concept of justice. What makes this point more complex—at least as it is depicted in the text of Judges—is that the oppression of women mirrors the neglect of the Divine.[46]

45. Josef Stern, in his article on the symbolism of circumcision, depicts an interesting inversion of the oppressive "writing" on women's bodies. "Maimonides on the Covenant of Circumcision and the Unity of God," in *The Midrashic Imagination*, ed. Michael Fishbane (Albany: SUNY Press, 1993). Stern portrays circumcision in its Kabbalistic understanding as the inscription of the name of God on the human body. This inscription, in turn, serves as a dynamic reminder of the human capacity to elevate and transcend one's own existence. In a strikingly self-serving and corrupt version of the inscription of the name of God on their own bodies, the men in the Book of Judges project their own violence as an inscription on the bodies of their (female) victims.

46. To be sure, these episodes in the Book of Judges are not the only examples of men severely misreading women, and thus failing to understand the moral and political import of

The Book of Esther inverts the moral and political paralysis described at the end of the Book of Judges. Esther, in her own text, reorders the heretofore-negative legacy of her own Benjaminite tribe by endowing the national life of her people with moral and political coherence. In addition, unlike the women in the concubine in Gibeah incident, the central female protagonist in the Esther narrative refuses the personal status of victim. Instead, by personally entering into the political fray within the strange and hermetically sealed environment of the Persian court, Esther is instrumental in imagining a new method of salvation, constructing a coherent plan for its achievement, and institutionalizing social and religious practices that would perennially reconstitute community for her own people. As the acknowledged heroine of the Esther narrative and the preeminent woman in terms of social and political power within the Persian Empire, Esther is in a prime position to demonstrate the positive results that accrue when the voice of a woman is heeded. Taken together, the end of the Book of Judges and the Book of Esther demonstrate two aspects of the same truth: national salvation comes about when women's voices are heard. Ignoring women's cries—silent or not—comes at a grievous cost to both personal and national welfare.

The Metaphor of the Text: Violence and Identity

Esther's letters address more than the splintered and far-flung Jewish community in Persia. By mandating these performative structures in perpetuity (Esther 9:28), Esther sets up the framework for the continuity of dynamic communal feeling. She knows from her experience that the strengthening of community is the best way to combat the unfriendly social and political surroundings of exile over which the Jews, as a group,

---

the challenges that they face. Another such case is found in the interaction between Eli and Hannah. The circumstances of their engagement is Hannah's silent prayer, which leads the high priest to classify her as a drunk. Eli's misinterpretation here is fundamental, as he literally misreads the privileged sacral text (the Urim v'Tumim), which, in the Midrashic reading, lights up the letters to describe Hannah as "proper" (*k'sh'r*) but which Eli misunderstands as "drunken" (*sh'k'r*). In the end, of course, Eli corrects his misapprehension and correctly predicts Hannah's future bearing of a son who, although as yet unbeknownst to him, would foretell the passage of power from his own family to what would eventually become a monarchic dynasty. This theme of Eli's severe misreading is carried through the narrative when it describes his weak and belated attempts to correct the gross misbehavior of his sons during Temple service (1 Sam. 2:22–25).

have no control. By utilizing metaphor to engage her own circumstances and devise creative solutions to the political challenges that she faces, Esther celebrates the evanescent nature of meaning and definition, realizing that this can turn problems into solutions. Esther discerns that reading life and its texts metaphorically clarifies how negative situations may be reversed and solutions effected (9:1, 22).[47]

This understanding comes to Esther not only from her own tribal misreading (the malefactors portrayed in the concubine in Gibeah episode are Benjaminites, from Esther's own tribe), but also as a result of a more distant tale, whose ramifications and traditions may well have structured Esther's comprehension of the importance of text and the centrality of metaphor to interpretation: the story of Jephtah's daughter from the Book of Judges. This is the narrative of a girl sacrificed because of her father's rash vow to God while praying for victory against the enemies of the Israelites. The bare bones of this story seem to have no connection at all to textual interpretation. The traditions that have accrued to this text, however, reflect some of the concerns that appear to motivate Esther in her more creative approach to textual interpretation.

In amplifying the tensions that surround Jephtah as he insists on fulfilling the imperatives of his vow, the Midrash supposes a series of dialogues between him and his daughter, in which she begs him to interpret the demands of his vow metaphorically rather than literally.[48] For Jephtah's daughter, the interpretative method utilized is a matter of her own survival. In the text of the Midrash, Jephtah remains unconvinced; in the broader sense, he cannot read, and his interpretation subsequently costs lives. By contrast, Esther's heightened awareness of the costs of interpretation, rooted in her own national culture, is focused on the fact that no interpretation is absolute, that interpretation can call reality itself into question. As the events in the Book of Esther demonstrate, things are not necessarily what they first appear to be, and one never can truly tell who is who.

47. In Handelman's words, "The boundaries between text and interpretation are fluid" (*Slayers of Moses*, 41).

48. This is the Midrashic reading: "[When Jephtah pronounced his vow], God was angry at him and said, 'If a dog or a pig or a camel had exited the house, would he have brought it before Me?' Therefore He prepared his [Jephtah's] daughter . . . and when he [Jephtah] wanted to sacrifice her, she cried and said, 'Did God write in the Torah that humans should be sacrificed? Rather, it specifies animal sacrifice and not human sacrifice.' [Jephtah] said, 'But I swore.' She answered, '[Is every vow to be taken literally?] Jacob swore to tithe everything to God, but he did not tithe his children!' . . . But he refused to listen to her" (Tanhuma Behukotai 5).

Despite the previous history of her nation/tribe in misinterpreting text, and her own contemporary experience with Haman's deadly manipulation of text in the Persian Empire, Esther does not give up on the ability of text to constitute meaning or even, in practical terms, to give coherence to communal life by establishing standards that create common practices and social cohesion. Instead, in her writing, Esther restructures the text. First, she transforms the text from a closed document into one open to reinterpretation.[49] Second, by using the text to mandate interpersonal and material exchange, Esther transforms the text into a basis for dynamic personal and social interaction, specifically reflected in the mandates to commemorate national survival by ongoing tangible practices of friendship and charity.[50] With this, Esther provides the model for re-presenting and creating community anew.

While Esther consciously attempts to reconstitute text as a life-giving instrument instead of a death-defining imperative, she cannot ignore the very real proclivities of texts to perpetuate evil. The multiple and therefore ambiguous nature of metaphor, which allows it to imagine answers to complex problems, also gives rise to difficulties in the course of realizing these solutions. The very flexibility of metaphor often means that the various solutions inherent in its sweep can contradict the fundamental premises constituting its structure. For example, the Book of Esther's denouement utilizes the mechanism of doubling in a way that problematizes the difference between good and evil, and even calls into question the moral value of maintaining national identity.

The ambiguous and doubling nature of metaphor is particularly evident in the introduction of violence into the conclusion of the Esther tale, where it is presented by Ahaseurus as the solution for the beleaguered Jews in the Persian Empire to overcome their enemies.[51] Coming as it does

49. As we have seen, Esther does not annul Ahaseurus's decree. Rather, she adds to and, by implication, interprets it. In this way, she manages to transform the essence of the text—from an immutable dead letter to a document offering dynamism and options to heretofore-rigid political structures—while still technically remaining within the bounds of legally sanctioned textual activity.

50. Esther 9:22. Cf. Susan Handelman, *The Slayers of Moses*, especially 37–42, where Handelman analyzes the (Hebrew) Biblical concept of text as life enhancing rather than life circumscribing.

51. Ahaseurus's ineptitude in dealing with difference is implicitly contrasted to other Biblical kings—such as Solomon—who efficiently harnessed the talents of different peoples and transferred populations in the service of large political/economic enterprises (1 Kings 5:27–33). To be sure, these projects had negative (political) consequences of their own (at least for

to counter the horrific implications of Haman's proposed ethnic cleansing and religious genocide, this proposal may be viewed as ineffective and even ironic. Instead of rejecting violence, whose introduction constitutes the central political and human (survival) dilemma for the Jews of the Persian Empire, Ahaseurus proudly (and magnanimously!) gives the Jews the same killing rights that he had already given their enemies. The doubtful moral or even political value of such mass killings to the stability of his empire does not seem to trouble him. Many modern critics have argued also that the fighting that ends the dramatic arc of the Book of Esther thus provides no resolution at all to the narrative's moral dilemma: the structure and justification of power through selective killings.[52] This point becomes

---

Solomon's dynasty; cf. 1 Kings 11:1–43), but nothing that approached the moral extremity or heinousness of ethnic/religious genocide.

52. Elliot Horowitz's *Reckless Rites* (Princeton: Princeton University Press, 2006) is one work that views the Biblical description of the violence at the end of the Book of Esther as being in the nature of a celebration (the book then goes on to describe and assess the thematic of violence as expressed in Jewish history [from pre-medieval times onward]), implicitly arguing that the book (in tandem with other Biblical texts) glorifies this violence. Horowitz quotes approvingly (the Jewish) Claude Montefiore's 1896 negative description of the Jews' battle against their enemies, cited at the end of the Book of Esther, as a "massacre of unresisting Gentiles" (quoted in *Reckless Rites,* 29). Horowitz also cites negative Christian assessments in much the same tone (the reference here is to the Reverend Adeney's remarks on the "savagery" of the Jews' actions, cited in *Reckless Rites,* 28). In addition, Horowitz also analyzes the historical development of the (artistic) depictions of the hangings of Haman and his sons, narrated in the Book of Esther; he concludes that the existence of these depictions is a function of the varying sensitivities of the Jews, in different historical periods, to the severity and suffering of this method of enforced death. Thus, Horowitz writes, "Jewish artists working during the interwar years rarely depicted the hanging of Haman, and none . . . the hanging of his sons" (102). Regarding the absence of illustrations of hanging in editions of the Book of Esther published in the United States in the post–World War II period, Horowitz theorizes that this may be due to the desire (of the editors/publishers of the period) to distance themselves from the specter of black lynchings in the South (106).

A few points regarding scholarly textual interpretation must be noted. First, the reception of a text over centuries does not, in and of itself, furnish proof regarding the tone or contents of that work. Jew and Gentile alike may well have read the Book of Esther as endorsing violence, but that conclusion reflects more on the reader than on the text itself. As noted earlier in this essay, men have been (purposefully?) misreading women and their texts for millennia. In the situation described in the Book of Esther, as the text itself makes abundantly clear, royal decrees are by definition irrevocable (8:5). This means that even the death of Haman does not remove the need of the Jews to arrange for their own robust defense, as the decree engineered by Haman (cleverly) outlives the personal fate of the prime minister himself (cf. 8:3): the diktat calls for all peoples of the Persian Empire to "be ready for this day" (3:14), to "annihilate all Jews . . . to take their spoils for plunder" (3:13). Even with the death of Haman, then, vigorous self-defense on the part of the Jewish population of the Persian Empire is vital to their continued physical survival. The text notes repeatedly that the Jews gathered in self-defense to "lay hands on/defend their lives against those who sought ill for them" (8:11; see also 9:2, 16).

more acute when considered in the context of the plurality of nationalities making up the Persian Empire, all of whom insist on living as separately identifiable groups (Esther 1:22). Moreover, in terms of the broader moral issues raised by the Esther narrative, one can question the moral justification of persistently maintaining a national identity if, in the end, violence becomes necessary for its survival; thus, the separate national entity can come to resemble the very enemy who had aimed to annihilate that identity.

For those critics of the text who condemn the Persian Jews for engaging in the same violence as their enemies, it is important to remember the valence of Ahaseurus's legal text: because ancient Persian law (as described in the text) prohibits the rescission of any royal edict (Esther 8:8), the victimized Jews in the Persian Empire would still be subject to the murderous impulses of whoever chose to rise against them on the specified dates (2:12–14). In this tortuous situation, the only way for the Jews to survive is to defend themselves, even with violence, against those enemies whose permission to murder the Jews had never been (and never could, by royal edict, be) withdrawn.

The ambiguity of metaphor means that solutions hold negative as well as positive implications. The necessity of the Persian Jews at all to engage in violence points to both the messiness of politics (enabled in this case by the deep-seated anti-Jewish feeling that seems to have existed in large areas of the ancient Persian Empire) and the fact that real-life events do not always end with perfect moral closure. Importantly, the text reveals that

---

Finally, regarding the depictions of the hangings of Haman and his sons, Horowitz conflates the two events. In the text itself, these are presented separately, because they represent different aspects of the narrative. Haman's hanging is directly ordered by King Ahaseurus and is depicted by the Biblical text as a matter of dramatic and moral closure: upon learning that Haman had planned to hang Mordecai, who had saved the king from the nefarious designs of the assassins Bigthan and Teresh, Ahaseurus orders that Haman himself be hanged forthwith (Esther 7:8–9). This swift reversal of fortune, central to the denouement of the plot, is typical of the elaborate twists and turns of the Esther narrative, and so it is understandable that this scene is often depicted in illustrated form. (In this context, similar prominence is also traditionally given to artistic depictions of Haman's crestfallen parading of Mordecai's triumphal procession through the streets of Shushan [6:11–13], but Horowitz unaccountably fails to take notice of this phenomenon.) By contrast, the hanging of Haman's sons does not occur in the context of a death decree. The Book of Esther recounts that Haman's sons are killed in battle (9:5–10), and it is only later that their bodies are hanged on the gallows. The symbolism inherent in hanging the bodies of one's enemies in the time of war is clear: it is a sign of victory (albeit an unappetizing one, to modern readers). In the context of the Biblical narrative, one could even say that this depiction of clear victory is actually a signal that the time for violence is approaching its close (the Book of Esther recounts that fighting lasts only one more day and is limited to Shushan; 9:12–15).

throughout this process, the Persian Jews remain aware of the ambiguity of the metaphor within which they operate. This is signaled in the text with the notation that even as the Jews defend themselves against their enemies, they steadfastly refuse to touch any of the enemy's booty (Esther 9:10, 15, 16). While this may seem of no great moment to the modern reader,[53] this is a point of great cultural significance, particularly within the provenance of the Biblical text. In the ancient world, stripping the enemy of his spoils was an accepted part of the conduct of war, even though Jacob had frowned on such behavior when manifested by his sons Simeon and Levi in their raid on Shekhem. In fact, it is this that causes him to curse them on his deathbed (Gen. 34:30; 38:5–7). That the Jews in Persia choose deliberately and concretely to repudiate this particular ancestral behavior, deriving no profit at all from the conduct of war (and, arguably, not even meeting their expenses in the campaign), is material evidence that the Jews do not succumb to the morally ambivalent opportunities available to them through the ambiguous doubling of Ahaseurus's "solution." With their morally calibrated actions, the Persian Jews combat the uncertainty of doubling by insisting on actualizing only its morally positive options. By extension, one may conclude that it is similarly feasible to combat the uncertainty that seems emblematic of human existence by consciously harnessing the power of metaphor to analyze and come up with novel solutions to ever-mutating challenges. In *The Reason of Metaphor*, Donald Miller analyzes metaphor and metaphorization in just such a way to reimagine modern social relationships and political solutions.[54]

53. Interestingly enough, while contemporary thinkers might want to claim that modern sensibilities are above crass looting, particularly in the course of ideologically motivated warfare, the ongoing judicial cases involving artworks wantonly seized from civilians by Nazi soldiers and leadership during World War II, only now being returned to (surviving heirs of) their rightful owners, give the lie to this conceit.

54. In *The Reason of Metaphor* (New York: Sage, 1992), Donald Miller writes of the contribution that metaphorical thinking can make to current political practice. After detailing how political differences in the approach to solving particular problems may be traced to the different metaphors utilized to view the problem (the point here is that the metaphor in play ("metaphors are negotiated" [110]) helps define the problem which, in turn, suggests the logical solution), Miller has this to say on the nature of political leadership: "The role of the 'wise' social policymaker . . . is to generate metaphors that not only integrate the conflicting situation, but that also allow some favourable redefinition by each party of its value position" (112). On the nature of existence and politics, Miller writes, "Relationships between Selves and Others . . . [conceptualized in metaphor] . . . are interminable. . . . Politics could be described as whatever constitutes the play between certain selves and certain others. . . . This critical function . . . [of metaphorization] . . . [involves] . . . asking fresh questions, imagining new associations . . . [and is] . . . engaged in a politics of irresolution" (253, 254, 257, 258).

The narrative in the Book of Esther emphasizes the positive aspect of the everlasting potential reversibility that is the hallmark of human existence. At the same time, however, life's ephemeral nature, exposed by the metaphor, has frightening implications. The very text that had previously appeared to anchor the world of meaning now is revealed as the very element that may unsettle its foundations. Particularly in situations of exile, like those described in the Book of Esther, this uncertainty of identity can appear scary. After all, firm identity is precisely what prevents undifferentiated assimilation into the host country. Peter Mechanic has pointed out the historical aspect of recognizable identity's paradoxical quality: while assimilation had been much sought after by the Israelites prior to their exile, this very assimilation is dreaded by those same Israelites when they are in exile.[55] In other words, once they are the unassimilable "outsiders" in a strange society, the Israelites fear losing this special status because it would deprive them of their national identity. This interpretation problematizes the desirability of "fitting in" and demonstrates that sameness is not always an unmitigated good. At the same time, this new realization can foster a sense of hope, which is, paradoxically, a function of this very same reviled/treasured outsider status. Because the Israelites are constituted as a nation even before their possession of a homeland, the fact that exile forcibly renders them outsiders need not imperil their future national existence. The Jews' status as strangers enables them perennially to "return."[56]

55. Peter Mechanic traces the phenomenon of assimilation to the traditional Israelite position as "outsiders" even in their national homeland. He notes, too, that their Prophets roundly excoriate the Israelites for this desire. "Outsiders or Insiders," in *The Other in Jewish Thought and History*, ed. Laurence J. Silberstein and Robert L. Cohn (New York: NYU Press, 1994), 52–53.

56. This same paradox informs the complex verse in Leviticus, when God addresses the Israelites, telling them, "For you are strangers with Me" (25:23). The notion of founding a national polity (the Land of Israel) on the basis of mutual strangeness prevents the dehumanization of one or another "disfavored" group. Paradoxically, suspending all citizens in the category of "strangeness" keeps alive the humanity of all, as no one can lay claim to a privileged state of greater importance or meaning.

It is possible to view that "return" as a perennial movement, always undertaken but never fully achieved. In that vein, certain readers of the Esther narrative have claimed that the foreign setting of the story, as well as the lack of any sustained effort or even mention of return to the Land of Israel, reveals a favorable view of exile as the proper venue for the Jewish nation. On the other hand, the very tentativeness of the political position of the Jews—Esther may well be queen, and Mordecai may find success in the end as prime minister, but they hold these positions entirely at the pleasure of a foreign king not responsible to them—is something against which Esther's recourse to politics constantly fights. The fact that the insecurity of life lived in exile reflects the tentativeness of the human condition in general does not make exile the preferred condition for the ultimate actualization of human potential. Similarly, the

As developed in the Book of Esther, metaphor has implications beyond the time-bound strictures of politics to encompass the larger scope of history, and time beyond history. In *The Exile of the Word*, André Neher has written about the implicit silence emanating from the metaphor (although Neher himself does not specifically classify this silence as an inherent part of metaphor), figuring it as the space of existential choice that allows the human being to define and extend the relationship between him/herself and God. For Neher, it is in the answer to the silence—or, as the Book of Esther reveals, in the perception of and reaction to the metaphor—that our humanity is revealed.[57]

The Pleasure of Her Text

The recalibration of the concepts of outsider and insider enabled by exile is an extension of Esther's renewed conception of text.[58] By rethinking the boundaries of text, Esther enables words to both function as deeds and create a reality of their own. At the same time, she makes her people envision the dynamic solutions that can be found even in negative situations embodying absence, like exile. By valorizing the literary trope of metaphor, Esther draws her reading public into the text and thus dynamizes it, making it perennially relevant.

To be sure, the material realities of Esther's own life do not allow her to escape completely into the liberating and polysemic potentialities of the text. For all her implied power and potential of access as queen, Esther (like her predecessor, Vashti) holds her position completely at the king's pleasure.[59] In the final analysis, Esther is a woman caught in the strictures that empire places on all its subjects, most especially its women. In *Torrid Zones*, Felicity Nussbaum elaborates on the ideological (in the form of domesticity) and the sexual (in terms of procreation) submission of women

---

fact that exile has something of value to impart to the Jewish people is not the same thing as claiming that exile represents the best actualization of their national existence in perpetuity.

57. Cf. "Silence as Energy," 91–137; "Silence as a Challenge," 141–239; and especially "The Variations of 'Yes' to Silence," 171–209, all in *The Exile of the Word* (Philadelphia: Jewish Publication Society, 1981).

58. This title of this section is borrowed from Alice Bach, "The Pleasure of Her Text," in *The Pleasure of Her Text*, ed. Alice Bach (Philadelphia: Trinity Press International, 1990).

59. That is why even after years of marriage to Ahaseurus, Esther fears entering the king's court without a prior invitation (Esther 4:11).

that is the foundation of the (masculine) propagation of empire.[60] Still, while Esther never forgets her "place" in relation to the absolute power of her husband, the king, it is also significant that she manages to subvert that power in her own way: in that context, it is particularly telling that the Esther narrative records no progeny that she bears to Ahaseurus.[61]

In the end, the ultimate masquerade is the one perpetrated by the text itself. Disguised as a rich tale of court intrigue, it reveals itself actually to be centered on the most basic issues of human existence and identity. The very pleasure of the text—its air of mystery and magical resolutions—is intimately connected to both its style and its purpose. Derrida has written that metaphor sets up a situation in which the recognition of sameness yields the experience of pleasure, although it is important to note that the very idea of Derrida's deconstructive techniques problematizes the notion of uninflected "sameness."[62] This is a point of some literary importance, because providing pleasure in the narrative ensures maintaining audience interest in the text. But the textual pleasure experienced by the audience also generates a reality of its own: the creation of a community as it reads and interprets texts. In valorizing this recognition—or re-cognition, which is to say, rethinking—Esther re-visions the text as the template for the creation of a community of meaning and discourse: the text serves as the ongoing structure for concrete legal standards, as well as providing a space for dynamic personal interaction with and re-presentation of community.

60. "I argue here that a particular kind of national imperative to control women's sexuality and fecundity emerged when the increasing demands of trade and colonization required a large, able-bodied citizenry, and that women's reproductive labor was harnessed to that task . . . the domestic virtue demanded . . . ensured the legitimacy of family and property . . . but regulated sexuality . . . was often an attempt to define and legislate . . . 'colonial domination.'" Felicity Nussbaum, *Torrid Zones* (Baltimore: Johns Hopkins University Press, 1995), 1–2. Also, underlining the instrumental function of childbearing in the imperial context, Nussbaum writes, "Increasing the number of children will . . . build the empire" (27).

61. To be sure, other interpretative traditions do attribute some offspring to Esther and Ahaseurus. Tellingly enough, however, this progeny is identified with Darius, the Persian king who officially permits the Jews of the time to rebuild their Temple (Leviticus Rabbah 13:5), which implies the subversion of imperial uniformity to permit (some measure of) authentic religious self-expression on the part of a distinct minority grouping within the empire.

62. Jacques Derrida, "White Mythology," 38. In this sense, Paul Ricoeur highlights a different aspect of metaphor and the "jouissance" (to borrow a term from Irigaray) encountered when one attains this "recognition": "If metaphor . . . consists . . . in reducing the *shock* engendered by two *incompatible ideas*, then it is in the *reduction of this gap or difference* that resemblance plays a role . . . [and] elicits a veritable creation of meaning" ("Metaphor and Symbol," 51–52; emphasis added). It is important to remember that the gap between differences is reduced, not obliterated.

To be sure, it may be argued that the Book of Esther does not provide a fixed political algorithm to resolve imperial conduct, where tensions may arise between the values promoting the moral cohesion of empire and those providing enough space for the expression of different views. (This issue is not altogether divorced from current debates on whether "liberal" ideologies provide enough common moral ground to enable a country to cohere, and whether "conservative" ideologies are able to promote enough freedom to allow human proclivities, and not just the realities of power, to express themselves.) The very lack of uniform solution, however, may be understood as emphasizing the need to focus on the antinomies of each circumstance in order to negotiate a workable solution fitting the particular issues at hand. In this sense, the Book of Esther's narrow specificity to its particular circumstances in the Persian Empire serves as an ideological warning to heed the particulars of practical possibilities. In this connection, the position of Isaiah Berlin on the relationship between the experience of difference and the truth of absolute values is illuminating. In "Alleged Relativism in Eighteenth-century Thought," he insists that pluralism can exist within a framework of absolute values.[63] Similarly, more than any particular reading given to a specific text, it is through the act of seeking meaning through the word, valorizing the polysemy of the word, and dynamically acting on the word, that Esther reimagines the salvation of her people.

---

63. See *The Crooked Timber of Humanity* (Princeton: Princeton University Press, 1990), 81.

CONCLUSION

In *Imagined Communities*, Benedict Anderson breaks new ground by suggesting that the (modern) idea of the nation (and national identity) is a construct of the imagination rather than a strict expression of an organic tie to land or history. To be sure, "imagination" is not as transparent a concept as Anderson's description might make it appear. The imagination itself is socially constructed, and its opacity is not easily assimilated by the inhabitants of the more complex modern world in which we live. More than ever before, we are aware that closely held truths, even memory itself, can be manipulated. Still, despite the imagination's lack of hermetic sealant, the acknowledged contribution of the imagination to the conception of nationhood opens up an important aspect of national identity. It emphasizes that nationality is a negotiated idea, one subject to variegated influences and changes. The idea of the nation—what it means, how it coheres, whom it includes—is in constant flux.[1]

Although the diversity attributed to the idea of national identity gives it a distinctly modern (as opposed to the nineteenth-century organic) cast, an important origin of this idea can itself be traced back to the most ancient

---

1. Certain writers have taken issue with the notion of "imagined" communities, understanding this term to relativize the fundamental issue of national identity; thus, David Hazony in "Crimes Against the Humanities," *Azure* 27 (Winter 2007) claims that "imagined community," in the opinion of its adherents, denotes "an artificial construct with no genuine basis in history" (38). As demonstrated above, however, the imagination involved in "imagined community" is itself nuanced and must be interrogated; that is to say, the notion of "imagination" is not transparent and can be subject to an infinitude of power manipulations, with created memories leading to wars of hatred and destruction.

of documents. Through its presentation of the etiology of many different nations, the Bible alerts us to the fact that there is no one model for
national identity. The sense of belonging, the idea of community, adheres
to no single prefabricated formula. Nations are defined not just by history,
geographic propinquity, or even cultural affinity.[2] Instead, in the pages of
the Bible, nationhood is represented as a concept that arises after the dis-
missal of humanity from Paradise and the subsequent Divine upending of
what might be termed humanity's largest architectural project (of that era,
at any rate). In the Bible's account, nationhood represents cleavage in both
senses of that term: humanity is torn asunder (they no longer universally
communicate), but at the same time, they cling more closely to the frag-
ment of humankind that they deem to be "their" own nation.

The Bible adds a further complication to this picture with the formation of another nation, the Israelites, whose identity is also described as a
spiritual endeavor. Interestingly enough, however, the Bible's comprehension of that project does not portray this specific nation solely in terms
of the Divine concept of its mission. Instead, the Bible depicts Israelite
nationhood as a constructed identity negotiated over time. As explored
throughout the pages of this book, the sense of the nation goes through
many iterations. For a dynamic sense of the nation to exist, the people who
make up the nation must contribute to the content and structure of that
idea. Often, it is the forgotten, disrespected groups or individuals who
make the most significant contributions in this regard. Importantly, politics in the Hebrew Bible is not limited just to leaders who utilize this arena
to display their own visions of power and possibilities. Instead, politics is
viewed as the space in which all people—rich as well as poor; those with
power, and those without; those traditionally ignored, as well as those hail-
ing from respected families; the citizen as well as the stranger—express
their senses of justice and visions of rectitude for the polity. At times, the
people and the leaders must in fact remake that nation's identity.

But how is this identity to be refashioned? Which good is primary?
Whose happiness is to be preferred? In *The Republic*, Plato famously contrasts individual and social happiness, which are presented as (at least

2. In "Is There a Historic Right to the Land of Israel?" Chaim Gans argues that "historical rights . . . [themselves] cannot justify the right to territorial sovereignty." *Azure* 27 (Winter 2007): 83. He also qualifies the role of history in determining general location, as well as
including a notion of substantive justice to determine the allocation of territory to landless
nations (see especially 84).

potentially) antithetical to each other.[3] Alternatively, in defining politics
as the product of constant conversation between people and their leaders,
and among the people themselves, the Hebrew Bible eschews the dual-
ism of classical Greek political thought in order to forge its own vision of
the polis as a moral field of dynamic personal and social challenge. Thus,
the Hebrew Bible does not view politics as the arena that pits the individual and society at inevitable odds with each other. More complicatedly,
throughout its different narrative sequences, the Hebrew Bible uses the
individual and social spheres as spaces that mutually encourage noncon-
formist thinking. Thus, for example, Ruth uses her personal situation to
think through the dilemmas of difference in the social setting, never forgetting the threats and challenges that difference can pose to social cohesion. By the same token, the last section of the Book of Ruth informs us
of the central role that difference plays in the political development of the
Israelite nation.

The care with which the development of the political arena is depicted
in the Hebrew Bible demonstrates that even earlier than the era of the
ancient Greek political theorists, the writers of the Hebrew Bible already
understood politics as the forum that allows the expression of the highest
level of moral development. For the Biblical writers, the quintessential
humanity that is expressed in the arena of politics is not (just) a function
of politics as the site of agency and power, although power and conscious
agency are inherent parts of every political scenario. In the narratives depicted by the Hebrew Bible, politics emerges as uniquely human by providing a space in which all human beings are free to express their desires
about power and their conceptions of justice. As the Biblical narrative
demonstrates, choices about power do more than affect social realities. In
addition, these choices influence the moral quality and content of individual lives. This, in turn, affects the community as a whole no less than their
rulers. For the Hebrew Bible, politics morally defines both the individual
and the social spheres within which it operates. This means that politics in
the Bible functions as a space that both enables and demands the full realization and responsibility of moral choice. Consequently, there is no obvious
checklist of political desiderata in the Biblical text: politics is seen fundamentally as a range of options to be achieved rather than an organizational

---

3. In *The Republic*, Plato utilizes the metaphor of a statue to argue that individual happiness
has little or no moral standing when compared to the well-being of society as a whole (110).

chart to be imposed. As a result, the minutiae of political structures are left indeterminately and frustratingly vague.[4]

The lack of emphasis on political institutions and organizations in the Bible explains why so many of the Bible's political narratives occur in the absense of an independent Israelite polity. In the Biblical text, politics preexists and survives the nation that it helps define. Thus, Joseph and Esther are manifestly political figures in both structure and content. The strong moral component of the Bible's political understanding also helps the modern reader comprehend why the Bible, despite the best efforts of some of its most fervent promoters, persists in never offering a formulaic solution for achieving the "best" polity. The Bible's emphasis on the ever-changing notions of political discourse, and the people's own evolving role in its development, reveal that politics in the Biblical view is an ongoing process of moral challenge and dynamism. Simplistic answers may appear obvious and readily applicable, but in the Biblical depiction, they inevitably fail: one may argue that the monarchy under Solomon represents the height of Israelite moral and political achievement, but Solomon gives way to the pettiness of Rehoboam and the rebellion of Jeroboam. Ironically, both of these kings of the divided Israelite kingdom end up manipulating the actual symbols of moral attainment in their ongoing efforts to maximize their own political power (see 1 Kings 12:4–14, 20, 25–33).

The Bible demonstrates that the best characterization of the nation is not one confined to a caste-driven portrait of uniqueness. Rather, the best definition is broad enough to encompass all the people that inhabit the nation's precincts. The myriad individuals that cohere within a larger concept of common purpose form the nexus of a nation. In this sense, thinking about the self is one way to come to grips with what constitutes the essence of national identity. In effect, then, nations evolve in tandem with their people. Put more succinctly, nationhood is an ongoing project. Ultimately, nations succeed to the extent that they express the humanity of the people that constitute them. It is the people's ongoing challenge to exercise their humanity in both their individual and social capacities so that the nation becomes the highest expression of their humanity, instead of, as has so often been the case historically, its lowest caricature.

---

4. In *The Poetics of Biblical Narrative*, Meir Sternberg makes a similar observation on the moral indeterminacy of the Biblical text, arguing that it makes the text morally demanding and thus perennially alive for its reader (179).

Eschewing a more precise description of nationality that might be more convenient, albeit constricting, the Bible's "estranged" sense of nationality is able to evoke the complex and changing sense of nationhood that best captures the highest human aspirations for political life. Importantly, the Bible's evocation of how national identity has been constructed by different groups in different times and places is not itself free of moral or political implications. As the Bible presents it, any group may decide to call itself a nation, but the real challenge is to maintain that identity over the vicissitudes of time, place, and fortune. This is not just a theoretical issue: one of the contemporary challenges to international stability remains the presence of "failed states" in various parts of the world.

In order to understand why a state has "failed," it helps to know how a state may succeed. Here, the Bible does offer one persistent theme: nations cohere—they embody the unity claimed by their title—if they establish a vibrant national discourse. This is particularly evident with regard to the Israelites, the nation most closely examined in the Biblical text. Meaningful dialogue cannot be imposed from the top, and false discourse dies without real impetus from the people on whose behalf individual leaders may claim to conduct it (this is a major theme of the concubine in Gibeah narrative). The importance of ongoing national discourse is so central to the Bible's understanding of national coherence that God is portrayed as acceding to the establishment of the Israelite monarchy simply because it represents, at the time, the concerted desire of the Israelite people (even though both God and His prophet, Samuel, consider this form of government morally deleterious).

Thus, we see that despite the Bible's presentation of reservations about one or another leader or method of governance, prime moral value still rests on the establishment of political discourse and the ensuing unity and quality of communal life (this is the dominant theme of the moral reckoning of the Tower of Babel episode). For the Bible, issues regarding the style of governance—in particular, the details of the arrangements of power that so bestir polities today all over the globe—are secondary to the ability of a political society to maintain an inclusive conversation about both its deepest values and its projected aims and actions. Thus, the Bible's narratives about establishing discourse occur in different places and in diverse times, almost irrespective of whether there is an independent polity that can act on the results of that discourse (significantly, the events of and the dialogue established within the Book of Esther take place during the course of a seemingly endless exile). In the Bible's view, questions of political power are subordinate to issues of political vision: the presence of dynamic discourse precedes and ultimately trumps the issue of brute dominance.

The question of political vision invariably leads to the question of how far that vision extends. Indeed, part of the complexity of the Biblical understanding of a justifiable and coherent politics is that the Biblical text persistently interrogates accepted notions of just what the polity is able to accomplish. In the Biblical text, the fact that nationhood is predicated on the problematic nature of the crisis of the Tower of Babel means that politics represents an ambiguity of possibilities: it always teeters on the blade of cleavage, in both senses of that term. Politics represents both unity (of the specific nation in its borders) and disunity (at the price of keeping all others out). But as subsequent Biblical narratives also make clear, the people regarded as "outsiders" are often really the ones at the very heart of society (this teaching represents both the opportunity and the tragedy of the concubine in Gibeah episode). Paradoxically, for the Bible, the best opportunities of politics make themselves available when the open discourse that activates them remains aware of its own animating dialectic, containing at once energizing and destructive implications. Politics, for the Bible, is a dangerous enterprise, due less to the power positions involved than to the risks of abandoning moral coherence.

The Bible derives a very costly and complex political lesson from this perception. This lesson is complex because it seems to muddy the waters of what can appear, at first, to be a very simple and clear choice; and it is costly because of the price it exacts from the people who ignore its challenge. A polity cannot cohere either morally or practically if it is based only on a self-contained (ethnic) and self-serving concept of nationality. From the Bible's moral perspective, a nation that couches its identity *only* on the sense of its own exclusivity (which can also extend itself to include the justifications of power-driven realpolitik), by definition, cannot engage in the open discourse required by a dynamic sense of national identity, which includes respect for others and inclusion of difference. Thus, in the Biblical view, constructing a polity based only on exclusion is in effect putting a lie into practice, because it claims to build community without providing for the real unity enabled by a full and open discourse—one that consists of not only a group of people and their imitative clones, but also those who are demonstrably Other. In addition, on the functional level, the Bible demonstrates that a nation characterized only by sameness and exclusion will inevitably fail to cohere, because nations whose people do not talk to each other are fated, one way or another, to disappear. For the Bible, politics exemplifies the moral and practical imperative of valorizing discourse. Put more simply, people must recognize each other in order to be able to talk to each other if they, singly and communally, are to survive.

To be sure, the Bible recognizes that the nurturing of discourse is not a simple process or an easily obtainable goal. The maintenance of discourse is a labor that, by definition, is never finished: the challenges of discourse alter over time and demand constant recalibration in order to keep the people aware of the new situations they must confront jointly if they are to grow together as a nation. Regardless of the actual structures of power, sustaining dynamic discourse means that the nation's leaders must uphold a strong current of responsiveness to the people if that discourse is to remain meaningful (a similar point is made in *Antigone*, a work written at a time historically close to the Biblical era, where Creon's failure to do this ultimately delegitimizes his rule). The validation of democratic values, of abiding moral significance in the Biblical narrative of power, runs deeper than the particulars of the titles given to the individual leaders in power.

The centrality of political discourse to the creation of national identity is a logical prelude to the Bible's view of leadership. Leadership is not a function of brute force. While people in power can dominate their subjects, this alone, in the Bible's estimation, does not transform them into legitimate leaders. Instead, the Bible offers observations about power that are open-ended, and thus troublesome, because they are not neatly packaged solutions to the pressing travails of politics. In the end, the Bible forces each individual, irrespective of status and function, to think about what constitutes authentic discourse, so that all people in concert may arrive at a language of political dialogue that expresses their respective essences as separate individualities as well as their common membership in the same corporate body.

The narratives of power in the Bible reveal that the space of the political can reflect, as expressed in *Leviathan*, the domain of Divine creativity within practical limitations, but also the ever-expanding sphere of human imagination and possibilities.[5] The ancient Biblical narratives about nationality and establishing communal discourse are not just stories of a bygone

---

5. "Nature (the Art whereby God hath made and governes the World) is by the *Art* of man, as in many other things, so in this also imitated, that it can make an Artificial Animal . . . for by Art is created that great LEVIATHAN called a COMMON-WEALTH, or STATE." Thomas Hobbes, "Introduction," in *Leviathan*, ed. C. B. Macpherson (New York: Penguin, 1968), 81.

era. Although current insular readings may choose to interpret Biblical theories of governance as espousing just one approach to politics, scholars as far back as the fifteenth century (e.g., Abarbanel) and as close to our own national heritage as Thomas Paine (in *Common Sense*) and the Congregational minister Samuel Langdon (in "A Government Corrupted by Vice") read the plain meaning of the Biblical text as suggesting a far more complex understanding of the requirements of legitimate government. Read dynamically, the Bible forms the key to help grapple with questions centering on the very deepest concerns of security and freedom that continue to challenge the lives of all on this planet.

BIBLIOGRAPHY

Abarbanel [Isaac Abrabanel]. *Commentary on the Bible*. Tel Aviv: HaPoel HaMizrahi, 1979.

Abrahams, Roger D., and Alan Dundes. "Riddles." In *Folklore and Folklife*, edited by Richard M. Dorson. Chicago: University of Chicago Press, 1972.

Ackerman, James S. "Joseph, Judah, and Jacob." In *Literary Interpretations of Biblical Narratives*, edited by Kenneth R. R. Gros Louis. Vol. 2. Nashville: Abingdon, 1992.

Ages, Arnold. "Why Didn't Joseph Call Home?" *Bible Review* (August 1993): 42–46.

Alter, Robert. *The Art of Biblical Narrative*. New York: Basic, 1981.

———. *The Art of Biblical Poetry*. New York: Basic, 1985.

———. "Samson Without Folklore." In *Text and Tradition*, edited by Susan Niditch. Atlanta: Scholars Press, 1990.

Alter, Robert, and Frank Kermode. *The Literary Guide to the Bible*. Cambridge, Mass.: Harvard University Press, 1990.

Amit, Yairah. *The Book of Judges: The Art of Editing*. Boston: Brill, 1999.

———. *History and Ideology: An Introduction to Historiography in the Hebrew Bible*. Sheffield: Sheffield Academic Press, 1997.

Anderson, Benedict. "Exodus." *Critical Inquiry* 20 (1994): 314–27.

———. *Imagined Communities*. New York: Verso, 1983.

Apfel, Roberta, and Lise Grondahl. "Feminine Plurals." In *Reading Ruth: Contemporary Women Reclaim a Sacred Story*, edited by Judith A. Kates and Gail Twersky Reimer. New York: Ballantine, 1994.

Appiah, Anthony. "The Uncompleted Argument: Du Bois and the Illusion of Race." In *The Idea of Race*, edited by Robert Bernasconi and Tommy L. Lott. New York: Hackett, 2000.

Aristotle. *Poetics*. In *Aristotle on Poetry and Style*. Translated by G. M. A. Grube. New York: Liberal Arts Press, 1958.

Arnold, Bill T., and H. G. M. Williamson. *Dictionary of the Old Testament Historical Books*. Downers Grove, Ill.: InterVarsity, 2005.

Aschkenasy, Nehama. "Language as Female Empowerment in Ruth." In *Reading Ruth: Contemporary Women Reclaim a Sacred Story*, edited by Judith A. Kates and Gail Twersky Reimer. New York: Ballantine, 1994.

———. *Woman at the Window: Biblical Tales of Oppression and Escape*. Detroit: Wayne State University Press, 1998.

Auerbach, Erich. *Mimesis*. Princeton: Princeton University Press, 1968.

Babuts, Nicolae. *The Dynamics of the Metaphoric Field: A Cognitive View of Literature*. Newark: University of Delaware Press, 1992.

Bach, Alice. "The Pleasure of Her Text." In *The Pleasure of Her Text*, edited by Alice Bach. Philadelphia: Trinity Press International, 1990.

———. "Rereading the Body Politic." In *Judges: A Feminist Companion to the Bible*, edited by Athalya Brenner. Sheffield: Sheffield University Press, 1999.

———. "Signs of the Flesh: Observations on Characterization in the Bible." *Semeia* 63 (1993): 61–79.

———, ed. *Women in the Hebrew Bible: A Reader*. New York: Routledge, 1999.

Bachrach, Rabbi Joshua. *Mother of Kings [Ima shel malkhut]*. Jerusalem: Yeshivat Ohr Etzion, 1984.

Bacon, Gershon C. "Haredi Conceptions of Obligations and Rights: Polish Jewry, c. 1900–1939." *Jewish Political Studies Review* 3, nos. 3–4 (1991): 85–95.

Bakhtin, M. M. *The Dialogic Imagination*. Austin: University of Texas Press, 1981.

Bal, Mieke. *Death and Dissymmetry: The Politics of Coherence in the Book of Judges*. Chicago: University of Chicago Press, 1988.

———. *Lethal Love: Feminist Literary Readings of Biblical Love Stories*. Indiana: Indiana University Press, 1987.

———. "Lots of Writing." In *Ruth and Esther: A Feminist Companion to the Bible (Second Series)*, edited by Athalya Brenner. Sheffield: Sheffield Academic Press, 1999.

———. "Metaphors He Lives By." *Semeia* 61 (1993): 185–207.

———. "Mythe à la Lettre: Freud, Mann, Genesis, and Rembrandt, and the Story of the Son." In *A Feminist Companion to Genesis*, edited by Athalya Brenner. Sheffield: Sheffield Academic Press, 1993.

———. "The Rape of Narrative and the Narrative of Rape: Speech Acts and Body Language in Judges." In *Literature and the Body: Essays on Populations and Persons*, edited by Elaine Scarry. Baltimore: Johns Hopkins University Press, 1988.

Bar-Efrat, Shimon. *Narrative Art in the Bible*. Sheffield: Almond, 1989.

Bar On, Bat-Ami. "Marginality and Epistemic Privilege." In *Feminist Epistemologies*, edited by Linda Alcoff and Elizabeth Potter. New York: Routledge, 1993.

Baskin, Judith R. *Midrashic Women: Formations of the Feminine in Rabbinic Literature*. Waltham, Mass.: Brandeis University Press, 2002.

Bauman, Richard. "'I'll Give You Three Guesses': The Dynamics of Genre in the Riddle-Tale." In *Untying the Knot: On Riddle and Other Enigmatic Modes*, edited by Galit Hasan-Rokem and David Shulman. New York: Oxford University Press, 1996.

Beal, Timothy K. *The Book of Hiding*. New York: Routledge, 1997.

Beal, Timothy K., and David M. Gunn, eds. *Reading Bibles, Writing Bodies: Identity and the Book*. New York: Routledge, 1996.

Bechtel, Lyn M. "Rethinking the Interpretation of Genesis 2.4b–3.24." In *A Feminist Companion to Genesis*, edited by Athalya Brenner (Sheffield: Sheffield Academic Press, 1993).

Beiner, Ronald. *Theorizing Nationalism*. Albany: SUNY Press, 1999.

Belfer, Ella. "The Jewish People and the Kingdom of Heaven: A Study of Jewish Theocracy." *Jewish Political Studies Review* 1, nos. 1–2 (1989): 7–37.

Bellis, Alice Ogden. *Helpmates, Harlots, and Heroes*. Louisville, Ky.: Westminster/ John Knox, 1994.

Benhabib, Seyla. "Subjectivity, Historiography, and Politics: Reflections on the 'Feminism/Postmodernism Exchange.'" In *Feminist Contentions*, edited by Linda Alcoff and Elizabeth Potter. New York: Routledge, 1993.

Berger, Harry, Jr. "The Lie of the Land: The Text Beyond Canaan." *Representations* 25 (1989): 119–38.

Berlin, Adele. "Characterization in Biblical Narrative: David's Wives." *Journal for the Study of the Old Testament* 23 (1982): 69–85.

———. "On the Use of Traditional Jewish Exegesis in the Modern Literary Study of the Bible." In *Tehillah le-Moshe*, edited by Michael Cogan, Barry L. Eichler, and Jeffrey H. Tigay. Winona Lake, Ind.: Eisenbrauns, 1997.

Berlin, Adele, and Marc Zvi Brettler. *The Jewish Study Bible*. New York: Oxford University Press, 2004.

Berlin, Isaiah. *The Crooked Timber of Humanity*. Princeton: Princeton University Press, 1990.

Berquist, Jon L. *Controlling Corporeality: The Body and the Household in Ancient Israel*. New Brunswick: Rutgers University Press, 2002.

Beuken, W. A. M. "I Samuel 18: The Prophet as 'Hammer of Witches.'" *Journal for the Study of the Old Testament* 6 (1978): 3–17.

Bhabha, Homi K. *Nation and Narration*. New York: Routledge, 1990.

Blackham, H. J. *The Fable as Literature*. London: Athlone, 1985.

Blidstein, Gerald J. "In the Shadow of the Mountain: Consent and Coercion at Sinai." *Jewish Political Studies Review* 4, no. 1 (1992): 41–53.

Bloom, Harold. *The Anxiety of Influence*. Oxford: Oxford University Press, 1973.

Boyarin, Daniel. *Intertextuality and the Reading of Midrash*. Bloomington: Indiana University Press, 1990.

Boyarin, Daniel, and Jonathan Boyarin. "Diaspora: Generation and the Ground of Jewish Identity." *Critical Inquiry* 19 (1993): 693–725.

———. "The Lie of the Land: The Text Beyond Canaan." *Representations* 15 (1989): 119–38.

Brass, Paul R. *Ethnicity and Nationalism: Theory and Comparison*. New York: Sage, 1991.

Brenner, Athalya, ed. *A Feminist Companion to Exodus to Deuteronomy*. Sheffield: Sheffield Academic Press, 1994.

———. *A Feminist Companion to Genesis*. Sheffield: Sheffield Academic Press, 1993.

———. *A Feminist Companion to Samuel and Kings*. Sheffield: Sheffield Academic Press, 1994.

———. *Judges: A Feminist Companion to the Bible (Second Series)*. Sheffield: Sheffield Academic Press, 1999.

———. "Naomi and Ruth." *Vetus Testamentum* 33, no. 4 (October 1983): 385–97.

———. *Ruth and Esther: A Feminist Companion to the Bible (Second Series).* Sheffield: Sheffield Academic Press, 1999.

Brenner, Athalya, and Fokkelien van Dijk-Hemmes. *On Gendering Texts: Female and Male Voices in the Hebrew Bible.* Leiden: E. J. Brill, 1996.

Brettler, Marc. *The Book of Judges.* New York: Routledge, 2002.

———. "The Book of the Judges: Literature as Politics." *Journal of Biblical Literature* 108, no. 3 (1989): 395–418.

———. *The Creation of History in Ancient Israel.* New York: Routledge, 1995.

Brisman, Leslie. *The Voice of Jacob.* Bloomington: Indiana University Press, 1990.

Bronner, Leila Leah. *From Eve to Esther: Rabbinic Reconstructions of Biblical Women.* Louisville, Ky.: Westminster/John Knox, 1994.

———. "Serah and the Exodus: A Midrashic Miracle." In *Exodus to Deuteronomy: A Feminist Companion to the Bible (Second Series),* edited by Athalya Brenner (Sheffield: Sheffield Academic Press, 2000).

Brown, Richard Harvey. *Society as Text.* Chicago: University of Chicago Press, 1987.

Brueggemann, Walter. "In Trust and Freedom: A Study of Faith in the Succession Narrative." *Interpretation: A Journal of Bible and Theology* 26, no. 1 (1972): 3–19.

———. *A Social Reading of the Old Testament: Prophetic Approaches to Israel's Communal Life.* Minneapolis: Fortress, 1994.

Butler, Judith. "Contingent Foundations: Feminism and the Question of 'Postmodernism.'" In *Feminist Epistemologies,* edited by Linda Alcoff and Elizabeth Potter. New York: Routledge, 1993.

Bynum, David E. "Samson as a Biblical Hero." In *Text and Tradition,* edited by Susan Niditch. Atlanta: Scholars Press, 1990.

Cacciari, Cristina. "Why Do We Speak Metaphorically? Reflections on the Functions of Metaphor in Discourse and Reasoning." In *Figurative Language and Thought,* edited by Albert N. Katz, Cristina Cacciari, Raymond W. Gibbs Jr., and Mark Turner. Oxford: Oxford University Press, 1998.

Caillois, Roger. *Man and the Sacred.* Translated by Meyer Barash. Chicago: University of Illinois Press, 195.

Camp, Claudia V. "Metaphor in Feminist Biblical Interpretation: Theoretical Perspectives." *Semeia* 61 (1993): 3–36.

———. *Wise, Strange, and Holy: The Strange Woman and the Making of the Bible.* Sheffield: Sheffield Academic Press, 2000.

Camp, Claudia V., and Carole Fontaine. "The Words of the Wise and Their Riddles." In *Text and Tradition,* edited by Susan Niditch. Atlanta: Scholars Press, 1990.

Canto, Monique. "The Politics of Women's Bodies: Reflections on Plato." In *The Female Body in Western Culture: Contemporary Perspectives,* edited by Susan Rubin Suleiman. Cambridge, Mass.: Harvard University Press, 1985.

Castelnuovo, Shirley. "The Jewish Experience of Oppression as Portrayed in the Hebrew Bible: Leadership and Survival Strategies." *Jewish Political Studies Review* 3, nos. 1–2 (1991): 33–47.

Chalcraft, David J. "Deviance and Legitimate Action in the Book of Judges." In *The Bible in Three Dimensions,* edited by David A. J. Clines, Stephen E. Fowl, and Stanley E. Porter. Sheffield: Sheffield Academic Press, 1990.

Clines, David J. A. "Reading Esther from Left to Right: Contemporary Strategies of Reading a Biblical Text." In *The Bible in Three Dimensions*, edited by David J. A. Clines, Stephen E. Fowl, and Stanley E. Porter. Sheffield: Sheffield Academic Press, 1990.

Coats, George W. "The King's Loyal Opposition: Obedience and Authority in Exodus 32–34." In *Canon and Authority: Essays in Old Testament Religion and Theology*, edited by George W. Coats and Burke O. Lang. Philadelphia: Fortress, 1977.

Cohen, Arthur A., and Paul Mendes-Flohr. *Contemporary Jewish Religious Thought: Original Essays on Critical Concepts, Movements, and Beliefs*. New York: Free Press, 1987.

Cohen, Jeremy. *"Be Fertile and Increase, Fill the Earth and Master It": The Ancient and Medieval Career of a Biblical Text*. Ithaca: Cornell University Press, 1989.

Cohen, Shlomith. "Connecting Through Riddles, or the Riddle of Connecting." In *Untying the Knot: On Riddle and Other Enigmatic Modes*, edited by Galit Hasan-Rokem and David Shulman. New York: Oxford University Press.

Cohen, Stuart A. "The Bible and Intra-Jewish Politics: Early Rabbinic Portraits of King David." *Jewish Political Studies Review* 3, nos. 1–2 (1991): 49–65.

Cohn, Robert. *The Shape of Sacred Space: Four Biblical Studies*. Chico, Calif.: Scholars Press, 1981.

Confino, Alon. *The Nation as a Local Metaphor: Württemberg, Imperial Germany, and National Memory, 1871–1918*. Chapel Hill: University of North Carolina Press, 1997.

Coogan, Michael D., ed. *The New Oxford Annotated Bible*. Oxford: Oxford University Press, 2001.

Cornell, Drucilla. "What Is Ethical Feminism?" In *Feminist Contentions*, edited by Linda Alcoff and Elizabeth Potter. New York: Routledge, 1993.

Cover, Robert M. "Nomos and Narrative." *Harvard Law Review* 97, no. 4 (1983): 4–68.

Craig, Kenneth M., Jr. *A Poetics of Jonah*. Macon, Ga.: Mercer University Press, 1999.

Crenshaw, James L. *Samson: A Secret Betrayed, a Vow Ignored*. Atlanta: Scholars Press, 1978.

Cross, Frank Moore. *From Epic to Canon: History and Literature in Ancient Israel*. Baltimore: Johns Hopkins University Press, 1998.

Culler, Jonathan. "Commentary." *New Literary History* 6, no. 1 (Autumn 1974): 219–29.

Dailey, Anne C. "The Judgment of Women." In *Out of the Garden: Women Writers on the Bible*, edited by Christina Büchmann and Celina Spiegel. New York: Fawcett Columbine, 1994.

Deese, James. "Mind and Metaphor: A Commentary." *New Literary History* 6, no. 1 (Autumn 1974): 211–17.

de Lauretis, Teresa. *Technologies of Gender: Essays on Theory, Film, and Fiction*. Bloomington: Indiana University Press, 1987.

de Man, Paul. "Pascal's Allegory of Persuasion." In *Allegory and Representation*, edited by Stephen J. Greenblatt. Baltimore: Johns Hopkins University Press, 1981.

Derrida, Jacques. *Of Grammatology*. 1974. Translated by Gayatri Chakravorty Spivak. Baltimore: Johns Hopkins University Press, 1976.

————. "White Mythology." *New Literary History* 6, no. 1 (1974): 5–74.

Diebner, Bernd-Jörg. "Le roman de Joseph, ou Israël en Égypte: Un Midrash post-exilique de la Tora." In *Le livre de traverse: De l'exegèse biblique à l'anthropologie*, edited by Marcel Detienne. Paris: Éditions de Cerf, 1992.

Dienstag, Joshua Foa. *Dancing in Chains: Narrative and Memory in Political Theory*. Palo Alto: Stanford University Press, 1997.

Donaldson, Laura E. "Cyborgs, Ciphers, and Sexuality: Re-theorizing Literary and Biblical Character." *Semeia* 63 (1993): 81–96.

Dostoevsky, Fyodor. *The Grand Inquisitor*. Edited and translated by Ralph E. Matlaw. New York: Penguin/Meridian, 1991.

Dundes, Alan. "Riddles." In *Folklore and Folklife*, edited by Richard M. Dorson. Chicago: University of Chicago Press, 1972.

Eilberg-Schwartz, Howard. "When the Reader Is in the Write." Review of *Golden Doves With Silver Dots: Semitics and Textuality in Rabbinic Tradition*, by Jose Faur. *Prooftexts* 7, no. 2 (1987): 194–205.

Eisenstadt, S. N. *The Origins and Diversity of Axial Age Civilizations*. Albany: SUNY Press, 1986. See esp. "Introduction: The Axial Age Breakthroughs—Their Characteristics and Origins"; and "Introduction: The Axial Age Breakthrough in Ancient Israel."

Elazar, Daniel J. "The Book of Joshua as a Political Classic." *Jewish Political Studies Review* 1, nos. 1–2 (1989): 93–150.

————. "Deuteronomy as Israel's Ancient Constitution: Some Preliminary Reflections." *Jewish Political Studies Review* 4, no. 1 (1992): 3–39.

————. "Religion in the Public Square: Jews Among the Nations." *Jewish Political Studies Review* 11, nos. 3–4 (1999): 1–10.

Elper, Ora Wiskind, and Susan Wusan Handelman, eds. *Torah of the Mothers: Contemporary Jewish Women Read Classical Jewish Texts*. Jerusalem: Urim, 2000.

Elshtain, Jean Bethke, ed. *The Family in Political Thought*. Amherst: University of Massachusetts Press, 1982.

Esther Rabbah. Edited by Abraham Steinberger. Jerusalem: Makhon Hamidrash Hamevoar, 1986.

Exum, J. Cheryl. "Aspects of Symmetry and Balance in the Samson Saga." In *Redating the Teacher of Righteousness*, edited by Barbara E. Theiring. Australian and New Zealand Studies in Theology and Religion 1. Sydney: Theological Explorations, 1979.

————. *Fragmented Women: Feminist (Sub)versions of Biblical Narratives*. Valley Forge, Pa.: Trinity Press International, 1993.

————. *The Historical Books*. Sheffield: Sheffield Academic Press, 1997.

————. *Plotted, Shot, and Painted: Cultural Representations of Biblical Women*. Sheffield: Sheffield Academic Press, 1996.

————. "Promise and Fulfillment: Narrative Art in Judges 13." *Journal of Biblical Literature* 99, no. 1 (1980): 43–59.

————. "The Theological Dimension of the Samson Saga." *Vetus Testamentum* 33, no. 1 (1983): 30–45.

————. *Tragedy and Biblical Narrative*. New York: Cambridge University Press, 1992.

————. "'You Shall Let Every Daughter Live': A Study of Exodus 1:8–2:10." *Semeia* 28 (1993): 63–82.

Exum, J. Cheryl, and David J. A. Clines. *The New Literary Criticism and the Hebrew Bible*. Sheffield: JSOT Press, 1993.

Exum, J. Cheryl, and Stephen D. Moore. *Biblical Studies/Cultural Studies: The Third Sheffield Colloquium*. Sheffield: Sheffield Academic Press, 1998.

Fewell, Danna Nolan, ed. *Reading Between Texts: Intertextuality and the Hebrew Bible*. Louisville, Ky.: Westminster/John Knox, 1992.

Fewell, Danna Nolan, and David M. Gunn. *Gender, Power, and Promise: The Subject of the Bible's First Story*. Nashville: Abingdon, 1993.

Fischer, Irmtraud. "The Authority of Miriam: A Feminist Rereading of Numbers 12 Prompted by Jewish Interpretation." In *A Feminist Companion to Exodus to Deuteronomy*, edited by Athalya Brenner. Sheffield: Sheffield Academic Press, 1994.

Fishbane, Michael. *The Exegetical Imagination: On Jewish Thought and Theology*. Cambridge, Mass.: Harvard University Press, 1998.

———. *The Garments of Torah: Essays in Biblical Hermeneutics*. Bloomington: Indiana University Press, 1989.

Fogelin, Robert J. "Metaphors, Similes, and Similarity." In *Aspects of Metaphor*, edited by Jaakko Hintikka. Boston: Kluwer, 1994.

Fokkelman, Jan P. "Genesis 37 and 38 at the Interface of Structural Analysis and Hermeneutics." In *Literary Structure and Rhetorical Strategies in the Hebrew Bible*, edited by L. J. Regt, J. de Waard, and J. P. Fokkelman. Winona Lake, Ind.: Eisenbrauns, 1996.

———. *Narrative Art in Genesis*. Amsterdam: van Gorgon, 1975.

———. "Structural Remarks on Judges 18 and 19." In *Sha'arei Talmon*, edited by Michael Fishbane, Emanuel Tov, and Weston W. Fields. Winona Lake, Ind.: Eisenbrauns, 1992.

Forrester, Duncan. "Biblical Interpretation and Cultural Relativism." In *Ways of Reading the Bible*, edited by Michael Wadsworth. Totowa, N.J.: Harvester, 1981.

Foucault, Michel. "Le non du père." *Critique* (March 1962): 195–209.

Fraade, Steven D. *From Tradition to Commentary*. Albany: SUNY Press, 1991.

———. "Interpreting Midrash 1: Midrash and the History of Judaism." Review of *Judaism and Scripture*, by Jacob Neusner. *Prooftexts* 7, no. 2 (May 1987): 179–97.

———. "Interpreting Midrash 2: Midrash and Its Literary Contexts." Review of *Midrash, Mishnah, and Gemara*, by Weiss Halivni; and *Midrash and Literature*, edited by Geoffrey Hartman and Sanford Budick. *Prooftexts* 7, no. 3 (Spring 1987): 284–300.

Fraser, Nancy. "False Antitheses: A Response to Seyla Benhabib and Judith Butler." In *Feminist Epistemologies*, edited by Linda Alcoff and Elizabeth Potter. New York: Routledge, 1993.

Freeman, Gordon M. "The Language of Jewish Political Discourse." *Jewish Political Studies Review* 1, nos. 1–2 (1989): 63–76.

Freud, Sigmund. *The Interpretation of Dreams*. 1899. Translated by James Strachey. New York: Basic, 1965.

———. "The Uncanny." 1919. In *Writings on Art and Literature*, edited by Neil Hertz, translated by Angela Harris. Palo Alto: Stanford University Press, 1997.

Frieden, Ken. "Dream Interpreters in Exile: Joseph, Daniel, and Sigmund." In *Mappings of the Biblical Terrain*, edited by Vincent Tollers and John Maier. Lewisburg, Pa.: Bucknell University Press, 1990.

Fritsch, Charles T. "God Was with Him." *Interpretation* 9, no. 1 (January 1955): 21–34.

Frye, Northrop. *The Great Code: The Bible and Literature*. New York: Harvest, 1982.

———. "Vision and Cosmos." In *Biblical Patterns in Modern Literature*, edited by David H. Hirsch and Nehama Aschkenasy. Chico, Calif.: Scholars Press, 1984.

Frymer-Kensky, Tikva. *Reading the Women of the Bible*. New York: Schocken, 2002.

Geary, Patrick J. *The Myth of Nations: The Medieval Origins of Europe*. Princeton: Princeton University Press, 2002.

Gellman, Jerome. "Radical Responsibility in Maimonides' Thought." In *The Thought of Moses Maimonides*, edited by Ira Robinson, Lawrence Kaplan, and Julien Bauer. New York: Edwin Mellen, 1990.

George, Mark K. "Constructing Identity in Samuel 17." *Biblical Interpretation* 7, no. 4 (1999): 389–412.

Gerstenfeld, Manfred. "Neo-paganism in the Public Square and Its Relevance to Judaism." *Jewish Political Studies Review* 11, nos. 3–4 (Fall 1999): 11–38.

Glouberman, Mark. "Inhumanity and Polity: An Essay on Plato's *Republic*." *Iyyun: The Jerusalem Philosophical Quarterly* 49 (July 2000): 235–81.

Goitein, S. D. "Women as Creators of Biblical Genres." *Prooftexts* 8 (1988): 1–33.

Goldin, Judah. "A Law and Its Interpretation." In *Tehillah le-Moshe*, edited by Michael Cogan, Barry L. Eichler, and Jeffrey H. Tigay. Winona Lake, Ind.: Eisenbrauns, 1997.

Good, Edwin M. *Irony in the Old Testament*. Philadelphia: Westminster, 1965.

Gordis, Robert. "Studies in the Esther Narrative." *Journal of Biblical Literature* 95, 1 (March 1976): 43–58.

Gordon, Paul. *The Critical Double: Figurative Meaning in Aesthetic Discourse*. Tuscaloosa: University of Alabama Press, 1995.

Gottwald, Norman K. *The Hebrew Bible: A Socio-literary Introduction*. Philadelphia: Fortress, 1985.

———. *The Politics of Ancient Israel*. Louisville, Ky.: Westminster/John Knox, 2001.

Grabbe, Lester L. *Ezra-Nehemiah*. New York: Routledge, 1998.

Graves, Robert. *The Greek Myths: Complete Edition*. 1955. New York: Penguin, 1960.

Greenstein, Edward L. "Deconstruction and Biblical Narrative." *Prooftexts* 19, no. 1 (1989): 43–71.

———. "On the Genesis of Biblical Prose Narrative." Review of *The Narrative Covenant*, by David Damrosch. *Prooftexts* 8, no. 3 (1988): 347–63.

———. "The Riddle of Samson." *Prooftexts* 1, no. 3 (1981): 237–60.

Grosby, Steven. *Biblical Ideas of Nationality: Ancient and Modern*. Winona Lake, Ind.: Eisenbrauns, 2002.

Grosjean, Jean. *Samson*. Paris: Gallimard, 1989.

Grosz, Elizabeth. "Bodies and Knowledges: Feminism and the Crisis of Reason." In *Feminist Epistemologies*, edited by Linda Alcoff and Elizabeth Potter. New York: Routledge, 1993.

Gunn, David M. "In Security: The David of Biblical Narrative." In *Signs and Wonders: Biblical Texts in Literary Focus*, edited by Cheryl Exum. Decatur, Ga.: Society of Biblical Literature, 1989.

———. *Judges*. Malden, Mass.: Blackwell, 2005.

———. "Reading Right: Reliable and Omniscient Narrator, Omniscient God, and Foolproof Composition in the Hebrew Bible." In *The Bible in Three Dimensions*, edited by David. J. A. Clines, Stephen E. Fowl, and Stanley E. Porter. Sheffield: Sheffield Academic Press, 1990.

———. "Samson of Sorrows." In *Reading Between Texts: Intertextuality and the Hebrew Bible*, edited by Danna Nolan Fewell. Louisville, Ky.: Westminster/John Knox, 1992.

Gunn, David M., and Donna Nolan Fewell. *Narrative in the Hebrew Bible*. Oxford: Oxford University Press, 1993.

Haack, Susan. "'Dry Truth and Real Knowledge': Epistemologies of Metaphor and Metaphors of Epistemology." In *Aspects of Metaphor*, edited by Jaakko Hintikka. Boston: Kluwer, 1994.

Halbertal, Moshe, and Avishai Margalit. *Idolatry*. Translated by Naomi Goldblum. Cambridge, Mass.: Harvard University Press, 1992.

Halivni, David Weiss. "From Midrash to Mishna: Theological Repercussions and Further Clarifications of 'Chate'u Yisrael.'" In *The Midrashic Imagination*, edited by Michael Fishbane. Albany: SUNY Press, 1993.

Halpern, Baruch. *The First Historians: The Hebrew Bible and History*. New York: Harper and Row, 1988.

Handelman, Don. "Traps of Trans-formation: Theoretical Convergences Between Riddle and Ritual." In *Untying the Knot: On Riddle and Other Enigmatic Modes*, edited by Galit Hasan-Rokem and David Shulman. New York: Oxford University Press, 1996.

Handelman, Susan. "Everything Is in It: Rabbinic Interpretation and Modern Literary Theory." *Judaism* 35, no. 2 (Fall 1986): 429–40.

———. *The Slayers of Moses*. Albany: SUNY Press, 1982.

Hanson, Paul D. "The Theological Significance of Contradiction Within the Book of the Covenant." In *Canon and Authority: Essays in Old Testament Religion and Theology*, edited by George W. Coats and Burke O'Connor Long. Philadelphia: Fortress, 1977.

Haran, Menahem. "The Berit 'Covenant': Its Nature and Ceremonial Background." In *Tehillah le-Moshe*, edited by Michael Cogan, Barry L. Eichler, and Jeffrey H. Tigay. Winona Lake, Ind.: Eisenbrauns, 1997.

Harding, Sandra. "Rethinking Standpoint Epistemology: What Is 'Strong Objectivity'?" In *Feminist Epistemologies*, edited by Linda Alcoff and Elizabeth Potter. New York: Routledge, 1993.

Harrison, Bernard. "Parable and Transcendence." In *Ways of Reading the Bible*, edited by Michael Wadsworth. Totowa, N.J.: Harvester, 1981.

Hasan-Rokem, Galit. "'Spinning Threads of Sand': Riddles as Images of Loss in the Midrash on Lamentations." In *Untying the Knot: On Riddle and Other Enigmatic Modes*, edited by Galit Hasan-Rokem and David Shulman. New York: Oxford University Press, 1996.

———. *Web of Life: Folklore and Midrash in Rabbinic Literature*. Palo Alto: Stanford University Press, 2000.

Hasan-Rokem, Galit, and David Shulman, eds. *Untying the Knot: On Riddles and Other Enigmatic Modes.* New York: Oxford University Press, 1996.

Havel, Václav. *The Art of the Impossible: Politics as Morality in Practice.* New York: Knopf, 1997.

Hazony, David. "Crimes Against the Humanities." *Azure* 27 (Winter 2007).

Hazony, Yoram. *The Dawn.* Jerusalem: Shalem, 1995.

Hobbes, Thomas. *Leviathan.* Edited by C. B. Macpherson. Harmondsworth: Pelican, 1968.

Holquist, Michael. "The Politics of Representation." In *Allegory and Representation,* edited by Stephen J. Greenblatt. Baltimore: Johns Hopkins University Press, 1981.

Honeyman, A. M. "The Occasion of Joseph's Temptation." *Vetus Testamentum* 2 (January 1952): 85–87.

Honig, Bonnie. *Democracy and the Foreigner.* Princeton: Princeton University Press, 2001.

Horowitz, Elliot. *Reckless Rites.* Princeton: Princeton University Press, 2006.

Humphreys, W. Lee. "A Life-style for Diaspora: A Study of the Tales of Esther and Daniel." *Journal of Biblical Literature* 92 (1973): 201–23.

———. "The Tragedy of King Saul: A Study of the Structure of I Samuel 9–31." *Journal for the Study of the Old Testament* 6 (1978): 18–27.

Hutner, Isaac. *Pahad Yitzhak.* New York: Noble Book Press, 1999.

Hyman, Ronald T. "Questions in the Joseph Story: The Effects and Their Implications for Teaching." *Religious Education* 79, no. 3 (Summer 1984): 437–55.

Ilan, Tal. "The Daughters of Zelophehad and Women's Inheritance: The Biblical Injunction and Its Outcome." In *Exodus to Deuteronomy: A Feminist Companion to the Bible (Second Series),* edited by Athalya Brenner. Sheffield: Sheffield Academic Press, 2000.

Irigaray, Luce. *Speculum of the Other Woman.* Ithaca: Cornell University Press, 1974.

Jacobus, Mary. *Reading Woman: Essays in Feminist Criticism.* New York: Columbia University Press, 1986.

Jagendorf, Zvi. "'In the Morning, Behold, It Was Leah': Genesis and the Reversal of Sexual Knowledge." In *Biblical Patterns in Modern Literature,* edited by David N. Hirsch and Nehama Aschkenasy. Chico, Calif.: Scholars Press, 1984.

Jobling, David. "Saul's Fall and Jonathan's Rise: Tradition and Redaction in I Sam 14:1–46." *Journal of Biblical Literature* 95, no. 3 (1976): 367–76.

———, ed. *The Sense of Biblical Narrative: Structural Analysis in the Hebrew Bible II.* Sheffield: JSOT Press, 1978.

———. "A Structural Study in I Samuel." In *The Sense of Biblical Narrative,* edited by David Jobling. Sheffield: JSOT Press, 1978.

Jobling, David, Peggy L. Day, and Gerald T. Sheppard, eds. *The Bible and the Politics of Exegesis.* Cleveland, Ohio: Pilgrim, 1991.

Jonte-Pace, Diane. *Speaking the Unspeakable.* Berkeley and Los Angeles: University of California Press, 2001.

Jordan, June. "Ruth and Naomi, David and Jonathan: One Love." In *Out of the Garden: Women Writers on the Bible,* edited by Christina Büchmann and Celina Spiegel. New York: Fawcett Columbine, 1994.

Josipovici, Gabriel. "The Bible: Dialogue and Distance." In *Ways of Reading the Bible*, edited by Michael Wadsworth. Totowa, N.J.: Harvester, 1981.

———. *The Book of God*. New Haven: Yale University Press, 1988.

———. *Text and Voice*. New York: St. Martin's, 1992.

———. *The World and the Book*. 2nd ed. New York: Macmillan, 1979.

Jowett, Benjamin, ed. *"The Republic" and Other Works*. New York: Anchor, 1973.

Kaivola-Bregenhoj, Annikki. "Riddles and Their Use." In *Untying the Knot: On Riddle and Other Enigmatic Modes*, edited by Galit Hasan-Rokem and David Shulman. New York: Oxford University Press, 1996.

Kaminetzky, Rabbi Jacob. *Emet L'Ya'akov*. New York: Amen L'Ya'akov, 1998.

Kant, Immanuel. *Perpetual Peace and Other Essays*. Edited and translated by Ted Humphrey. Indianapolis: Hackett, 1983.

Kates, Judith A., and Gail Twersky Reimer, eds. *Reading Ruth: Contemporary Women Reclaim a Sacred Story*. New York: Ballantine, 1994.

Kedourie, Elie. *Nationalism*. London: Hutchinson, 1985.

Keegan, Terence J. "Biblical Criticism and the Challenge of Postmodernism." *Biblical Interpretation* 3, no. 1 (March 1995): 1–14.

Kellner, Menachem. "Politics and Perfection: Gersonides v. Maimonides." *Jewish Political Studies Review* 6, nos. 1–2 (Spring 1994): 49–82.

Kenik, Helen Ann. "Code of Conduct for a King: Psalm 101." *Journal of Biblical Literature* 95, no. 3 (1976): 391–403.

Kepnes, Steven. *Interpreting Judaism in a Postmodern Age*. New York: New York University Press, 1996.

———. "A Narrative Jewish Theology." *Judaism* 37, no. 2 (Spring 1988): 210–17.

Kermode, Frank. *The Genesis of Secrecy: On the Interpretation of Narrative*. Cambridge, Mass.: Harvard University Press, 1979.

Kidd, Colin. *British Identities Before Nationalism*. Cambridge: Cambridge University Press, 1999.

Kimelman, Reuven. "Abravanel and the Jewish Republican Ethos." In *Commandment and Community*, edited by Daniel H. Frank. Albany: SUNY Press, 1995.

———. "The Seduction of Eve and the Exegetical Politics of Gender." *Biblical Interpretation* 1 (Fall 1996): 1–39.

Kimhi. Commentary in *Mikraot Gedolot*. New York: MP Press, 1974.

Klagsbrun, Francine. "Ruth and Naomi, Rachel and Leah: Sisters Under the Skin." In *Reading Ruth: Contemporary Women Reclaim a Sacred Story*, edited by Judith A. Kates and Gail Twersky Reimer. New York: Ballantine, 1994.

Klein, Lillian R. *The Triumph of Irony in the Book of Judges*. Sheffield: Almond, 1988.

Kolodny, Annette. "Dancing Through the Minefield." In *Feminisms: An Anthology of Literary Theory and Criticism*, edited by Robyn R. Warhol and Diane Prince Herndl. New Brunswick: Rutgers University Press, 1991.

———. "A Map for Rereading; or, Gender and the Interpretation of Literary Texts." *New Literary History* 11 (1979–80): 451–67.

Kramer, Phyllis Silverman. "Miriam." In *Exodus to Deuteronomy: A Feminist Companion to the Bible (Second Series)*, edited by Athalya Brenner. Sheffield: Sheffield Academic Press, 2000.

Kreisel, Howard. *Maimonides' Political Thought*. Albany: SUNY Press, 1999.

Kristeva, Julia. *Strangers to Ourselves*. Translated by Leon Roudiez. New York: Columbia University Press, 1991.

Kugel, James L. *The Bible as It Was.* Cambridge, Mass.: Harvard University Press, 1997.

———. "The Bible's Earliest Interpreters." Review of *Biblical Interpretation in Ancient Israel,* by Michael Fishbane. *Prooftexts* 7, no. 3 (September 1987): 269–83.

———. *The Idea of Biblical Poetry: Parallelism and Its History.* Baltimore: Johns Hopkins University Press, 1998.

———. *In Potiphar's House: The Interpretive Life of Biblical Texts.* 1990. Cambridge, Mass.: Harvard University Press, 1994.

LaCocque, André. "The Different Versions of Esther." *Biblical Interpretation* 7, no. 3 (July 1999): 301–22.

LaCocque, André, and Paul Ricoeur. *Thinking Biblically: Exegetical and Hermeneutical Studies.* Chicago: University of Chicago Press, 1998.

Lasine, Stuart. "Interdeterminacy and the Bible: A Review of Literary and Anthropological Theories and Their Application to Biblical Texts." *Hebrew Studies* 27, no. 1 (1986): 48–81.

Leiman, Sid Z. "Masorah and Halakhah: A Study in Conflict." In *Tehillah le-Moshe,* edited by Michael Cogan, Barry L. Eichler, and Jeffrey H. Tigay. Winona Lake, Ind.: Eisenbrauns, 1997.

Lemche, Niels Peter. "David's Rise." *Journal for the Study of the Old Testament* 10 (1978): 2–25.

Levenson, Jon D., and Baruch Halpern. "The Political Import of David's Marriages." *Journal of Biblical Literature* 99, no. 4 (1980): 507–18.

Levinas, Emmanuel. *The Exile of the Word.* Philadelphia: Jewish Publication Society, 1981.

———. *Of God Who Comes to Mind.* Translated by Bettina Bergo. Palo Alto: Stanford University Press, 1998. Originally published as *De Dieu qui vient à l'esprit* (Paris: Librairie philosophique J. Vrin, 1986).

———. *Totality and Infinity.* Pittsburgh, Pa.: Duquesne University Press, 1961.

Levine, Baruch A. "The Next Phase in Jewish Religion: The Land of Israel as Sacred Space." In *Tehillah le-Moshe,* edited by Michael Cogan, Barry L. Eichler, and Jeffrey H. Tigay. Winona Lake, Ind.: Eisenbrauns, 1997.

Levinson, Bernard M. "Deuteronomy's Conception of Law as an 'Ideal Type': A Missing Chapter in the History of Constitutional Law." *Maarav* 12, nos. 1–2 (2005): 1–38.

———. "The First Constitution: Rethinking the Origins of Rule of Law and Separation of Powers in Light of Deuteronomy." *Cardozo Law Review* 27 (February 2006): 1853–88.

———. "The Reconceptualization of Kingship in Deuteronomy and the Deuteronomistic History's Transformation of Torah." *Vetus Testamentum* 51, no. 4 (2001): 511–34.

Levinson, Bernard M., Otto Eckart, and Walter Dietrich. "Recht und Ethik im Alten Testament." *Altes Testament und Moderne* 13 (2004): 15–45.

Licht, Robert A. "Communal Democracy, Modernity, and the Jewish Political Tradition." *Jewish Political Studies Review* 5, nos. 1–2 (Spring 1993): 95–127.

Low, Anthony. *The Blaze of Noon.* New York: Columbia University Press, 1979.

Lowenthal, Eric I. *The Joseph Narrative in Genesis.* New York: Ktav, 1973.

Machiavelli, Niccolò. *The Prince.* Edited and translated by Robert M. Adams. New York: Norton, 1977.

Malamat, Abraham. "Organs of Statecraft in the Israelite Monarchy." *The Biblical Archaeologist* 28 (1965): 34–65.

Malbim, Rabbi Meir Leibush. Commentary on Bible with Mekhilta and Sifrei (Torah/Prophets). New York: MP Press, 1974.

Margalith, Othniel. "More Samson Legends." *Vetus Testamentum* 36, no. 4 (1986): 397–405.

Marx, Anthony W. *Faith in Nation: Exclusionary Origins of Nationalism*. New York: Oxford University Press, 2003.

Matlock, R. Barry. "Biblical Criticism and the Rhetoric of Inquiry." *Biblical Interpretation* 5, no. 2 (April 1997): 133–59.

Matthews, Victor H. "The Anthropology of Clothing in the Joseph Narrative." *Journal for the Study of the Old Testament* 65 (March 1995): 25–36.

———. *Judges and Ruth*. New York: Cambridge University Press, 2004.

Matthews, Victor H., and James C. Moyer. *The Old Testament: Text and Context*. Peabody, Mass.: Hendrickson, 1997.

McCracken, David. "Character in the Boundary: Bakhtin's Interdividuality in Biblical Narratives." *Semeia* 63 (1993): 29–42.

McEntire, Mark. *The Blood of Abel: The Violent Plot in the Hebrew Bible*. Macon, Ga.: Mercer University Press, 1999.

Mechanic, Peter. "Outsiders or Insiders." In *The Other in Jewish Thought and History*, edited by Laurence J. Silberstein and Robert L. Cohn. New York: New York University Press, 1994.

Melamed, Abraham. "The Attitude Toward Democracy in Medieval Jewish Philosophy." In *Commandment and Community*, edited by Daniel H. Frank. Albany: SUNY Press, 1995.

Mendenhall, George E. *Ancient Israel's Faith and History*. Louisville, Ky.: Westminster/John Knox, 2001.

Merkin, Aryeh, ed. *Midrash Rabbah*. Tel Aviv: Yavneh, 1986.

Meyers, Carol. *Discovering Eve: Ancient Israelite Women in Context*. New York: Oxford University Press, 1988.

Midrash Bahayai. Jerusalem: Blum, 1988.

Mikra'ot Gedolot: Pentateuch. New York: MP Press, 1969.

Miller, David L., ed. *Jung and the Interpretation of the Bible*. New York: Continuum, 1995.

Miller, Donald. *The Reason of Metaphor*. New York: Sage, 1992.

Miller, Nancy K. "Rereading as a Woman: The Body in Practice." In *Reading Woman: Essays in Feminist Criticism*, edited by Mary Jacobus. New York: Columbia University Press, 1986.

Milne, Pamela J. "The Patriarchal Stamp of Scripture: The Implications of Structuralist Analyses for Feminist Hermeneutics." In *A Feminist Companion to Genesis*, edited by Athalya Brenner. Sheffield: Sheffield Academic Press, 1993.

———. *Vladimir Propp and the Study of Structure in Hebrew Biblical Narrative*. New York: Almond, 1988.

Milton, John. *Samson Agonistes*. 1957. Edited by F. T. Prince. Oxford: Oxford University Press, 1999.

Miscall, Peter D. "The Jacob and Joseph Stories as Analogies." *Journal for the Study of the Old Testament* 6 (1978): 28–40.

Mittleman, Alan. "From Private Rights to Public Good: The Communitarian Critique of Liberalism in Judaic Perspective." *Jewish Political Studies Review* 5, nos. 1–2 (Spring 1993): 79–93.

———. "Max Weber's Conception of Covenant in Ancient Judaism, with Reference to the Book of Judges." *Jewish Political Studies Review* 6, nos. 1–2 (Spring 1994): 9–25.

———. *The Scepter Shall Not Depart from Judah: Perspectives on the Persistence of the Political in Judaism*. Lanham, Md.: Lexington, 2000.

———. "Two Orthodox Jewish Theories of Rights: Sol Roth and Isaac Breuer." *Jewish Political Studies Review* 3, nos. 3–4 (Fall 1991): 97–107.

Morgenstern, Mira. "A Life of Faith and a Life of the Mind." In *Still Believing: Muslim, Christian, and Jewish Women Affirm Their Faith*, edited by Victoria Lee Erikson and Susan A. Farrell. Maryknoll, N.Y.: Orbis, 2005.

———. *Rousseau and the Politics of Ambiguity*. University Park: Pennsylvania State University Press, 1996.

Müllner, Ilse. "Lethal Differences: Sexual Violence as Violence Against Others in Judges 19." In *Judges: A Feminist Companion to the Bible (Second Series)*, edited by Athalya Brenner. Sheffield: Sheffield Academic Press, 1999.

Naveh, Gila Safran. *Biblical Parables and Their Modern Re-creation*. Albany: SUNY Press, 2000.

Neher, Andre. *The Exile of the Word: From the Silence of the Bible to the Silence of Auschwitz*. Translated by David Maisel. Philadelphia: Jewish Publication Society, 1981.

Nel, Philip. "The Riddle of Samson." *Biblica* 66 (1985): 534–45.

Neuberger, Benjamin. "Does Israel Have a Liberal Democratic Tradition?" *Jewish Political Studies Review* 2, nos. 3–4 (Fall 1990): 85–97.

Niditch, Susan. *Folklore and the Hebrew Bible*. Minneapolis: Fortress, 1993.

———. "Samson as Culture Hero, Trickster, and Bandit: The Empowerment of the Weak." *Catholic Biblical Quarterly* 52 (1990): 608–24.

Nietzsche, Friedrich. *The Birth of Tragedy and the Genealogy of Morals*. Translated by Francis Golffing. New York: Doubleday, 1956.

Noble, Paul. "A 'Balanced' Reading of the Rape of Dinah: Some Exegetical and Methodological Observations." *Biblical Interpretation* 4, no. 2 (1996): 173–204.

Novak, David. *Covenantal Rights: A Study in Jewish Political Theory*. Princeton: Princeton University Press, 2000.

Nussbaum, Felicity. *Torrid Zones*. Baltimore: Johns Hopkins University Press, 1995.

Och, Bernard. "The Garden of Eden: From Re-creation to Reconciliation." *Judaism* 37, no. 3 (Summer 1988): 340–51.

Orlinsky, Harry M. *Essays in Biblical Culture and Bible Translation*. New York: Ktav, 1974.

Ostriker, Alicia. "The Nursing Father." In *Out of the Garden: Women Writers on the Bible*, edited by Christina Büchmann and Celina Spiegel. New York: Fawcett Columbine, 1994.

———. "The Redeeming of Ruth." In *Reading Ruth: Contemporary Women Reclaim a Sacred Story*, edited by Judith A. Kates and Gail Twersky Reimer. New York: Ballantine, 1994.

Ozick, Cynthia. "Hannah and Elkanah: Torah as the Matrix for Feminism." In *Out of the Garden: Women Writers on the Bible*, edited by Christina Büchmann and Celina Spiegel. New York: Fawcett Columbine, 1994.

———. "Ruth." In *Reading Ruth: Contemporary Women Reclaim a Sacred Story*, edited by Judith A. Kates and Gail Twersky Reimer. New York: Ballantine, 1994.

Pagis, Dan. "Toward a Theory of the Literary Riddle." In *Untying the Knot: On Riddle and Other Enigmatic Modes*, edited by Galit Hasan-Rokem and David Shulman. New York: Oxford University Press, 1996.

Paine, Thomas. *Common Sense and Other Political Writings*. Edited with an introduction by Nelson F. Adkins. 1953. Indianapolis: Bobbs-Merrill, 1976.

Pardes, Ilana. "Beyond Genesis 3: The Politics of Maternal Naming." In *A Feminist Companion to Genesis*, edited by Athalya Brenner. Sheffield: Sheffield Academic Press, 1993.

———. *The Biography of Ancient Israel: National Narratives in the Bible*. Berkeley and Los Angeles: University of California Press, 2000.

———. *Countertraditions in the Bible: A Feminist Approach*. Cambridge, Mass.: Harvard University Press, 1992.

———. "Rachel's Dream of Grandeur." In *Out of the Garden: Women Writers on the Bible*, edited by Christina Büchmann and Celina Spiegel. New York: Fawcett Columbine, 1994.

Pateman, Carole. *The Disorder of Women*. Palo Alto: Stanford University Press, 1989.

Pava, Moses L. "Joseph and the Use of Insider Information." *The Torah-U-Madda Journal* (1993): 134–47.

Pepicello, W. J., and Thomas A. Green. *The Language of Riddles: New Perspectives*. Columbus: Ohio State University Press, 1984.

Peyser, Caroline. "The Book of Exodus: A Search for Identity." In *Torah of the Mothers*, edited by Ora Wiskind Elper and Susan Handelman. New York: Urim, 2006.

Pines, Shlomo. "Truth and Falsehood Versus Good and Evil: Study in Jewish and General Philosophy in Connection with the Guide of the Perplexed I, 2." In *Studies in Maimonides*, edited by Isadore Twersky. Cambridge, Mass.: Harvard University Press, 1990.

Plato. *The Republic*. Edited and translated by Francis MacDonald Cornford. 1941. New York: Oxford, 1977.

———. *The Symposium*. Edited and translated by Benjamin Jowett. New York: Anchor, 1973.

Polish, David. "Rabbinic Views on Kingship—A Study in Jewish Sovereignty." *Jewish Political Studies Review* 3, nos. 1–2 (Spring 1991): 67–90.

Polzin, Robert. *David and the Deuteronomist*. Bloomington: Indiana University Press, 1993.

———. *Moses and the Deuteronomist*. Bloomington: Indiana University Press, 1980.

———. *Samuel and the Deuteronomist*. 1989. Bloomington: Indiana University Press, 1993.

Prickett, Stephen. "Towards a Rediscovery of the Bible: The Problem of the Still Small Voice." In *Ways of Reading the Bible*, edited by Michael Wadsworth. Totowa, N.J.: Harvester, 1981.

————. *Words and the Word: Language, Poetics, and Biblical Interpretation.* 1986. New York: Cambridge University Press, 1989.

Propp, Vladimir. *Morphology of the Folktale.* Translated by Laurence Scott. Austin: University of Texas Press, 1968.

Radday, Yehuda T., and Athalya Brenner, eds. *On Humor and the Comic in the Hebrew Bible.* Sheffield: Almond, 1990.

Rashkow, Ilona M. *Taboo or Not Taboo: Sexuality and Family in the Hebrew Bible.* Minneapolis: Fortress, 2000.

Reiner, Gail Twersky. "Her Mother's House." In *Reading Ruth: Contemporary Women Reclaim a Sacred Story,* edited by Judith A. Kates and Gail Twersky Reimer. New York: Ballantine, 1994.

Reinhartz, Adele. "Anonymity and Character in the Books of Samuel." *Semeia* 63 (1993): 117–41.

Reis, Pamela. "Dead Men Tell No Tales." *Conservative Judaism* 44, no. 2 (Winter 1992): 57–61.

Ricoeur, Paul. "Metaphor and Symbol." In *Interpretation Theory.* Fort Worth: Texas Christian University Press, 1976.

Robinson, Ira. "The Evolution of Divine Worship According to Maimonides." In *The Thought of Moses Maimonides,* edited by Ira Robinson, Lawrence Kaplan, and Julien Bauer. New York: Edwin Mellen, 1990.

————. "Individual and Community: Rights and Obligations as Reflected in Two Nineteenth-century Responses." *Jewish Political Studies Review* 3, nos. 3–4 (Fall 1991): 75–84.

Rogerson, J. W. "'What Does It Mean to Be Human?': The Central Question of Old Testament Theology." In *The Bible in Three Dimensions,* edited by David A. J. Clines, Stephen E. Fowl, and Stanley E. Porter. Sheffield: Sheffield Academic Press, 1990.

Rosenak, Michael. "The Akedah—and What to Remember." In *Tehillah le-Moshe,* edited by Michael Cogan, Barry L. Eichler, and Jeffrey H. Tigay. Winona Lake, Ind.: Eisenbrauns, 1997.

Rosenberg, Joel. *King and Kin: Political Allegory in the Hebrew Bible.* Indianapolis: Indiana University Press, 1986.

Rotem, Judith. *Distant Sisters: The Women I Left Behind.* Philadelphia: Jewish Publication Society, 1997.

Rousseau, Jean-Jacques. *Émile; or, On Education.* Translated by Alan Bloom. New York: Basic, 1979.

————. *Oeuvres complètes.* Paris: Gallimard, 1955–.

Sacks, Robert D. *A Commentary on the Book of Genesis.* Lewiston, N.Y.: Edwin Mellen, 1990.

Sacs, Maurice. "An Anthropological and Postmodern Critique of Jewish Feminist Theory." *Jewish Political Studies Review* 6, nos. 1–2 (Spring 1994): 153–65.

Safran-Naveh, Gila. *Biblical Parables and Their Modern Re-creation: From "Apples of Gold in Silver Settings" to "Imperial Messages."* Albany: SUNY Press, 2000.

Sandmel, Samuel. *The Enjoyment of Scripture.* New York: Oxford University Press, 1972.

Sarna, Nahum M. *Understanding Genesis.* New York: McGraw-Hill, 1966.

Sasson, Jack. "Who Cut Samson's Hair? (And Other Trifling Issues Raised by Judges 16)." *Prooftexts* 8, no. 3 (1988): 333–39.

Scheffler, Israel. *Beyond the Letter: A Philosophical Inquiry into Ambiguity, Vagueness, and Metaphor in Language*. Boston: Routledge and Kegan Paul, 1979.

Schimmel, Sol. "Joseph and His Brothers: A Paradigm for Repentance." *Judaism* 37, no. 1 (Winter 1988): 60–65.

Schneidau, Herbert N. *Sacred Discontent: The Bible and Western Tradition*. Baton Rouge: Louisiana State University Press, 1976.

Schniedewind, William M. *How the Bible Became a Book*. New York: Cambridge University Press, 2004.

Schor, Rabbi Gedaliah. *Ohr Gedalyahu*. New York: Keren Zikhron Gedalyahu, 1986.

Schwartz, Howard. *Reimagining the Bible: The Storytelling of the Rabbis*. New York: Oxford University Press, 1998.

Schwartz, Regina M. *The Curse of Cain: The Violent Legacy of Monotheism*. Chicago: University of Chicago Press, 1997.

———. "Joseph's Bones and the Resurrection of the Text: Remembering in the Bible." In *The Book and the Text*, edited by Regina M. Schwartz. New York: Blackwell, 1990.

Schweid, Eliezer. "Religion and Modernity in Our Day." *Jewish Political Studies Review* 8, nos. 1–2 (Spring 1996): 3–36.

Segal, Eliezer. "Law as Allegory: An Unnoticed Literary Device in Talmudic Narratives." *Prooftexts* 8, no. 2 (1988): 245–56.

Segal, Jerome M. *Joseph's Bones: Understanding the Struggle Between God and Mankind in the Bible*. London: Penguin, 2007.

Shaw-Frank, Laura. "From Under the Palm Tree: The Model of Devorah." *Jewish Orthodox Feminist Alliance Journal* (Winter 2004): 3–4.

Shulman, Harvey. "The Political and the Sacred: Political Obligation and the Book of Deuteronomy." *Jewish Political Studies Review* 3, nos. 3–4 (Fall 1991): 23–58.

Sicker, Martin. "Democracy and Judaism: The Question of Equality." *Jewish Political Studies Review* 5, nos. 1–2 (Spring 1993): 57–78.

Simon, Ulrich. "Samson and the Heroic." In *Ways of Reading the Bible*, edited by Michael Wadsworth. Essex, N.J.: Harvester, 1981.

Simon, Uriel. "A Balanced Story: The Stern Prophet and the Kind Witch." *Prooftexts* 8 (1988): 159–71.

Slivniak, Dmitri M. "The Book of Esther: The Making and Unmaking of Jewish Identity." In *Derrida's Bible*, edited by Yvonne Sherwood. New York: Palgrave Macmillan, 2004.

Smith, Anthony D. *The Antiquity of Nations*. New York: Polity, 2004.

———. *Myths and Memories of the Nation*. New York: Oxford University Press, 1999.

Smith, Carol. "Delilah: A Suitable Case for (Feminist) Treatment?" In *A Feminist Companion to Judges*, edited by Athalya Brenner. Sheffield: Sheffield Academic Press, 1999.

———. "Samson and Delilah: A Parable of Power?" *Journal for the Study of the Old Testament* 76 (1997): 45–57.

Sohn, Seock-Tae. "'I Will Be Your God and You Will Be My People': The Origin and Background of the Covenant Formula." In *Ki Baruch Hu: Ancient Near Eastern, Biblical, and Judaic Studies in Honor of Baruch A. Levine*, edited by Robert Chazan, William Hallo, and Lawrence Schiffman. Winona Lake, Ind.: Eisenbrauns, 1999.

Sokoloff, Naomi B. "Feminist Criticism and Hebrew Literature." Review of *Eve's Journey*, by Nehama Aschkenasy. *Prooftexts* 28, no. 1 (1988): 143–56.

Soloveitchik, Rabbi Dr. Joseph B. "In the Days of Mordecai and Esther." RCA Hashkafa Unit, 2nd series, no. 4, lecture transcribed by Rabbi Abraham Besdin (5734/1973–74).

Sophocles. *Antigone*. Edited and translated by David Franklin and John Harrison. New York: Cambridge University Press, 2003.

Sparshott, F. E. "'As' or the Limits of Metaphor." *New Literary History* 6, no. 1 (1974): 75–94.

Speiser, E. A., ed. *The Anchor Bible: Genesis*. New York: Doubleday, 1964.

Sperling, S. David. *The Original Torah: The Political Intent of the Bible's Writers*. New York: New York University Press, 1998.

Stein, Arnold. *Heroic Knowledge: An Interpretation of "Paradise Regained" and "Samson Agonistes."* Minneapolis: University of Minnesota Press, 1957.

Stein, Dina. "A King, a Queen, and the Riddle Between: Riddles and Interpretation in a Late Midrashic Text." In *Untying the Knot: On Riddle and Other Enigmatic Modes*, edited by Galit Hasan-Rokem and David Shulman. New York: Oxford University Press, 1996.

Stein, Kenneth. "Exegesis, Maimonides, and Literary Criticism." *Modern Language Notes* 88 (1973): 1134–51.

Steinberg, Naomi. "The Deuteronomic Law Code and the Politics of State Centralization." In *The Bible and the Politics of Exegesis*, edited by David Jobling, Peggy L. Day, and Gerald T. Sheppard. Cleveland, Ohio: Pilgrim, 1991.

Steiner, Richard C. "The 'Aramean' of Deuteronomy 26:5: *Peshat* and *Derash*." In *Untying the Knot: On Riddle and Other Enigmatic Modes*, edited by Galit Hasan-Rokem and David Shulman. New York: Oxford University Press, 1996.

Steinmetz, Devora. "A Portrait of Miriam in Rabbinic Midrash." *Prooftexts* 8, no. 1 (January 1988): 35–65.

Stern, David. *Midrash and Theory*. Evanston: Northwestern University Press, 1996.

———. *Parables in Midrash: Narrative and Exegesis in Rabbinic Literature*. Cambridge, Mass.: Harvard University Press, 1991.

Stern, Josef. "Maimonides on the Covenant of Circumcision and the Unity of God." In *The Midrashic Imagination*, edited by Michael Fishbane. Albany: SUNY Press, 1993.

———. *Problems and Parables of Law*. Albany: SUNY Press, 1998.

Stern, Yedidia Z. "Living with Normative Duality: The Values at the End of the Tunnel." *Jewish Political Studies Review* 12, nos. 3–4 (Fall 2000): 95–112.

Sternberg, Meir. *The Poetics of Biblical Narrative*. 1985. Bloomington: Indiana University Press, 1987.

Strauss, Leo. "Interpretation of Genesis." *Jewish Political Studies Review* 1, nos. 1–2 (Spring 1989): 77–92.

Suleiman, Susan Rubin. "Writing and Motherhood." In *The (M)other Tongue: Essays in Feminist Psychoanalytic Interpretation*, edited by Shirley Nelson Garner, Claire Kahane, and Madelon Sprengnether. Ithaca: Cornell University Press, 1985.

Sweeney, Robert. "A Survey of Recent Ricoeur-Literature By and About 1974–1984." *Philosophy Today* (Spring 1985): 38–71.

Talmage, Frank. "Apples of Gold: The Inner Meaning of Sacred Texts in Medieval Judaism." In *Jewish Spirituality from the Bible Through the Middle Ages*, edited by Arthur Green. New York: Crossroad, 1987.

Tanhuma (Midrash). Edited by Jacob Weinfeld. Jerusalem: Eshkol, 1975.

Tanner, Tony. "Julie and 'La Maison Paternelle.'" In *The Family in Political Thought*, edited by Jean Bethke Elshtain. Amherst: University of Massachusetts Press, 1982.

Tolbert, Mary Ann. "Defining the Problem: The Bible and Feminist Hermeneutics." *Semeia* 28 (1983): 113–26.

Trible, Phyllis. *Texts of Terror*. Philadelphia: Fortress, 1984.

———. "Two Women in a Man's World: A Reading of the Book of Ruth." *Soundings* 59, no. 3 (Fall 1976): 251–79.

Tur-Sinai. "Shimshon v'Hidato/Samson and His Riddle." In *Iyyunim b'Sefer Shoftim* [*Considerations on the Book of Judges*]. Jerusalem: Kiryat Sepher, 1966.

van Praag, Herman M. "The Downfall of King Saul: The Neurobiological Consequences of Losing Hope." *Judaism* 35, no. 4 (Fall 1986): 414–28.

Vincent, Andrew. *Nationalism and Particularity*. New York: Cambridge University Press, 2002.

von Rad, Gerhard. *Genesis: A Commentary*. Philadelphia: Westminster, 1972.

Wadsworth, Michael. "Making and Interpreting Scripture." In *Ways of Reading the Bible*, edited by Michael Wadsworth. Totowa, N.J.: Harvester, 1981.

Walzer, Michael. *Exodus and Revolution*. New York: Basic, 1985.

Walzer, Michael, Menachem Lorberbaum, Noam J. Zohar, and Ari Ackerman, eds. *The Jewish Political Tradition*. Vol. 2. New Haven: Yale University Press, 2003.

Walzer, Michael, Menachem Lorberbaum, Noam J. Zohar, and Yair Lorberbaum, eds. *The Jewish Political Tradition*. Vol. 1. New Haven: Yale University Press, 2000.

Weber, Max. *Ancient Judaism*. 1952. Translated and edited by Hans H. Gerth and Don Martindale. New York: Free Press, 1967.

———. "Politics as a Vocation." In *From Max Weber*, edited by Hans H. Gerth and C. Wright Mills. New York: Oxford University Press, 1975.

Weinfeld, Moshe. "Zion and Jerusalem as Religious and Political Capital: Ideology and Utopia." In *The Poet and the Historian: Essays in Literature and Historical Biblical Criticism*, edited by Richard Elliot Friedman. Chico, Calif.: Scholars Press, 1983.

Weinhouse, Linda. "Faith and Fantasy: The Texts of the Jews." *Medieval Encounters* 5, no. 3 (1999): 391–408.

Weiss, Gershon. *Samson's Struggle*. New York: Kol HaYeshiva, 1983.

Wessels, J. P. H. "The Joseph Story as a Wisdom Novelette." In *Old Testament Essays*, edited by J. A. Loader and J. H. le Roux. Vol. 2. Pretoria: UNISA, 1984.

Westermann, Claus. *Genesis: A Practical Commentary*. Translated by David E. Green. Grand Rapids, Mich.: Eerdmans, 1987.

Wharton, James A. "The Secret of Yahweh: Story and Affirmation in Judges 13–16." *Interpretation* 27, no. 1 (1973): 48–66.

White, Hugh C. *Narration and Discourse in the Book of Genesis.* Cambridge: Cambridge University Press, 1991.

Widengren, Geo. "King and Covenant." *Journal of Semitic Studies* 2, no. 1 (January 1957): 1–32.

Wildavsky, Aaron. *Moses as Political Leader.* 1984. Jerusalem: Shalem, 2005.

———. "Survival Must Not Be Gained Through Sin." *Journal for the Study of the Old Testament* 62 (1994): 37–48.

———. "What Is Permissible so That This People May Survive: Joseph the Administrator." *PS* (December 1989): 779–88.

Willis, John T. "Cultic Elements in the Story of Samuel's Birth and Dedication." *Studia Theologica* 26, no. 1 (1972): 33–61.

Wolfson, Elliot R. "Circumcision and the Divine Name: A Study in the Transmission of Esoteric Doctrine." *The Jewish Quarterly Review* 78, nos. 1–2 (1987): 77–112.

Yee, Gale A., ed. *Judges and Method: New Approaches in Biblical Studies.* Minneapolis: Fortress, 1995.

Yuter, Alan J. "Positivist Rhetoric and Its Functions in Haredi Orthodoxy." *Jewish Political Studies Review* 8, nos. 1–2 (Spring 1996): 127–88.

Zakovitch, Yair. *The Life of Samson (Hayyei Shimshon): A Critical-literary Analysis.* Jerusalem: Magnes, 1982.

———. "Through the Looking Glass: Reflections/Inversions of Genesis Stories in the Bible." *Biblical Interpretation* 1, no. 2 (1993): 139–52.

Zemach, E. M. "Metaphors and Ways of Life." In *Aspects of Metaphor,* edited by Jaakko Hintikka. Boston: Kluwer, 1994.

Zerubavel, Yael. *Recovered Roots.* Chicago: University of Chicago Press, 1995.

Zornberg, Avivah. "The Concealed Alternative." In *Reading Ruth: Contemporary Women Reclaim a Sacred Story,* edited by Judith A. Kates and Gail Twersky Reimer. New York: Ballantine, 1994.

———. *Genesis: The Beginning of Desire.* Philadelphia: Jewish Publication Society, 1995.

———. *The Particulars of Rapture.* New York: Doubleday, 2001.

INDEX